NO
LIMIT

NO LIMIT

The Rise and Fall of Bob Stupak
and Las Vegas' Stratosphere Tower

John L. Smith

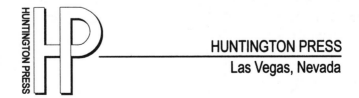

HUNTINGTON PRESS
Las Vegas, Nevada

**No Limit—The Rise and Fall of Bob Stupak
and Las Vegas' Stratosphere Tower**

Published by
Huntington Press
3687 South Procyon Avenue
Las Vegas, NV 89103
(702) 252-0655 Phone
(702) 252-0675 Fax
e-mail: lva@vegas.infi.net

ISBN 0-929712-18-8

Library of Congress Catalog Card Number: 96-79031

Cover Photos: Ed Foster (Stratosphere Tower), Mark Lawson Shepard
(Bob Stupak), Jason Cox (Author Photo)
Cover Design: Scott Sullivan
Production: Jason Cox
Interior Design: Bethany Coffey & Jason Cox

Printing History
1st Edition—July 1997

In memory of Prince L. Smith Jr., 1927-1996.

Acknowledgments

For a man who has sought publicity most of his life, Bob Stupak was extremely reluctant to have his life story told. In fact, he initially declined to be interviewed for this book. Thankfully, he changed his mind, and the story is much better for the half-dozen question-and-answer sessions to which he submitted. It is my hope that I've rendered his life accurately, for I admire his tenacity, not only in the casino but in life as well. It should be noted, however, that this is not an authorized biography. Any mistakes that may have found their way into this book are my responsibility.

Getting the straight story on anyone in Las Vegas is always difficult, but fortunately not every casino operator in the city took the Fifth when it came to Bob Stupak. Although many were extremely helpful, Klondike casino owner John Woodrum was a veritable guide to Stupak's amazing story. Thanks also to Lyle Thompson of Vacation Village, Michael Gaughan of the Gaughan family casinos, and other casino operators who prefer to remain anonymous. And thanks to Richard Schuetz of Stratosphere for taking time to help. Unfortunately, Grand Casinos' maven, Lyle Berman, declined to be interviewed; perhaps he was too busy writing his own amazing success story.

The anecdotes of numerous police officers, paramedics, tow-truck drivers, business leaders, stock analysts, elected officials, and working stiffs greatly contributed to this story. I thank them for their patience and consideration. You will find their names and insights throughout this book. Particular thanks to former Stupak spin doctor Dan Hart, ex-Las Vegas City Councilman Scott Higginson, City Councilman Arnie Adamsen, Las Vegas Mayor Jan Laverty Jones, Phyllis McGuire, Lou Adams, and Eddie Baranski.

A book on Bob Stupak would not have been possible without the work of dozens of journalists, editors, and photographers who have chronicled his immensely colorful life and times. Among the many: Ed Becker, Dave Berns, Myram Borders, Rex Buntain, Jeff Burbank, Monica Caruso, Sandra Chereb, Carol Cling, Jeffrey Cohan, Aaron Cohen, Roger Dionne, Chuck DiRocco, Mike Donahue, John G. Edwards, Steve Falcone, Tanya Flanagan, Jeff German, Rene Germanier, Joshua Good, Marian Green, Susan Greene, Adrian Havas, Mary Hynes, George Knapp, Wayne C. Kodey, Sergio Lalli, Jim Laurie, George McCabe, Sean McKinnon, Pete Mikla, Tom Mitchell, Jane Ann Morrison, Bruce Orwall, Dave Palermo, Mike Paskevich, Merlyn Potters, Gary Rotstein, Diane Russell, Jim Rutherford, Jeff Scheid, Cathy Scott, Adam Steinhauer, John Stearns, Howard Stutz, Gary Thompson, Mike McCuen, Richard Velotta, Michael Ventura, Ed Vogel, Susan Voyles, Lynn Waddell, Mike Weatherford, Ken White, and Andy Zipser.

Librarians in Las Vegas and Pittsburgh also lent their time and expertise during the research of the manuscript. I especially would like to thank Padmini Pai and Pamela Busse of the *Las Vegas Review-Journal,* as well as the archivists at the *Pittsburgh Post-Gazette* and Carnegie Public Library of Pittsburgh.

The editorial expertise of Deke Castleman and Anthony Curtis of Huntington Press cannot be overstated. They took my ragged first draft, whipped it into shape, and had faith in my ability to deliver a manuscript in a few short months. Among the hard-working crew at Huntington that I gladly count as allies: Len Cipkins, Bethany Coffey, Jason Cox, Virginia Castleman, June Flowers, Jacqueline Joniec, Jim Karl, and Beverly Ware. I hope to work with them again soon. Thanks, too, are due my sister Cath Cassidy for her 11th-hour editing expertise.

Finally, thanks to my wife, Patricia, and daughter, Amelia, for their love and understanding. I am as rich as Rockefeller to have you.

The old dice scuffler approached the crap game and leaned on the rail.

"What are you doing back here?" I asked. "You know you can't beat the game, and you're down to your last few bucks."

"Son," the broken-down shooter said, "I have to make a bet every day. How else will I know when the good luck comes back?"

— old Las Vegas story

"You have to create your own celebrity in this business."

— Bob Stupak

Table of Contents

A View from the Top

It is one of those big blue spring days that sun-baked Las Vegans live for. A whispering breeze takes the edge off the warm afternoon and wisps of clouds feather across the limitless desert horizon.

All in all, a good day to die.

I'm strapped into a NASA-goes-to-the-carnival contraption called the Big Shot, which is bolted to the top of the Stratosphere Tower, which stretches 1,149 feet into the glorious April air. As such, it is the tallest freestanding structure west of the Mississippi. That makes me just about the tallest freestanding columnist for as many miles around.

Stratosphere, the casino-resort-tower at the north end of the Las Vegas Strip, is set to open in three days, and I've been invited to test my stomach and fear of heights against a ride that is accurately described as the world's tallest Heimlich maneuver. Riding next to me? Stratosphere's big-idea man himself, Bob Stupak.

Any machine whose operators make you remove your slip-on shoes, eyeglasses, loose jewelry, and wobbly denture plates before experiencing it qualifies as a thrill ride. Anyone who travels anywhere with Bob Stupak qualifies as a thrill seeker. The ride is more like taking a double dose of syrup of ipecac with a mad scientist than taking a spin on the giant teacups with Walt Disney.

The Big Shot launches 16 citizens out of their shoes with the force of four Gs up 160 feet to near the top of the tower in less time than it takes to beg God for forgiveness.

Then you drop like a dead man at negative one G, only to be caught a few feet from a certain messy demise on the platform below—and propelled upward again. The ride takes 31 seconds from start to finish. There's no telling how much time it takes off your life.

Bob Stupak, still looking frail after nearly killing himself in a motorcycle accident a year earlier, knows something about the precious value of life. He once set speed records on a motorcycle, and was traveling with his son, Nevada, at 60 miles per hour when he rammed his Harley-Davidson into the side of a perfectly good Subaru. Not even Stupak liked his odds of recovering from that accident, which shattered his face and spirit and left him in a month-long coma.

But only in Las Vegas could a guy like Stupak find a Florence Nightingale in the form of McGuire Sisters legend Phyllis McGuire. Perhaps somewhere inside Stupak's cracked skull was what naysayers and hunch players had learned over the previous 25 years—that it never pays to bet against the quintessential Las Vegas huckster.

To go from a heartbeat from the Big Hereafter to riding the Big Shot on a gorgeous spring afternoon is vintage Bob. Sitting next to him as he mugs for the cameras moments before blast-off, the accident's effects are still noticeable. But they don't keep him from smiling and selling his project to anyone willing to listen.

"You look nervous," Stupak says to me. "Loosen up. We haven't lost a rider yet."

Nervous? The tower is a full 1,145 feet taller than the threshold of my acrophobia. I feel like Jerry Lewis doing a remake of "The Right Stuff." Whatever stuff I have is doing the mambo in my stomach. Television camera crews from Los Angeles train their lenses on Stupak as he tosses off one-liners and prepares to take the Big Shot to the top of the tower, where those who manage to keep their eyes open can glimpse Lake Mead and can take in every inch of the Strip before free-falling back toward the concrete launching platform and what would appear to be certain death.

Stupak's hulking personal valet, Brendan, snaps photographs of his boss hamming it up with gawkers, reporters, and construction workers. Then we're ready.

"Every ride starts the same way," Stupak says. "Repeat after me: Hail Mary, full of grace—" and then he cackled like Vincent Price on laughing gas.

Our chairs shoot up the side of the tower.

"Top of the world!" Stupak yells, mocking his anxiety-riddled guest. Who does this guy think he is, James Cagney?

We're at the top in a finger snap, then enter a free fall, then climb, then fall, climb, and fall again before gently returning to the launching pad.

Somewhere between my breathless cry for absolution and the second drop, I begin to enjoy myself. I stop squinting long enough to catch the expansive Las Vegas Valley and the unadulterated glee on Stupak's scarred face.

At this moment, I know I'll write a story about Bob Stupak.

Providing, that is, I don't vomit on his shoes.

If P.T. Barnum had a hedonistic twin, Bob Stupak might be the guy. He is one of the last of the great Las Vegas wild men. In an era in which corporations have placed their publicly traded USDA Grade A stamp on the city, at a time in which gaming's most notorious party animals have begun posturing as elder statesmen of Las Vegas casino society, Bob Stupak is still tearing up the neon-lighted streets with his big ideas, big bets, and big mouth. He is a man bereft of hypocrisy, pretense and, some say, table manners, a guy incapable of passing up an intriguing wager. He is a man capable of betting the price of a four-bedroom house on the most innocuous proposition, a fellow who would lay $1 million on the Super Bowl and not only win the wager but get ten times that in publicity.

Stupak is a gambling man and a carnival-style promoter of the first order. His "Free Vacation" promotions attracted thousands of customers, as well as the intense scrutiny of fraud investigators from across the country who just knew there had to be something crooked about the deal. After all, Bob Stupak is the guy who once promised a stuntman $1 million to jump off the top of his 24-story Vegas World Hotel—propelling the casino operator to international tabloid celebrity—then charged the fearless flier a $975,000 landing fee. More than once, Stupak's huckster's heart had nearly cost him his coveted Nevada gaming license. If, as Damon Runyon once wrote, life is 6-to-5 against, Stupak has enjoyed the longest run of luck in the history of a city that makes suckers out of even its most savvy players.

And there's the Stupak who was voted Mr. Las Vegas by his ally, Mayor Jan Jones. Following his accident, the huckster emerged as a philanthropist with the fastest checkbook in a place that prides itself on its big-hearted spenders. Stupak gave away more than $1 million before the last bandage was removed from his battered body. He knew he had enjoyed the greatest good fortune. Maybe he was hedging his spiritual bets.

Stupak is annually voted the Most Embarrassing Las Vegan by newspaper readers. In a pitchman's paradise the caliber of southern Nevada, where candidates for the title proliferate the landscape, it is a mighty statement.

With the improbable construction of the Stratosphere Tower, in spring 1996, Bob Stupak finally was about to make the score of his life in the city that eats dreams like 99-cent breakfasts. The fact his triumph was on the edge of a crime-riddled neighborhood known as Naked City made the emerging success story all the more incredible.

On a clear day from the tower's observation platform, the keen-eyed can see all of Naked City—every dilapidated rooftop, small-time drug deal, and street-corner hustle. Naked City has been a starting point for Las Vegas immigrants for decades.

Other Las Vegas neighborhoods have crime rates as high, but no other is as notorious; even changing the neighborhood's name to the kinder, gentler Meadows Village hasn't improved its reputation as a gang-infested shooting gallery.

To the south, the tower offers an incredible view of the Strip and the heart of the city built by Las Vegas' notorious founding fathers. There's the Las Vegas Country Club, the Desert Inn, and the Stardust, built by Moe Dalitz and his associates. There's Caesars Palace and Circus Circus, two of the amazing ideas to take shape from the mind of Jay Sarno. And there are the wildly successful Mirage and Treasure Island resorts, the creations of the gaming industry's premier player, Steve Wynn.

Looking north to downtown, Fremont Street's clog of casinos jut from under a ponderous metal canopy whose two million lights were designed to reinvigorate the area and return Glitter Gulch to its past glory. But the so-called Fremont Street Experience is downright plain compared to Stupak's flashy tower.

If you gaze with a forgiving eye, Las Vegas appears almost handsome from so high above the street. Boomtowns are not by nature attractive places. They are full of the dust and bluster of breakneck progress, and Las Vegas fits the profile. Boomtowns have the thrown-together look of a stripper late for her curtain call: hair mussed, too much rouge, and buttons undone. They are riddled with road construction, exposed water lines, and the kind of energy that attracts Joad families from across the land. As such, Las Vegas perennially ranks among the fastest-growing cities in the nation, with approximately 4,000 newcomers arriving each month.

As the last great American boomtown, Las Vegas suffers from all those infrastructural maladies and offers every ounce of the promise. For the immigrant with no English, the autoworker with no assembly line, the desperate hunch player with a fatally flawed dice system, it is the place for fresh starts, second chances, and last stands. The community is a national leader in job creation, personal-income growth, and suicide.

The Big Shot ride epitomizes Stupak's improbable, even death-defying rise in Las Vegas. It is as if all the energy he has expended during his extraordinary life and career has been manifested in the nation's tallest freestanding observation tower and a couple of thrill rides to end all thrill rides.

Any city can have the tallest observation tower. Only in Las Vegas would such a structure merely qualify as a piece of mundane architecture unless it had a NASA blast-off simulator and a rooftop roller coaster. But that's Bob Stupak for you.

In the corporate era, where gaming stocks trade on Wall Street and casino bosses carry Ivy League degrees and a bravado that often passes for brilliance, the individual operator is an anomaly. Sadly, the city's personality has changed. It has largely reinvented itself as a sort of Stepford with a casino-based economy: ceaselessly prosperous, but quiet. A little too quiet. Most of the city's genuine characters have gone the way of the Dunes, Sands, and Silver Slipper. The seasoned racketeers who migrated to Las Vegas ahead of the law and settled into a respectability have faded into the landscape. In the corporate company town, there isn't much room for personality—not with billions of dollars at stake. Even Stupak needed to bail out his big idea with eight-figure assistance from Grand Casinos Inc. and its founder, Lyle Berman. True to Stupak's nature, he met Berman across a poker table.

Of all the risky proposition bets Bob Stupak ever placed, by far the most daring was his idea to remake the Las Vegas skyline by constructing the incredible Stratosphere Tower.

Even in a town built on long odds, this venture was a million-to-one shot.

The Cruelest Month

The 1989 Harley-Davidson rushed south on Rancho Road past Charleston Boulevard, accelerating its two riders, a father and son, into the warm desert night. The Las Vegas weather in March often is chilled, windy, and wet, but the last night of the month was dry. It was thirty minutes before April Fool's Day, 1995.

The father motored past a convenience store, service station and, just east on Charleston, the University Medical Center. The neighborhood was familiar. So was the tandem ride. The old man had been speeding his three children around on high-performance motorcycles since they were old enough to hang on.

He knew these streets better than those in his hometown. He had been a Las Vegas resident for more than 20 years and had spent much of his adult life within a couple miles of downtown. When you've ridden bikes at speeds topping 120 miles per hour, the act becomes second nature. Accomplished riders have something akin to a sixth sense that enables them almost to feel and avoid dangerous situations.

The driver put the big bike through its paces as he had done with so many motorcycles. Although he hadn't competed in three decades, he had owned motorcycles since he was 15 and had drag-raced them against the best riders in the country. Along the way he had collected a truckload of trophies and more than his share of close calls. Clipping the Harley beyond the posted

35-mile-per-hour limit over dry asphalt was a simple enough feat.

As a token testament to safety and Nevada law, he wore a European-style half helmet strapped to his neck.

He shifted, the bike hit its stride, and in a moment the two men were traveling more than 60.

The young woman in the northbound Subaru had no time to react as she began her left turn from Rancho Road onto Mason Avenue.

Slicing through the night, the Harley rider locked up the brakes a heartbeat before broadsiding the Subaru. The impact knocked the automobile backward and sent the riders glancing off the car, over the top and onto the road. They landed together, the driver taking the brunt of the impact on his face, the passenger's landing cushioned by the driver's body.

It was 11:35 p.m.

Las Vegas Fire Department Station No. 5 stands at Hinson Street and Charleston, approximately one mile west of Rancho Road. When dispatch reported an accident with injuries on Rancho at Mason, the stationhouse came to life. Within seconds, paramedics Bryan Alexis and Ian Adams were dressed, in their rescue unit, and driving eastbound on Charleston.

They arrived at the accident scene within five minutes and were greeted by attendants from Mercy Ambulance, whose offices are in the neighborhood near the medical center.

Mercy paramedic supervisors Bob Kenney and Marla Malone were on duty that night and, hearing the call, rolled onto the accident scene almost out of reflex. They were the first paramedics to arrive and were joined moments later by Mercy paramedic August Corrales and his partner, Tricia Wacker.

Through absolute chance, within 15 minutes of the accident, six veteran paramedics were on hand to give aid to the fallen bikers and the slightly injured automobile driver. The older biker's luck wasn't all bad. He was still alive.

Although their actions sometimes look chaotic to the un-trained eye, paramedics follow a set pattern when arriving at an accident scene to optimize efficiency and maximize victims' odds of survival. After the initial triage observation, in which those whose injuries are deemed the most severe are quickly assessed, paramedics set their priorities. In this case, the woman in the Subaru was shaken up and showered with glass when her side window popcorned from the impact of the Harley and its rid-ers. The motorcycle's passenger was next to the sidewalk, moan-ing. He appeared to have a broken leg. Otherwise, the attention of as many as six paramedics was focused on the fallen rider. Wacker briefly attended to the wounds of the rider's son before returning to the most severely injured victim.

"We had just dropped a patient off at the hospital and were getting ready to go out. We were just down the street," Wacker recalled. "Immediately when we got out of the truck we did a scene survey. Knowing that he was critical, we just moved him to the ambulance and to the hospital as rapidly as we could."

The Harley rider was nearly dead. His neck was cut from ear to ear, and his head was noticeably swollen. The half helmet had kept his brains from spilling onto Rancho Road, but had not saved him from bearing the brunt of the impact with the asphalt. His face was pulverized.

In his six and a half years as a firefighter and five years as a paramedic, Bryan Alexis had viewed dozens of fatalities and fig-ured he had experienced every sort of grisly accident imagin-able. But he had never seen a living person with a head so swol-len and a face so devastated.

So distorted was the face that Alexis, his partner, and the other paramedics failed to recognize it.

"We pulled up and I quickly went over there, and I started to assess him," Alexis said. "The appearance was just so bad. We tried to block that out. He was probably 10 to 15 feet away from the motorcycle. It appeared that he wasn't going to make it. We immediately tried to immobilize him."

Massive bleeding made the process difficult. The driver was unconscious. His heartbeat was faint, his breathing shallow. He was a few minutes from being beyond help. The clock was running in what emergency-room physicians and paramedics commonly call the Golden Hour, the precious time from the moment a serious accident occurs until the patient is delivered to the trauma unit. The paramedics set to work, cutting off the rider's clothing and prepping him for the short ride to the emergency room. His arms and left leg appeared to be broken, but that was the least of the paramedics' concerns.

What really startled Alexis was the throat gash.

"The laceration appeared to be from ear to ear, kind of like a Colombian necktie," he said. "It was like someone cut his throat, but when I looked at the helmet he'd been wearing I saw that the strap around his neck is what caused the massive laceration. His teeth were broken. There was so much trauma. It was probably the worst I've ever seen. No, it definitely was the worst."

There was no time to treat him at the scene, so the paramedics slipped a cervical collar around his neck, rolled him to one side, and placed a back board underneath him. Then they loaded him into the ambulance for transport to the trauma unit at University Medical Center with Alexis and Wacker in the back.

Had the accident occurred even a mile farther away from the hospital and Station No. 5, their speed might not have made a difference. En route, Alexis grabbed a large-bore needle and administered a massive infusion of saline solution, which has the same consistency as blood. It not only replaces the fluids that are rapidly being lost, but also helps slow shock in traumatized patients. With his blood pressure dropping, it was the only way to keep him alive until the ambulance reached the hospital.

Keeping him breathing was the other immediate problem. Normally, Alexis would use a laryngoscope to insert a tracheal tube down the throat of the patient. But the patient's face and neck were too far gone. The veteran paramedic couldn't see the precise area between the vocal cords to insert the tube.

But he had to act quickly or he would have a dead man on

his hands. He did his best to locate the base of the throat and slipped in the tracheal breathing tube. With the tracheal tube inserted, the lungs were inflated, oxygen flowed, and blood was prevented from leaking down his throat. The free-hand medical attention kept the patient breathing, but barely.

"It was the first time for me," Alexis said. "We just opened it up and went for it."

"We had him packaged and in the rig in no more than ten minutes. When we arrived at the hospital, we took the patient with us and transferred him into a bed. We did our best, but I really didn't think he was going to make it."

Corrales said, "It was really a shared effort to take care of him. We didn't know he was a celebrity, not that it would have mattered. What happened is just something we typically do. Listening to people talk about what the CATscans were, he did not have a high likelihood of survival."

And all that time, none of the paramedics knew who they were treating. The face was unrecognizable.

When the younger rider arrived at the hospital, his ankle obviously broken, he asked, "How's my dad? How's my dad?"

"Is this your father over here?" he was asked.

"That's my dad," the young man said. "That's Bob Stupak."

Back on the street, as police accident investigators attempted to piece together events, the greater irony loomed large in the background. From where the rider had come to rest on the asphalt, glancing to the east he would have had a splendid view of his life's greatest achievement as it rose more than 1,000 feet into the desert night.

But he could not see, of course. By early April Fool's Day, the fallen rider was headed for a deep coma as trauma specialists worked to save his life.

Lucky Bob Stupak was dying almost as fast as he lived.

ONE

A Gambler's Son

The boy fought sleep. It was after 2 a.m., long past his bedtime, and as he sat at the kitchen table he strained to listen for the telling sounds in the chilly Pittsburgh night: the low rumbling of the Cadillac pulling into the driveway, the heavy thud of the car door shutting, the click of the front door opening.

The boy was no more than six, and he waited through the night for his father to return home from work. He was young, but he knew his father's job was different. While other dads toiled in the smoking steel mills during the prosperous few years after the end of World War II, the boy's father labored in a smoky mill of another kind. Where other men went to work before dawn in dungarees, the boy's father dressed sharper than a banker and often left for work as the sun went down.

The two-story house on the South Side at 2017 Sarah Street was silent. The boy was nodding off. But when the front door opened, the kid sprung into action. He popped the question before his father had time to remove his hat and overcoat.

"Can we throw 'em, dad?" he asked. "Can we throw the dice?"

"Of course we can," the father said, smiling.

With that, the kitchen-table crap game was open for business.

Where other fathers and sons might toss a baseball, Chester Stupak and his boy, Bobby, pitched dice. It was the boy's introduction to the seductive world of random numbers. Years later Bob Stupak would recall that, while other children were concentrating on addition and subtraction, he had long since graduated to multiplication, division, and something rarely taught in any elementary school, the 36 combinations possible on a pair of dice. Not to mention bedtime stories that featured the Runyonesque adventures of Pittsburgh's favorite dice dealer.

"Tell me a story, dad," young Bobby said. "Tell me just one."

Baby-faced Chester Stupak grinned and, as if he had memorized the stories of Runyon himself, recounted the exploits of the night's big winner, a mouthy Malone who talked a good game but crapped out in the end and had to ask the old man for a few bucks. Which he received despite his arrogance. There was no need to humble a fellow when he was down; the best way to keep customers was to treat them with a little respect and make them think the owner was a bit of a soft touch. The tales were sanitized, to be sure, for despite what Runyon might write, the gambling racket was no place for children. But Nathan Detroit had nothing on Chester from Pittsburgh.

In Greek mythology, Palamedes invented dice and money to pass the time during the battle of Troy, and surely one of Chester's ancestors must have been there. Chester Stupak was a proud Polish American who possessed a legendary gift for dice and the numbers lottery that became Pittsburgh institutions. If he had a mythical connection to the dice, he also possessed a keen understanding of customer relations. He refined the art on his way to winning friends and influencing people throughout Allegheny County from the end of the war well into the 1980s.

Pittsburgh was in the action from the start. At the confluence of the Allegheny and Monongahela rivers, where the Ohio River is formed, the Indians founded the village of Shannopin in the late 17th century. It became a crossroads for fur traders and adventurers and emerged as an incorporated city in 1816.

With large mineral deposits, abundant coal fields in western Pennsylvania and West Virginia, and river access, Pittsburgh was ideally located in the heart of America's industrial coming of age. The city was shrouded in the smoky cloak of progress, and its steel mills provided economic hope and back-breaking work for generations of immigrant laborers.

The son of immigrant Poles, Chester Stupak was born June 7, 1914, on Pittsburgh's South Side. The muscular, seething city on the South Side of the Monongahela defined his world, as it did thousands of immigrants from Eastern Europe, many of whom lived within walking distance of the domed St. John the Baptist Ukrainian Catholic Church on South 7th Street. Ordinary row houses lined the neighborhood; up on 27th Street the mills belched black smoke and swallowed up laborers each morning.

Young Chester might have joined those mill workers had he not had the odd fortune of losing his life savings as a teenager to a sharp-shooting dice dealer with a back-alley crap game. In that early humiliation, he discovered something irresistible in the dice and came away with the knowledge that a gambler's reputation might be soiled in a blue-collar town, but his hands stayed clean.

If one man could take all his money with such ease, then couldn't anyone provide the dice and rope the players?

Chester walked to a dime store, purchased a pair of dice, and went into business for himself. He remained in Pittsburgh's gambling rackets the rest of his life.

The enterprise entailed more than providing a place to play and a bankroll to cover the action. There was also the mob to consider. Only a fool took men like Frank Amato, John LaRocca, Joe Sica, and Tony Ripepi lightly. But in the World War II era, Pittsburgh was run by an even greedier gang in the form of the city's elected leaders. Their thirst for greenbacks was unquenchable. Between the mob and the politicians, the illegal dice business was far more complicated than either eighter-from-Decatur or seven-come-eleven.

Winning money was the easy part; hanging on to it took considerable finesse.

Bob Stupak often boasts that his father, Chester Stupak, operated Pittsburgh's longest-running crap game, from 1941 to

1991. But the man was more than a simple gambling boss with a penchant for the galloping dominos. Baby-faced Chester Stupak was a man of stature in Pittsburgh's backroom casino circles. He was to illegal numbers and card rooms what Carnegie was to steel. Although Chester never would be able to brag that he was bigger than U.S. Steel, he could boast of being the most active, visible, and elusive operator in the city's history. He was a man of many talents and the envy of Pittsburgh gamblers.

Chester slipped indictments the way Pittsburgh-born fighters Harry Greb and Billy Conn slipped punches. Whether he was suspected of operating a casino out of the back of a shuttered brewery or accused of offering a beat cop a couple thousand to look the other way, Chester enjoyed an uncanny run of legal luck.

It is no wonder that cops, judges, and journalists suspected that he was hedging his bets by corrupting courtroom proceedings. The final results rarely varied: Chester Stupak, his youthful face grinning from the front page of the *Pittsburgh Post*, managed to dodge the charges.

At various times in its history, Pittsburgh has been known as the Smoky City and "Hell With the Lid Off." Before its urban redevelopment movement turned it into one of the nation's sparkling cities, Pittsburgh was much maligned. When asked what needed to be done with the city, architect Frank Lloyd Wright replied, "Abandon it." But Pittsburgh boomed during World War II. Much of the rest of the nation might have suffered from rationing, but by Armistice Day there was plenty of money floating around in America's steel town. At times, it must have seemed as if Chester Stupak had his hands on most of it.

In Pittsburgh, his dice game was an immediate success. Not that he didn't experience the usual irritations in the form of police raids, undercover investigators, revenue agents, and the like. But that was the cost of doing business in an illegal racket.

Unlike some of his competition, namely the strong, silent types who operated on behalf of the local mob families, Chester Stupak brought more than a pair of dice and a bankroll to the party. He brought a sense of humor and a philosophy that endeared him not only to the shortstop players who hit him up for a double sawbuck, but also to the local authorities who found him as irresistible as he was incorrigible. The fact they regularly received gifts from good old Chester kept the politicians and police officers pacified.

When it came to the game, Chester had few peers and no limit. It was one of many tales he told his son.

"But what if somebody comes in and bets too much?" a young Bob Stupak once asked his father.

"What's the difference?" Chester said. "You cover the bet. The money eventually comes back to you."

Chester recalled the night at his jam-packed Lotus Club when Moon Miller came bouncing through the door with his pockets stuffed with cash. The Lotus Club had operated under the nose of the police for decades, and Moon Miller knew the way to the action as well as anyone.

"Ten thousand across, Ches!" Miller called through the house.

The crowd stirred. The dice skittered across the tables. Everyone in the Lotus Club was listening.

Had Moon Miller been hitting the hard stuff?

Had he knocked over a savings and loan?

"Ten thousand across, Ches," Miller shouted.

The guys and dolls watched through the smoke. Moon Miller was calling for a bet that, in those years shortly after the war, would have paid for three houses in the suburbs.

The pressure was on, but Chester Stupak just smiled. After some negotiations, he accepted Miller's wager—and proceeded to lose a bundle. The players talked about it for months afterward as they traveled from all over the county to get to Chester's big dice game.

Bobby asked, "What about all that money? Weren't you

sweating it?"

"It didn't make no difference," he said. "Besides, I didn't lose. I've beaten Moon Miller out of that much money and more over the years. And I'll beat him again. This was nothing but a good advertisement."

Even though every player and police officer in Pittsburgh knew where Chester's action took place, the law was decidedly blind to Chester's crap game, which surely is a testament to his charisma and his cash. The unwritten rules were followed to the letter: no trouble, no violence, and nothing spilled out into the street where decent folk might be offended. And no fully marked crap tables, either. After all, the cops had a reputation to protect. In the outer county, on a farm or in a vacant house, Chester might have a roulette wheel, crap tables with a full layout, and a numbers bank that would impress a New York lottery boss. But at the Lotus Club, or wherever Chester rolled his dice inside the city limits, he kept things simple and unobtrusive. He would use a pool table, divide it with a string, and drop the dice. Players had to shoot across the string. The game was on.

Chester kept his family close to him in business. One relative was the custodian of the Lotus Club, and Chester's wife, Florence, would always be counted on to help out with the numbers accounting. While at school, young Bobby often would go to the Lotus for lunch, carrying in a bag of burgers from the White Castle on 16th Street. As he ate, he often saw the waning moments of crap games that had been going since the previous evening.

Dice became Chester's calling card. When he opened a supper house called Club 19 with a game in back, engraved invitations bore a pair of dice and directions to the action.

Not long after Club 19 opened in Washington County, a Pittsburgh newspaper reporter began writing scathing articles about Chester's roulette and crap games. With a call, Chester discovered that far from being a bastion of journalistic integrity, the reporter was said to have had a piece of a mob gambling club nearby. Chester inadvertently had cut into the scribe's action.

With one eye on his rear-view mirror, Chester picked up and moved. He wasn't afraid of a little bad publicity; he was concerned about steering clear of the knee-breakers.

"He kept waiting for the heat to go away, but it never did," his son recalled. "The boys had the area locked up."

Perhaps one reason for Chester Stupak's great fortune was his ability to run honest games and to remain within handshake distance of Pittsburgh's notorious ward bosses, who at times held a grip on the city's vice rackets. From after-hours nightclubs to red-light brothels, the political insiders offered protection for illegal activities—for a price.

And they had competition from traditional racketeers. Mafia-type activity in the area dates as far back as the 1890s, when Sicilian-born John Bazzano Sr. assumed the role of boss of the mob family that operated in Pittsburgh and southwestern Pennsylvania. Bazzano grew fat during Prohibition, ordering the execution of rivals in the gambling and bootlegging businesses, before being ice-picked to death in 1932.

By then, the neighborhoods were riddled with hoods of every stripe.

In 1950, numbers activity in Pittsburgh topped $100 million a year, according to law-enforcement estimates. Turning to lottery sales and backroom casinos was not only a lucrative move, but it also eased pressure from the cops and district attorney. A numbers racket they could handle; blood in the street embarrassed them.

"The august, dignified, black-robed jurists for years have shown a benevolent attitude toward organized racket crime and the criminals behind it. As much as any one factor, the easy sentences imposed by both Allegheny County judges and the 'gypsy' jurists imported from surrounding counties, upon convicted racket criminals, are responsible for the breakdown of law enforcement against organized crime in Allegheny County," respected investigative reporter Ray Sprigle wrote in his groundbreaking 1950 series on the city's underground gambling empire.

"In recent years the racket has developed a new angle," Sprigle wrote. "In some wards, by and with the consent of the ward chairman, a group of small-fry mobsters will make a deal with a topflight racket syndicate to operate as a subsidiary of the well-financed big syndicate."

Unlike Philadelphia, where much of the gambling racket was run by the Bruno crime family, and Reading, where a Bruno faction operated multimillion-dollar backroom casinos, Pittsburgh's mob didn't quite measure up. Not that the city was without its home office of La Cosa Nostra. On the contrary, until 1956 Pittsburgh was known as the domain of Frank Amato, who managed to achieve a modicum of success under Pittsburgh's close-knit system.

Then came John Sebastian LaRocca, a sort of Rodney Dangerfield of mob bosses. Try as he might to shake down local businessmen, according to Carl Sifakis' *The Mafia Encyclopedia*, he was nearly laughed out of the city.

"A much-overrated mobster, John LaRocca was often described as the Mafia boss of southwestern Pennsylvania and Pittsburgh," Sifakis wrote. "Some knowledgeable observers, however, have tended to regard him as the leader of the Mickey Mouse Mafia East, a play on the description of several west coast crime families because of their general ineffectiveness and their inability to protect their own turf from incursions by the New York and Chicago mobs."

LaRocca simply could not compete with the "Ward Syndicates" in several of the traditional rackets, and he never gained the reputation of Bruno or western Pennsylvania crime boss Russell Buffalino.

LaRocca, however, was quite successful in extracting his percentage of the profits garnered by a group of gambling junket operators who shipped high rollers from Pittsburgh to Las Vegas. Not that millionaire status boosted his image with the New York bosses.

Legendary mob informant Vincent Teresa scoffed at LaRocca's boss status. To Fat Vinny, LaRocca was "a mob guy from Pittsburgh who some people say is a boss but he isn't."

LaRocca, whose criminal career began in 1922, died in 1984. He was 82 and left a legacy as an also-ran in the underworld. The mob never could compete with Pittsburgh's political bosses.

Perhaps he should have taken a lesson from lucky Chester Stupak.

Although the mob was capable of applying considerable pressure, there was plenty of room and plenty of action to go around. With few cops watching them and fewer politicians crowing about the evils of gambling, it was obvious to even casual observers that men like Chester Stupak had powerful friends. Chester accepted it as the cost of doing business, but in later years he stopped greasing palms.

"Whoever he had to pay, the last twenty years he stopped paying," Bob Stupak said years later. "Whenever I would come back to Pittsburgh for a visit, I'd always ask the cab drivers if there was any action in town where a guy could shoot dice. About ninety percent of the time they would say, 'Oh, there's Chester's joint on the South Side.' The last fifty years, if anybody opened up a crap game they'd be closed in five minutes by the IRS, the CIA, whoever. But my dad operated with no trouble. He was an institution. When he died, it was over."

It didn't hurt to have the father of the district attorney as a dear friend. When the son got the bright idea to break up Chester's game in the name of justice and bold newspaper headlines, the father set him straight.

"The day you raid Chester's game is the day I don't have a son anymore," he said.

It helped to be able to shake hands and slap backs with the chief of police and most of his men. It also helped to have a sense of humor when the time came for the election-year roust. Chester understood that, occasionally, he would have to allow the local authorities an opportunity to do their best Claude Rains skit from *Casablanca*. Rains, the worldly local police chief, steps into the backroom casino at Rick's Cafe American and exclaims that he is "shocked, shocked!" to see illegal gambling going on, even as he accepts his piece of the action. So, too, it was with Pittsburgh authorities and lucky Chester Stupak.

His first arrest came in 1946 when Allegheny County detectives noticed his involvement with a growing gambling and numbers operation. He was hauled in for operating an illegal lottery, but once reduced, the charges amounted to little more than a traffic citation. A check of police records years later revealed no disposition in the case.

By 1950, his reputation was well established. The cops occasionally took playful shots at him, but for many years he appeared unbeatable in court. After all, everybody knew about Chester and his dice game.

Regulars referred to a Stupak casino as Chester's Place. The original Chester's Place sat above L&M Upholstery on the second floor of a brick building located at 93 Sixteenth Street near Carson Street in the city's 17th Ward. It was a big, airy room without plush carpet or chandeliers. The room was dominated by three pool tables marked for craps.

Although homely by Vegas standards and illegal under Pennsylvania law, Chester's Place ran wide open day and night. If it lacked a neon sign announcing its location, perhaps it was because no gambler on the South Side needed directions to find its door. No bouncers, no B girls, no problems. Just plenty of action and a boss who seldom found reason not to smile.

Then his place became the subject of a long expose by enterprising *Pittsburgh Post-Gazette* writer Sprigle.

LAW DOESN'T FOOL WITH CHESTER
'THE LAW' DOESN'T BOTHER TO BOTHER 'CHESTER'S PLACE,'
THAT BIG GAMBLING JOINT ON THE SOUTH SIDE, WHERE THE DICE ROLL
EVERY NIGHT REGARDLESS OF WHETHER THE 'HEAT' IS OFF OR ON

So this is "Chester's Place," for years famous all over Pittsburgh. Whenever the heat goes on and the joints all over town go dark, Chester's Place can be depended upon to keep right on clipping the boys for their paychecks.

... In every other section of Pittsburgh and Allegheny County the rackets are operated as rackets are supposed to be operated. No matter how wide-open they run, the boys at least try to give visiting newspapermen an impression of stealth and clandestinity. But not on the South Side.

There the numbers racket runs like a legal and respectable business. Nobody questions the stranger who wants to buy a slip or two, either on the races or the stocks.

Sprigle's series of articles on Pittsburgh's rackets led to many law-enforcement inquiries, numerous arrests, and the extreme discomfort of the city's elected leaders.

For Chester, it was the first time he was publicly accused of being less than his own man. Nick "Yee" Terleski and James Bova, both of whom carried lengthy police records, were said to be Chester's uninvited silent partners in the city's most celebrated crap game. Years later, his proud son would remember things differently.

"My dad never had no partners. Some people might have thought he did, but he didn't," Bob Stupak said. "When the cops came in to raid the place, they'd have to arrest somebody. They'd pick a two-dollar guy, a small bettor, even though everyone knew it was Chester's game. My old man would act like another player. The cops would ask, 'Whose place is this?' and a guy would stand up and say, 'This is my place.' The police knew, but they went along with it. The two-dollar player would take a fall, my old man would pay all the attorney's fees, but it was always a customer who took the beef. There was no jail time involved. It's just something the police did from time to time. The two-dollar player got instant recognition in the neighborhood and in the papers. He was a big guy for a few days."

If he lacked partners, he did have plenty of pals. For a man in a racket as hard as Pittsburgh steel, Chester Stupak was one soft touch.

"My dad was a George. You know, a generous guy," Bob Stupak said. "He gave away fucking money like it was water. He was the easiest fucking mark in the world. I wish I had the money he gave away. A guy would approach him and start in with a story. He didn't want to hear the story. He'd say, 'Here's twenty.' Occasionally, somebody would come up to him and try to hit him up for a hundred, which was a lot of money in those days. My dad would say, 'I can't loan you a hundred, but I'll give you fifty.'

"He was always giving money to shortstops. Shortstops come in with a little bit of money. You can always count on them to be busted and looking to borrow. You can't loan them a hundred or two hundred because they can't afford to pay you back and they'll stop coming into your place. So you give them half. Never loan them what they want; always give them half."

Besides, the money had an uncanny way of returning to Chester's tailored pockets.

Young Bobby Stupak, so awed by the wonder of the dice, was determined to make his way in the racket. Although his sisters, Nancy and Linda, would heed their father's wishes and attend college, Bobby developed an allergic reaction to authority and conventional learning at an early age.

"I was always daydreaming and looking out the window," he recalled years later. "I daydreamed of glory."

And he placed bets at every opportunity. Young Bobby began playing the numbers lottery at age nine. It's where he made his first score. He took a penny to a neighborhood grocery and handed it to the clerk. When his one-cent number turned up a winner on the thousand-number game, he won $6.

"Boy, was I taking the worst of it," Stupak remembered. "Six hundred for one on a 999-to-1 shot."

From that point on, he bet a little every day.

It was something else he shared with his father.

After Sprigle's series, Chester Stupak had a difficult time keeping his name out of the newspapers. He had become a soft touch for the police. Chester was indicted on gambling and liquor charges in December 1953. When the non-jury trial finally commenced in Judge Francis J. O'Connor's courtroom, the defense called for delay after delay. At one point, the judge permitted Chester time away from the rigors of trial to complete a Caribbean cruise. In the end, "the lucky gambler," as the press called him, was acquitted of all charges.

Even before that case was adjudicated, Stupak was again arrested on gambling charges. His luck held, and a grand jury threw out the case.

The police kept at it. Chester, meanwhile, was franchising his action at a rapid rate. By day, he ran a pinball machine outfit on the South Side. By night, the dice rolled nonstop. By the summer of 1957, he had converted a Peters Township lumber yard into a gambling den called Club 19, and another satellite casino opened up in the basement of a private home just outside the city limits on Becks Run Road.

In December 1957, Stupak was operating out of the swanky Ozark Club in the Pittsburgh suburb of West Brownsville when his one-man parade was interrupted by a police battering ram at the door. On the way to charging Stupak with keeping a gambling house, state troopers tore apart the Ozark Club, collecting evidence and intimidating everyone but the proprietor.

Then District Attorney Michael Hanna began interrogating the troopers who pulled the raid.

"You would have thought you were on trial," a trooper told a reporter.

Hanna was later accused of wrecking the investigators' "perfect case" against the smiling Stupak.

William McKee, the lieutenant who led the raid, said, "It was a good case, there's no doubt about that. We've done our part. The boys did a good job, no matter what anybody says."

Whatever went on, the result was the same: a grand jury tossed out the charges against Chester—and assigned the cost of repairing his illegal gambling hall to the county.

Then came the John James bribery case, which made banner headlines in Pittsburgh's newspapers, and surely led the police to believe that this time they had their man. In September 1958, Chester was back in court, with his partner in the numbers racket, Henry Katz, for allegedly offering hush money to James, a Pittsburgh patrolman. Far from a corrupt cop, James had been cited for bravery numerous times. He had been shot twice and stabbed once while on duty. He was a family man with a daughter at Duquesne University. James was working undercover and his effort resulted in the arrest of 17 persons connected to Pittsburgh's underground gambling rackets. Stupak and Katz were charged with bribery, conspiracy, operating a lottery, and corrupting an officer.

The first bribe attempt came in September 1956 and the first actual cash transaction occurred months later at the Chez Dee Club in Brentwood, where Stupak slyly slipped the cop $300 under the table.

Once the news got out that he had accepted bribes from the biggest gamblers in Pittsburgh and that the state had used legal but controversial phone recordings to gather further damning evidence, James emerged as a hero to some upstanding members of the community. The wiretaps would help convict several of the accused, and James' strong character hurt other defendants.

But Chester Stupak was no ordinary racketeer. Stupak and Katz hired bulldog defense attorney Louis Glasso and the fight was on. Glasso objected to the secretive nature of the case. He objected to the use of the wiretaps. He objected to the amount of money the cop accepted. He went so far as to say that defendant Katz, a longtime gambler who already had a federal tax-stamp conviction, had been lured into operating a numbers game by the officer.

"It's a terrible thing to befriend a man, eat his food, drink his drinks, and then turn on him," Glasso said.

He did not claim Stupak and Katz had not offered bribes, or that their offers were rejected. The defendants admitted as much when they took the stand in their own defense. It was, they said with a shrug, the cost of doing business.

But their attorney assured the court that the defendants had been entrapped by the deceptive cop. James promised them protection from police raids, they claimed. So they felt justified in paying him a total of $8,800.

At home, Chester's children saved newspaper clippings and—far from being mortified—laughed at the press accounts about their father. The press became obsessed with Chester's tailored suits, custom shoes, and youthful appearance.

"We got a kick out of the publicity," Bob Stupak remembered years later. "When he appeared for a court date, I just remember the jacket he had on. My sisters and me, we all laughed at the stories. He was considered dapper, and he wore a Palm Beach sports jacket to court. The press commented on it. When he got home he said, 'What the hell did I wear that goddamn jacket for?' He took the case seriously.

"My old man, he had more shoes than I'll ever have in my life. My dad got up in the morning, showered and shaved, and put on a suit. When he came downstairs for breakfast, he was dressed for the day in a suit and tie. I mean, he was well-dressed for breakfast! I don't think I saw him six times in my whole life that he didn't have a tie on. He had a wardrobe from here to China. My old man's closet was gigantic. He had more shoes than you'd see in a shoe store, more shirts, more jackets. I don't think I ever saw my dad casual."

So of course the press often commented on Chester's daily fashion statement. Although only 5-feet-7, he was a big man on the street. Imagine how the reporters crowed at his acquittal.

If the patriarch of the Stupak family was ridiculed by polite society, little Bobby never noticed. By the time he was old enough to understand what was being said about his dad, he no longer belonged to the straight world.

"When I was a kid, I thought that's what big people did—you throw dice against the wall," Bob Stupak recalled years later. "That's the way I was raised forever."

It was common for Chester and his friends to play a private game at the Sarah Street house until early in the morning. When young Bobby would come downstairs for breakfast, they would still be at it, smoking and watching the action. Florence had long ago accepted her husband's calling. The rackets supported their family in comfort; the publicity and threat of jail were facts of the life they led.

Only a square would fail to appreciate why Chester would offer money to a cop, or why it was a business expense in Pittsburgh. After all the payoffs he had made over the years, it was argued that setting up good old Chester was downright dishonest.

The 12-member jury thought so, too.

On September 13, 1958, Stupak and Katz were found not guilty on all charges. The acquittal stood even after one juror reported to the judge that she had been offered a $300 bribe if she voted on the side of the defense.

Chester Stupak, the dapper Houdini of the Pittsburgh legal system, was free again.

Lou Adams managed Chester's Lotus Club for six years. The Lotus was a members-only operation that featured a restaurant, bar, and dance floor. But members came for the action that went on upstairs. For obvious reasons, Chester was listed only as a member. Adams and Stupak usually were tipped to police racket-squad raids. They kept a hulking former police detective at the front door to keep out the riffraff and to spot undercover cops trying to blend into the scene.

"Everybody knew he was the owner, but he didn't have his name on paper," Adams said. "Chester, although a little man, had a big heart. He was a real gentleman and one of the finest guys I've ever met. As to fortitude, Chester didn't let anybody screw him or fool him."

It did not mean he ruled the Lotus with an iron fist. On the contrary.

"His theory was, 'You can't gamble if you don't have a game,' and these guys were part of the game," Adams said. "Invariably the shortstops always came back when they had money. It was an investment."

But there were limits to his generosity. He was no sucker.

Chester was upstairs at the Lotus late one night rolling dice head-to-head with two wiseguys when Adams heard a shot ring out. Rushing upstairs, Adams passed one of the shooters desperately trying to escape. When he arrived at the scene, diminutive Chester Stupak had wrestled the second, much larger man into submission. It turned out that Chester had beaten them on the square out of several thousand dollars. They shot at him and somehow missed.

"They shot at him point-blank and hit the wall," Adams said.

Instead of calling the police, Chester cooled down, obviously realizing that desperate men are dangerous men. Instead of throwing them out on the street, he bought them a drink. The gun-shooting crap shooters lived a long time, but they never crossed Chester Stupak again. And they continued to regularly lose their bankrolls at the Lotus Club.

The hustlers weren't the only ones who took a shot at Chester's cash reserves.

"A lot of police used to take advantage of Ches's generosity," Lou Adams said. "At Christmas, we used to give the regular beat man a ten-dollar bill and a bottle of booze. I'd buy ten or twelve cases of booze at Christmas just to give away. It was part of doing business, an expenditure for the heat, and most of the police were very cooperative. But at Christmas, we'd have cops from the North Side and the Hill District showing up at our door. They weren't even from the South Side, but Ches made sure we took care of them anyway."

Adams also recalled top Pittsburgh law-enforcement officials receiving up to $1,000 per month from generous Chester Stupak. The cost of doing business was expensive, indeed. Add to that the $50,000 tribute extracted from Stupak by local mob bosses, and it's no wonder Chester was such a popular man on the South Side.

Robert Stupak was born April 6, 1942, and was hard to handle from the time he was a toddler. Florence Stupak was a strong-willed mother who managed to keep the Stupak girls in line, but had a devil of a time with young Bobby, who took to skipping class at an early age at St. Adalbert Catholic School. Adalbert of Prague's life's work was characterized by failure, but his impact on others was great, Alison Jones writes in *Saints*. Adalbert was the patron saint of Polish people, but he wasn't having much luck with young Bob Stupak.

One morning at the home on Sarah Street, Florence Stupak let her 3-year-old son Bobby out to play in the yard while she worked in the kitchen. A few minutes later, she returned to find him missing and began to fret. Then she heard his small voice in the distance and really began to panic.

Her condition worsened when she spotted him at the top of the rickety fire escape that ran up the side of the three-story house. He was more than 30 feet above the ground, laughing as he climbed. When he reached the top, he ran around the roof, leaned over the side and giggled as his mother looked on in horror. Within minutes, family and friends gathered around the fire escape and made their plan to rescue the boy.

Young Bobby Stupak had attracted his first crowd.

By the time he was old enough to go to church, he began shirking his duties.

"He used to fall asleep in church. At St. Adalbert's, he had to go to mass every morning," Florence recalled. "The sister told him he wasn't allowed to have a rosary because his mind would wander. He had to take a prayer book with him to school every morning. He was always losing his prayer book.

"One day, he just couldn't find it. So, I had a little telephone book we kept our numbers in. It looked like a prayer book, so I gave him that to take to church."

Little Bobby Stupak faked it flawlessly.

He was less successful at shining his mischievous light at the church. One Saturday, the day before Easter, one of the sisters emerged from the convent to find young Bobby exiting the church.

Had some miracle of faith taken place? Had the child had an epiphany? Had he made a conversion or even an attempt at penance?

No. She soon discovered that he'd lit every candle in the church. The Easter candle-lighting ceremony would be ruined unless someone acted quickly. Instead of calling the local authorities or the priest of the parish, the nun wisely dialed up Florence Stupak, who settled the debt and saved her son's place at St. Adalbert's.

As a scrawny seven-year-old, Bobby landed his first job as a paperboy, hawking the *Pittsburgh Press* and *Post-Gazette* on the street corner. It took weeks to convince the vendor to give the undersized kid a chance, but Bobby finally was handed five copies at four cents apiece. He would sell each paper for a nickel and pocket a penny.

His first day on the job, he felt the pain of failure. He sold four papers but couldn't give away the fifth. Instead of admitting defeat, he stuffed the unused newspaper through a sewer grate and handed over his small change with a smile. He took no profit, but gained the confidence of the vendor.

"There was no way I was going to admit I couldn't do the job," he recalled decades later. "I couldn't face defeat. I couldn't let him know."

His mother might have wanted him to study hard and one day merge into the straight business world, but he would have none of it. He preferred Hollywood gangsters to the squares at St. Adalbert's. In the early years, Florence usually knew where to find her boy and often called on Lou Adams to leave the Lotus Club to comb the South Side for her wayward 11 year old.

"Bobby loved the movies," Adams said. "When he was a kid, it wasn't unusual for Bobby to sit through two showings. His mother used to call me at 11, 11:30 at night knowing where

Bobby was. She'd ask me to go get him. There were only two theaters on the South Side. So I'd go down on Carson Street where the movies were.

"The first month he opened his club in Vegas years later, I went to see him. The first thing he said to me was, 'Lou, did my mother send you to find me?'"

School, when he found his way to class, bored him. Long-time friends remember young Bob as a quiet classmate who was making book when other kids were reading them. He was a skinny boy equipped with plenty of tough talk, an endless supply of cigarettes, and a regular need for forged absence slips to give to school officials.

The law demanded that he attend school until he was 16, and he struggled to comply. Stupak became a regular customer for truant officers, who saw more of him than many of his teachers.

"I got nailed a few times," he recalled years later. "Your friends would write you up a note to take in the next day."

Three months shy of his 16th birthday, with parole clearly visible, Bob Stupak spent most of his time riding his motorcycle and working on his side jobs. He was not the kind to bag groceries at the corner store. To him, a side job meant hustling suckers, hawking discount watches from bar to bar, and watching the action on the South Side.

St. Basil's and the 9th grade beckoned, but when the chance arose to quit school, Bob Stupak took it. He purchased an even faster Harley, much to his mother's chagrin.

"When he'd go to school in the morning, I used to pray that telephone wouldn't ring," Florence said. "When he started riding motorcycles, I could barely stand it. Even today when I see anybody riding a motorcycle I bless them and make a sign of the cross. I think to myself how crazy they must be. I can't stand motorcycles. When he would go out, I couldn't sleep until I'd hear the door close and look at him and know he was okay."

With his bike racing as fast as his mind, he slicked back his hair and hit the street in the heart of the James Dean era. But the

Pittsburgh Kid was a rebel with an angle.

He carried with him an unofficial degree in math and accounting and the sort of bravado that comes from being a gambler's son. He was at home on the South Side, fed off its energy, worked its lucrative netherworld. The South Side was filled with loansharks and bookmakers, con men and rough customers, and young Bob Stupak was awed by the action. He knew every cab driver and saloon bookie. He hustled a buck in pool halls and bowling alleys in Pittsburgh and Steubenville, Ohio, 39 miles away. He played the numbers every day.

Then he met Truman Beckett at Magno's restaurant and moved up a notch on the street. In partnership with Beckett, Stupak got into the cheap-watch business, selling them at a 60 percent markup; he also became something of a small-time loanshark.

Then Bob Stupak's life started moving even faster. He began drag racing motorcycles for trophies and glory. He crashed his motorcycle often enough to break both knees. No one questioned the skinny kid's courage.

"Nobody else would go to that extreme," Stupak said years later.

Meanwhile, Florence Stupak was counting her rosary beads.

"She went out and watched me race a couple times and it cooled her off a little bit," Bob Stupak recalled. "I won when she watched, but she still didn't like it."

The result was more than one near-death experience, a couple of menacing tattoos on his skinny arms, and a six-foot trophy. He toured for a while on the drag racing circuit from Pennsylvania to Daytona, Florida. But glory was one thing; money was something else.

Bobby Stupak craved both in the worst way, and in the time of Elvis nothing assured more of both than the title of pop singer. His trips to the clubs of Steubenville had shown him where the action was, and he made up in confidence what he lacked in talent. If another Polish kid, Bobby Vinton, could make it big in pop music, then why couldn't Bobby Stupak?

But first he needed to do something about the name. "Stupak" was too ethnic and didn't exactly flow off the tongue. It was the name of a Polish kid from Pittsburgh, not a suave singing sensation or rock 'n' roll idol.

That's when it hit him. If he was going to be a star, why not advertise the fact?

And so Bobby Star was born.

He crooned love songs and snappy ballads and pulled off a genuine coup after a few short months. Through agent Marty Wax, he signed a recording contract with United Artists.

"I went into this big office in New York and it was just like you'd imagine," Stupak recalled. "Mike Stewart was the president of United Artists at the time and he said, 'Kid, I'm going to make you a big, big star.'"

Mike Stewart was a man who could get things done in New York's payola-riddled record business. He had taken four Canadians and, largely on the strength of his image-making ability alone, turned them into wholesome international singing stars called the Four Lads. If the Four Lads could succeed with their saccharine sound, surely so could one tough Polish kid.

On his way to certain stardom, the teen idol in the making needed to work on his act and his songwriting skills. He played clubs in Pittsburgh and Steubenville with mixed results. His voice wasn't smooth enough for love ballads, not strong enough for rock 'n' roll. He had the hair and the attitude, but little else.

What he needed was a gimmick. Some stars had swiveling hips. Other cool cats groomed their pompadours to perfection.

Bobby Star attracted attention with a cat of another kind—a full-grown cheetah plucked directly from the Bird and Animal Kingdom of New York. The crowds might not compare his voice to Bobby Vinton's, but Bobby Star would be remembered around the clubs of Steubenville for his rebellious streak. When one club owner banned the animal from the stage, Bobby Star seized the moment.

With television cameras capturing the action, he coolly strutted out the door of the club and onto the sidewalk, then tied the animal to a parking meter. He dropped a dime in the slot and went back about the business of being a star.

"It was too much," he recalled many years later. "We had the television stations and the newspapers covering it like it was a big deal. They loved it. There are a lot of things you can do with a gaff to get yourself known.

"When I stopped singing and started hollering I became good. I did a lot of hollering. It was okay. The kids liked it."

But something happened on the way to the top. Bobby Star was not lacking in bravado, but he was a little short on talent. His first single, "Together," fell apart immediately.

"When they released it, it was a bomb and I couldn't get in the fucking door again," Stupak said. "I was under contract, but I was done as far as they were concerned. Then I got pissed off. I walked away from something that guys would have cut off their left toe to have."

In all, he recorded eight songs for United Artists, none of which made Bobby Star shine. His attempt at a sentimental Christmas standard became a ditty called "Jake the Flake." With lyrics such as: "Here comes Jake/Jake the Flake/Jake the little white snowflake/Comin' down from the sky/To make our Christmas all white," it wasn't exactly "White Christmas."

It wasn't long before his star began to dim. Like motorcycle racing before it, singing became a low priority. He faded from the music business and at 19 years old, weighed his options. Although it promised to give him valuable insight into the psyche of the gambler, working around his father's crap game did not figure to put Bob Stupak on the fast track to business success. Running numbers and roping suckers for moneylenders was good for laughs and spending cash, but it wasn't a career for a big dreamer. Drag racing on motorcycles provided the thrills, but there wasn't much money in it and the teenager's knees already were damaged by his red-lining style. And he really wasn't much of a crooner. No, the young hustler definitely needed some straightening out.

Too late for the monastery, disinterested in university life, and with America's involvement in Vietnam a few years away, he joined the National Guard and went on active duty from November 1959 to May 1960. His service status also served to cool any problems he might have had at the time with Pittsburgh law enforcement and heat from some shadowy members of the city's illegal gambling community. At Fort Knox, Kentucky, and Fort Sill, Oklahoma, Stupak was a raw recruit, just another skinny kid growing up on the cusp of the 1960s.

He never distinguished himself in battle or saw a moment's action, but Private Stupak still managed to stand out in the sea of drab green fatigues and butch haircuts.

He was the private with the crap game. Bob Stupak may have left his childhood behind when he joined the army, but he brought his dice with him.

Once settled in at Fort Knox, he quickly realized two things. First, though his fellow soldiers hailed from all over America, most seemed willing to gamble at a moment's notice. Second, they barely understood how many dots there were on each die.

"Nobody knew that there were three ways to make a four on the dice, four ways to make a five, and six ways to make a seven," Stupak said. "They had no knowledge at all of these little cubes they were gambling with."

There was no need to shave the dice. Stupak merely adjusted the odds. The shooters figured they were getting a great deal when he offered them even money on some propositions; little did they know that the odds of making some rolls were far greater. Stupak escaped the service at the first opportunity, but he carried the lesson in human behavior with him back to Pittsburgh, then halfway around the world to Australia.

The outcome of the Stupak-Katz state trial infuriated U.S. Attorney Hubert Teitelbaum, who immediately vowed to pursue the pair. But Teitelbaum's take was different. He claimed to have specific knowledge of high-ranking Pittsburgh officials who had been accepting bribe money from gamblers for years. He also spotted an obvious flaw in Chester Stupak's business: the operator had neglected to purchase a $50 federal gambling tax stamp and did not appear to have been paying his annual 10-percent tribute to the U.S. government.

When it was implemented, the federal tax stamp at first confused and then confounded illegal gamblers and bookmakers. If they identified themselves as racketeers by purchasing the stamp, they set themselves up for future investigation. If they failed to pay their measly $50, they risked a certain federal violation and the dangerous intrusion of the Internal Revenue Service. Use of the tax stamp eventually was struck down in 1965 by the United States Supreme Court in the Marchetti and Grosso case. Convictions based on the law were overturned, but that came years too late for some big-city bookies and dice operators.

In 1963, the federal government was ready to try its luck against Chester Stupak.

After all he'd been through, it's difficult to imagine such a giant being felled by a glorified clerical error. But that is precisely what happened.

Stupak had leased a section of a building at 2124 E. Carson Street from his friend of 25 years, Ambrose Lewis. A hotel operator, Lewis was called as a witness and had to admit that he had made space available in the building for what Stupak called his Yip-Yip Club. Lewis and other witnesses testified that, yes, Stupak definitely operated a dice game at the club. But no one remembered any illegal lottery.

"The Yip-Yip Club was a nice clean place where ordinary folks could come and try their luck," Lewis said. His testimony began to take on the flavor of a testimonial for his old friend, Chester.

Had the witnesses known that the federal tax stamp was required for bookmaking and numbers, but not for craps?

A dice game violated state laws, but this was a federal case. Their collective memory proved most fortuitous for Chester. Although the press commonly called Stupak a numbers banker whose Pittsburgh empire encompassed the north and south sides of the city, he denied he was ever anything more than a dice dealer.

But the signs were right for conviction. Stupak had admitted paying off a police officer to protect a numbers network. The cop, John James, was on hand in an attempt to persuade a new jury of Stupak's grave transgression.

With federal authorities such as U.S. Attorney General Robert Kennedy making big headlines for their pursuit of gamblers and members and associates of organized crime in the early 1960s, raiding dice dens became a favorite pastime of police and a popular editorial subject for journalists.

By January 1964, Chester barely had time to hang up his coat before hearing the cops at the door of one of his operations. In fact, it was his own coat that incriminated him after police used a steel-tipped battering ram to bust down the door of the converted Bauerlein Brewery. When the authorities got around to scooping up the dice, chips, cards, and tables, they also found a sports jacket no one was interested in claiming. The ever dapper Chester Stupak had left a laundry ticket with his name on it inside the pocket of the coat.

In late 1964, more than 18 years after Chester's first gambling arrest, Federal Judge Herbert P. Sorg sentenced him to four months in prison, assessed a $2,500 fine, and placed the gambler on one year's probation.

The legal assault was far from finished. In 1966, the Pennsylvania State Police hooked up with Internal Revenue Service agents, and Stupak was on the run again. Agents seized a $10,000-a-day numbers operation from a garage at the farm of Stupak associate William Donovan. Not only was Chester arrested, but police grabbed his nephew, James Stupak, as well.

Chester was as unflappable as ever. When confronted by the police, he shrugged and said, "This is the first time I've ever been here."

But police had spotted him going in and out of the garage for weeks. He wound up serving six months in jail.

Bob Stupak saw first hand what operating illegally could do even to an accomplished angle-shooter like his father. Cross the line, and the authorities eventually will get you. Not everyone can be bought or cajoled. Even the best hustlers pay the price sooner or later.

Young Bob Stupak was nothing if not resourceful. For years he had noticed a decades-old racket that operated just inside the law. The hook was simple, really. An enterprising soul approaches restaurants, cafes, and nightclubs with a pitch: For the promise of discounts on meals and services, their establishment is included at no charge in a big book of valuable coupons offered to prospective customers. The restaurant owner benefits by the increased business and the consumer gets to eat on the cheap. The man who puts the two together makes money by selling the coupon books, with their estimated hundreds of dollars of value, for less than a sawbuck.

Stupak's first book was a crude little number that offered discounts on goods, services, and entertainment from Pittsburgh's "most respected" establishments. That is, those establishments he could enlist in his program. The first book featured $100 in value and sold for $6.95. It was immediately successful and led to more expansive versions that included free car washes, two-for-one meals, movie tickets, bowling, and beauty-parlor services.

"I'd put a book together, then go out on the road and sell it," Stupak remembered. "I'd come home as soon as I built up a bankroll."

Where motorcycles and nightclub singing had failed to provide him with the money his nonstop lifestyle and growing gambling habit demanded, the coupon books promised scads of fast cash. He quickly turned himself into the uncrowned king of discount coupons. Coupon books had been a Pittsburgh street business since the 1920s, but Stupak was well on his way to reestablishing the system and hustling it as never before.

Chester, of course, didn't need to promote his business. His action was still wide open, which by the mid-1960s had begun to make Pittsburgh police and prosecutors more than a little nervous. Between election-year political grandstanding and federal revenue agents sniffing for scandal, smiling Chester Stupak was being squeezed. The beat cops might have wanted to ignore his second-floor crap game and countryside casino, but they could not ignore the presence of federal law enforcement. Once again they were forced to crack down on the Mayor of the South Side.

About the time Chester was convicted for the first time, Bob Stupak began making trips to Las Vegas.

"The first time I came to Vegas, it was '64," Stupak recalled later. "I sat down in a restaurant at 4 a.m. and the waitress said, 'What are you having, sir? Breakfast, lunch, or dinner?' It was 4 a.m., and she was asking, 'Breakfast, lunch, or dinner?' I thought, 'God made this town for me.'

"That's when I became absolutely mesmerized with Las Vegas. It seemed like the city was tailor made for me."

But he would quickly learn another valuable lesson: Las Vegas was not a town for the impatient or faint of heart.

Bob Stupak began his Las Vegas education not long after that first visit. The occasion was a score with a coupon book worth $250 that he sold like crazy for $12.95. He was making plenty of money and decided to spend some. That meant a dice trip to Las Vegas. He packed a bag and grabbed the first early-morning jet heading west. He called ahead and booked a room at Caesars Palace, but by the time he arrived at McCarran Field a little after noon, his clothes looked like he had slept in them. At the airport, he laid out a couple hundred bucks and bought himself the classic Vegas-Guy uniform: wild sports shirt with an open collar, gaudy pants, and white shoes.

"After changing right there at the airport, I felt like an altogether different guy," Stupak said many years later. "I was just excited about being there."

Resembling a cross between a pimp and a professional golfer, Stupak hit Caesars running. He dumped his bags at the bell desk, toked the bellman, took out a $10,000 marker, and drank in the scene.

For men with the true heart of a gambler, the air is different in Las Vegas. For card and dice junkies, its alkaline waters are more rejuvenating than the baths at Lourdes.

Stupak hit the tables the way a boozer hits the juice.

And the tables hit him back.

Caesars Palace, the home of his hero Frank Sinatra and enough Wiseguys to fill a Hall of Fame mug book, was rapidly busting him out. He bet and lost, bet and lost, bet and lost, lost, lost.

"Soon I took out markers for everything I had, and I blew it all," Stupak said. "I was flat busted—blew my credit entirely."

The $10,000 gone, he shuffled back to the credit manager and managed to get another $2,000. In a few moments, he went quiet again. Now he was down $12,000.

It was not yet 1 p.m. He had been in Las Vegas less than one hour. It had taken him longer to get his bags and hail a cab to the hotel than it had to exhaust his entire credit line plus 20 percent. He felt as if every sharp gambler in the place was watching him.

"Here I was in my new clothes at Caesars, and I was flat broke," he recalled in his 1985 book *Stupak on Craps*. "I didn't even get to my room, didn't have a drink, didn't go to the bar, didn't go to dinner, didn't go to a show. I didn't do anything. The only thing I did was get mad at myself, at Las Vegas, at the world."

He returned to the bell desk, where the bellhop clearly remembered him and his $5 tip. After all, less than 60 minutes had elapsed. He ordered his bags, shook off the bellhop's bewildered look, left the building, and refused to change his mind about leaving Las Vegas. His Vegas vacation had cost $12,000 plus airfare and had lasted all of an hour. At those prices, he couldn't afford to change his mind.

He stewed over the loss all the way back to Pittsburgh and for days afterward. The Pittsburgh Kid had acted like the biggest sucker ever to chew a hayseed. He had tossed his accomplished money-management skills like snake eyes the minute he walked through the door. He had allowed the scent of the action and the speed of the city to cloud his thinking, something that happened to tourists, but was not supposed to affect a genuine wise-guy gambler like Stupak.

It was then he realized that the only way he was ever going to make a consistent score in a Las Vegas casino was to own one.

Bob Stupak's life left little time for sleep. He dealt coupon books during the day, staked crap games after dark. The popularity of the coupons enabled him to generate fast cash and live a deceivingly high lifestyle. He drove a canary-yellow Cadillac with matching interior. When he pulled up to the Stardust Lounge in Pittsburgh with a date on one arm and a $2,000 wad of cash in one pocket, he never failed to be noticed. Other men scuffled for their livings, and the young Stupak seemed to come by his so easily.

It didn't hurt that he peeled off a $100 bill and bought a round of drinks for the house. Surely his source of cash was as infinite as it was illegal.

In reality, everything he owned was either in his pocket, on his back, or in the trunk of the Cadillac. But there was no need to let anyone in on the secret, especially not the small-stakes crapshooters who couldn't resist taking a shot at the young punk with the yellow ride and the ready cash. So, he obliged them. He picked them up like school children, escorted them to the basement of his family's Brownsville Road home, and cleaned them out as fast as he could. Then he drove them back to the Stardust, bought them a drink, and bid them goodnight.

"You couldn't miss the car in those days," he said. "I had $2,000 in my pocket and the Cadillac. As far as they were concerned, I had millions. It was all show business. Everybody wanted to take a shot. Why? Because I had the bankroll."

And the patter to go with it. In a pinch, he made up rules as he went along, brushing off doubters with, "These are downtown Vegas rules."

"I had a lot of fun with that," he said. "I broke a lot of guys. And I got broke myself once. A bunch of guys cleaned me out of my whole fucking bankroll, then flew to Vegas and came back empty. Oh, that pissed me off. But most of the time it was okay."

It kept him in spending cash, which he often deposited at the region's racetracks. The horses didn't always run his way, but as usual, Bob Stupak had an angle worked out that narrowed the odds against him considerably. He booked the bets of his pals, who spent freely and believed that, since Stupak was the youngest in the bunch, he ought to be in charge of running the wagers to the betting window. Instead, he handled the bets himself, disappeared until after the race was over, paid off the winners at track odds, and pocketed the losing bets. At Pittsburgh Meadows and Waterford Park, there was no easier way to make a small score.

"I never had a steady job," Bob Stupak once said of his youth. "All the jobs I had were self-inflicted."

If he had held a steady job, his life might have taken an entirely different course. While running the street, Stupak met and fell in love with Gerry Bova, the daughter of a Western Union worker. He bought her a two-and-a-half-carat diamond ring and the couple was engaged to be married. Instead of going down the aisle, though, the experience led to a trip halfway across the world.

"She said she couldn't marry anyone without a job," Stupak recalled.

Not long after that, Bob Stupak got into yet another motorcycle accident. He received a $3,200 insurance settlement and had a decision to make: he could either buy a new racing motor-cycle or take his coupon book parade on the road. He decided to buy the bike, but it already had been sold to someone else.

By this time, not yet 24, Stupak was working a number of angles in Pittsburgh, but the town was growing too familiar. On the advice of his father, Bob Stupak struck out for Australia.

The son of a gambler could not have picked a more fitting destination. By some accounts, Australians bet more than any other English-speaking people. Whether on the two-up coin-toss, the annual Melbourne Cup race, or in one of a growing number of casinos, Aussies have always had plenty of ways to risk their money. Although not always lawful—two-up, for example, was illegal until 1983—gambling is woven into the fabric of the nation.

"Gambling is, quite simply, the national passion and the most obvious dislocating force at every level," Australian author Richard Walsh once wrote.

Australian novelist Frank Hardy observed in *The Four-Legged Lottery*: "Gambling in Australia. Where else in the world are jockeys more revered than musicians or scientists? Where else in the world are the people's clubs dependent for their existence on poker machines? Where else in the world is a famous racehorse stuffed and enshrined in a museum?

"... From the very beginning, life was a gamble among the convicts and settlers. Our country was pioneered in the spirit of a gambler's throw."

Years later, Stupak would put it simply. He wasn't dodging the law or the draft when he set off for Australia.

"I wanted adventure," he said.

With the $3,200 insurance settlement, plus a wad of cash from his father, Bob Stupak set out to conquer Australia one coupon-book buyer at a time.

"I went over on a shoestring, but I started making money almost immediately," he said later. "I've just been very lucky in business."

Lucky, but more than a little unorthodox by Australian standards. Aussie authorities had a devil of a time figuring out where all Stupak's money came from—and where it was going. His accounting procedures were to say the least unusual and, more importantly, his method of paying taxes odd. Melbourne officials might have been new to the coupon game, but they knew plenty about taxes and were well capable of following a paper trail where one existed.

Stupak wasn't the only American seeking fortune in Australia. Bally Corporation had sent its emissaries Down Under in an attempt to expand its slot machine empire. But Stupak's goals were not quite as expansive. His coupon club was ideally suited to his cocky personality. He knew that he wasn't really selling value to either the restaurant owner or the patron; he was selling the idea of value. And he was selling himself, which was fast becoming his greatest skill.

Victoria police were almost immediately suspicious of Stupak's game, but as they watched his one-man empire grow, it became apparent that merchants and consumers were participating freely in his coupon program. His books, filled with two-for-one meal deals, were becoming increasingly popular, especially after he generated enough of a following to advertise and expand his discount services.

Years later, even the most experienced detectives with Victoria's Major Fraud Group would recall no problems with Stupak's program worthy of opening a large-scale investigation. Their files, in fact, failed to retain even his name.

The Melbourne Office of Fair Trade and Business, the city's version of the Better Business Bureau, also gave Stupak a pass. The office, responsible for investigating illegal and unsavory businesses, had no record in its expansive database of Stupak, who was fast becoming known as the Yankee Invader in some Aussie circles.

His coupon books were catching on, but Stupak was impatient. He wanted the success to come more quickly and was encountering opposition from Australian business owners who were reluctant to trust a Yank. So he enlisted chapters of the

Junior Chamber of Commerce in cities across the country to participate in his "Business Sampler" program, which not only offered the usual goods-and-services coupon pitch, but also generated income for the service organizations.

He accomplished this feat in a way that, by late-1960s standards, was nothing short of progressive. Instead of the usual face-to-face sales meetings, in which his youthful appearance and Junior Elvis wardrobe were bound to alienate some skeptics, he produced a movie that extolled the vast virtues of the Business Sampler program. The self-produced soundtrack was hip, the voice-over respectfully Australian. The star, of course, was Bob Stupak.

And it worked.

From Adelaide to Sydney, hundreds of businesses warmed up to his snazzy coupon pitch. Sitting at the top of the pyramid, he raked in the cash.

As in Pittsburgh, the money came and went. He threw lavish parties, ate at the best restaurants, tipped a week's pay, and established himself as an American playboy.

The major criticism of Stupak's operation was the loose accounting. He was, after all, the son of a backroom casino man who kept the day's winnings in his head and hip pocket. Though it was no sin in the Australia of the late 1960s, such shoddy practices would qualify as trouble spots when he eventually moved back to the United States and attempted to open a casino in Las Vegas.

Stupak traveled widely through Australia during the seven years he made it his home. It was there he met and became infatuated with Annette Suna. In his mid-20s, he was more interested in making money than settling down, but when Annette became pregnant, he found himself faced with a tough decision. He thought of moving on, even returning to the United States, but instead the young hustler couldn't leave behind the woman who carried his child.

"I was Catholic and so I did the Catholic thing," Stupak recalled years later. "I married her."

It wasn't an understated elopement, but a grand affair. Stupak was in love with the camera and managed to finagle permission from authorities to shoot footage for the wedding movie from the top of the Sydney Harbor Bridge. After the wedding, the Stupaks embarked on a world tour. They traveled in style from the tropics to Europe. Bob Stupak's ingenuity and eighth-grade education had taken him around the world at an age most young men were just getting out of college.

He was 25. His daughter, Nicole Stupak, was born several months later. Both Bob and Annette knew the relationship would not last; they were married less than two years. But Bob was proud of his baby girl and promised to remain in contact. Years later, Nicole Stupak would go to work for her father in Las Vegas.

While living in Australia, Stupak also met the woman who would become his second wife, Sandra Joyce Wilkinson. Blond-haired and outgoing, she adored the infinitely confident American who courted her. Sandy Stupak eventually would emerge as a fixture at the Las Vegas poker tournaments to which Stupak would become addicted. (She was nicknamed "Lady Maverick" after winning a high-stakes Texas hold 'em poker game in 1984 at Binion's Horseshoe.) Like many of the women in Bob Stupak's life, she was seen as a classy, calming influence, albeit an ultimately unsuccessful one. Stupak married her in 1971 and they remained together until 1985. She gave him two children, Nevada and Summer, and supported his wild acts of self-promotion.

"Bob has always been Bob. You know, rough around the edges and as cocky as can be," a longtime friend of Stupak recalled. "But Sandy, she was a nice lady. She knew how to act in public. And I think she had a head for figures. She wasn't obnoxious, as Stupak could be on occasion. I think she did her best to complement him, but that wasn't always easy. Bob could be pretty wild, drinking and carrying on. With Bob, you never knew which set of manners he was going to bring with him. But Sandy, she was a nice lady. Pretty, too."

Bob Stupak resided in Australia off and on for seven years before returning to Pittsburgh. All the while he dreamed of going back to the Strip and breaking into gambling's major leagues. By 1971, he had plenty of Australian dollars to exchange and big plans for a casino of his own. But it would take more than a bankroll and bravado to make it in Las Vegas.

TWO

The Million-to-One Shot

On its best day, Bob Stupak's Million Dollar Historic Gambling Museum & Casino was a gaudy little slot joint built on the site of an auto dealership.

For its owner, the homely operation represented the sort of legitimacy that had eluded Chester Stupak most of his life. Although it was true, as his son liked to brag, that everyone on the South Side of Pittsburgh adored smiling Chester Stupak, the dapper man's lengthy arrest record precluded him from making the transition from lovable Pennsylvania outlaw to legitimate Nevada casino man. The state's unofficial gaming-license grace period, during which former bookmakers, bootleggers, and leg-breakers could be approved, had ended years earlier. Although once-notorious men such as Moe Dalitz, Benny Binion, and Israel "Icepick Willie" Alderman found refuge in Nevada's state-regulated industry, Chester Stupak would never be able to join them. If he were ever to walk into a Stupak casino in Las Vegas, it would have to be owned by his son.

Using the bankroll he built in Australia and collected from Chester Stupak and his friends—a total of $120,000 cash and another $180,000 in personal assets—Bob Stupak moved to Las Vegas in 1971. Unlike his father, he would do it right: face the licensing scrutiny and obtain the state's official approval. It wouldn't be easy. The politics of gaming is a most intricate system that far transcends the regulatory process and state statutes.

It wasn't a simple matter of filling out the right forms; Stupak had to meet the right people, hire the proper attorney, weave his way through a hundred potential pitfalls, and project a business-like manner that was far from his own partying persona.

After arriving in Las Vegas, Stupak had trouble settling on a residence that fit his ambition. He was used to full maid service in Australia's best hotel suites, but he had to nurse his bankroll if he was going to survive in southern Nevada. He stayed a few days in a downtown apartment, then attempted to land a cut-rate deal from Marv Silbman at Caesars Palace.

"I'm not coming to gamble," Stupak assured the wily casino man. "I just need a place to stay until I get settled."

Silbman made him an offer too good to refuse: $10 a day at the sweetest resort on the Strip. Full service for a sawbuck.

Stupak couldn't believe his luck.

But Silbman knew human nature too well. In no time, Stupak was down at the tables blowing his bankroll at breakneck speed. After a few days, Stupak pried himself away from the crap tables long enough to relocate to the Bali Hai Motel, where the temptations were considerably reduced.

For the first few weeks, Stupak couldn't get out of his own way. He bought a shiny new Cadillac for $9,000 and had it delivered to Caesars, but before he drove it a mile a valet attendant accidentally smashed into it with a guest's vehicle. The car was totaled.

He continued to throw his money around, but got sloppy one night while hanging out with a local party girl. He wound up getting robbed at gunpoint of $13,000. The money was quickly recovered by police, only to be released to the defendant by a slippery local judge. For Stupak, the loss was an expensive wakeup call. He wasn't in Pittsburgh any more.

Stupak had some money and street savvy, but he was a long way from Vegas respectability. He needed to learn the local playing field, and quickly, if he was going to succeed. Rather than joining the Chamber of Commerce, he devised a plan to become acquainted with the real Las Vegas. He took out a classified advertisement in the local newspapers:

> Investments Wanted. Australian businessman with six to
> seven figures to invest looking for business opportunities.

Stupak was inundated with inquiries from every grifter and
wiseguy in the city, as well as a few legitimate entrepreneurs.
Within months of taking out his advertisement, he heard about
local musician Paul Lowden's desire to put together a group of
investors to purchase the struggling Hacienda on the south end
of the Strip. Stupak contacted Lowden and immediately agreed
to invest in the project. It was, he thought, an ideal way to gain
entry into the Las Vegas of his dreams. But as the deal drew
nearer, Lowden grew more distant. Instead of making good on
his deal with Stupak, Lowden found another investor in Allen
Glick, whose Argent Corp. would go on to own not only the
Hacienda but the Stardust, Fremont, and Marina as well, before
government investigators uncovered a massive casino skimming
operation connected to the Chicago mob and other Midwestern
organized crime groups. Lowden, whose company today owns
the Santa Fe Hotel and Casino in Las Vegas, was never impli-
cated in the case.

Although the Hacienda deal fell through, Stupak benefited
greatly from the experience by meeting former Nevada Governor Grant Sawyer, an attorney associated with the sale and,
through Sawyer, respected Las Vegas attorney Ralph Denton.
Denton would remain Stupak's attorney for the next 25 years.

He continued to build his contacts.

While negotiating for the purchase of Nishon's Cocktail
Lounge and Supper Club, owned by Nish Kerkorian, Stupak became acquainted with attorney Harry Reid. Reid represented
Kerkorian, older brother of Kirk Kerkorian, and was able to
smooth introductions to Clark County Sheriff Ralph Lamb, one
of the most powerful elected officials in the state and chairman

of the board that issued southern Nevada's liquor and gaming licenses. Stupak wisely maintained friendly relationships with Reid, who went on to become Nevada's senior U.S. Senator, and Lamb, who was sheriff until 1979 and remains one of the most recognizable men in the community.

At the restaurant, which Stupak renamed Chateau Vegas, the new owner attempted to solve the many mysteries of restaurant ownership, while simultaneously playing Nish Kerkorian at gin, trying to beat the old owner out of the $220,000 note he held on the club.

"Neither one of us was a particularly good gin player," Stupak recalled. "On a scale of one to ten, Nish was about a two. I was about a three, but that was enough of an edge for me."

Creating a place with atmosphere, one that assured Stupak of being cast in just the right light, wasn't easy. But the Chateau Vegas filled the bill.

With its shadowy ambience and casino clientele, the restaurant on Convention Center Drive not far from the Strip was popular with a late-night crowd that included some of the city's most notorious characters. The idea of owning a popular restaurant was one thing; turning a profit in one was something else. It was a lesson Stupak learned quickly.

"It took me about two months to find out that was a mistake," he said later. "The place always seemed to be full and my accountant kept telling me how much I was losing. I knew it would only be a matter of time before I sold it."

Everyone in Las Vegas knew the real action was on the Strip, and Stupak itched to invest there. But without a local mentor or friendly savings and loan to guide him, he found himself playing in the equivalent of a high-stakes dice game. With the Teamsters Central States Pension Fund lending millions to its favorite entrepreneurs, Las Vegas was rapidly expanding. Stupak believed the action was destined to expand north of Sahara Avenue.

Then came what he perceived to be his big break. Using his own bankroll and money borrowed from Chester and his Pittsburgh pals, Bob Stupak purchased a 1.5-acre parcel on the site of the old Todkill/Bill Hayden Lincoln Mercury dealership for $218,000.

While a long way from the heart of the Strip or the center of Glitter Gulch, the joint's location at 2000 Las Vegas Boulevard made some sense. Thanks to poor planning by city road survey-ors, that spot on the boulevard was something of a crossroads. Several busy arterials—Main Street, Las Vegas Boulevard, and St. Louis Avenue—converged in a tangle of asphalt chaos at Bob Stupak's front door. He might have lacked the college educa-tion of the city's best known young operators and the political juice and big-time financing of its established bosses, but by purchasing the land he figured he'd pulled off a genuine coup right under their noses.

His few Las Vegas contacts immediately chided him.

"Hey, when I came here to live, I wanted a joint," Stupak recalled years later. "I wanted to find a place on the Strip. I rode up and down and there was a for sale sign right here. So I bought the property. I'd been here about six months. And I thought I was on the Strip. So I told some guys I bought 2000 Las Vegas Boulevard. And they said to me, 'You stupid schmuck. You're not on the Strip! The Strip starts at Sahara Avenue.'

"I said, 'I don't see no signs saying the Strip stops here!'

"When I opened up, the Stardust was at the heart of the Strip. I was a lot closer to the Stardust than the Hacienda, or even the Tropicana or Marina."

But he failed to appreciate the fact that the Strip defied com-mon geographical explanation. Las Vegas Boulevard might stretch across the city, but the Strip's boundaries were clearly, if unofficially, defined and Sahara Avenue was its northernmost border. It was a stretch of road controlled by a small group of hardened casino men, some of whom had connections in the American underworld. They protected their territory and per-centage of the industry as if it were sacred turf, as if their lives depended on it. Bob Stupak was in miles over his head.

To those unfamiliar with Nevada's regulatory process,

Stupak's late 1973 licensing investigation might have been a source of wonderment. When he visited Pittsburgh, chief investigating agent Gary Reese found plenty of illegal gambling in Bob Stupak's life. But establishing the source of Stupak's bankroll would prove a challenge.

Reese was an accomplished investigator, but even a blind man could have found Chester Stupak's lovably notorious dice operation. Coming from the only state in America where gambling was legal, Reese recoiled at the sight of wide-open wagering. Could the local police actually not know about Chester's Place?

Of course not. Reese later recalled the lukewarm greeting his agents received from local authorities. In part because of their status as something other than traditional law enforcement, in part because they were walking into a way of operating that was far different than Nevada's regulatory system, they kept a low profile and pretended not to be flabbergasted by the Pittsburgh style of gambling.

"It didn't resemble one of our casinos," Reese said. "But it was wide open. But how can you punish a son for the activities of his father?"

Bob Stupak, meanwhile, called his father and told him to prepare for visitors from Nevada.

"They went to the game," Bob Stupak recalled. "They had no trouble getting into the club. He was nice to them because of me. They hung around and the whole bit.

"When they left they went right to the police station and put the police on the spot. I don't blame them for going to investigate, but they didn't have to go to the police. My dad's crap game wasn't exactly a secret on the South Side."

Then there were Stupak's Australia years to consider. Stupak's licensing investigation came at the same time Nevada gaming agents were preparing to travel to Australia to investigate Bally Corporation, whose slot machine expansion had come under scrutiny by that country's law enforcement. The exhaustive investigation eventually would lead to the forced retirement of a key Bally official who had maintained longtime relationships with organized crime figures. Stupak was on the back burner, and Reese later recalled the agents spending only a few days investigating the Australian coupon business and what readily appeared to be a poorly designed accounting system.

Although the Control Board might have been concerned with Stupak's tax and accounting problems, it had little difficulty recommending approval of his gaming license.

Bob Stupak was approved to operate the Million Dollar Historic Gambling Museum on November, 15, 1973, and received his license the following February. That month he insured the museum at 2000 Las Vegas Boulevard through the Fireman's Fund American Corporation for $200,000 and added policies for $80,000 in personal property, $5,000 in office equipment, and $100,000 in cash. It was little enough coverage for a place that would boast of having $1 million on display.

The casino's signs began a Stupak tradition. In a city known throughout the world for its overstated billboards and gaudy signage, the tiny Million Dollar Historic Gambling Museum immediately took its place among the most brazen. Before the joint had opened its doors, the proprietor had workers paint an enormous sign the length of the building, featuring a buxom bikini-clad babe straddling the M and tossing cash at passersby.

BOB STUPAK'S WORLD FAMOUS
MILLION DOLLAR HISTORIC GAMBLING MUSEUM
WORLD'S BIGGEST JACKPOT

Another billboard read:

SEE WHAT A $100,000.00 BILL LOOKS LIKE

"The name was about 10 feet longer than the casino," Stupak would recall years later.

The Million Dollar Historic Gambling Museum might have lacked a prime location, big advertising budget, and even a handful of hotel rooms, but it did not lack for overstatement.

In a city jammed with hyperbolic sales pitches, Stupak borrowed from everyone. He appeared to admire Horseshoe patriarch Benny Binion most. Binion's customers stood in line to get their picture taken in front of $1 million under glass, so Stupak designed a "wall of cash." He also installed a special altar for players daring enough to try his big slot machine, which was touted as offering the "World's Richest Jackpot." The big payoff: $250,000.

"There's no place in the world where anyone can put a dollar in a slot machine, pull the handle, and have the chance of winning a quarter of a million dollars," he said, falling into the long tradition of Las Vegas operators whose gift for numbers was surpassed only by their gift of gab.

Photographs of legendary Las Vegans, including Bugsy Siegel, peered at tourists from the walls that were not covered in cash. Stupak also offered suckers a gratis gander at a rare $100,000 bill, or at least a reasonable facsimile. (Alas, Stupak later admitted the bill was a fake.) Stupak's clip joint touted the world's only two-reel slot machine, and another that paid off in automobiles. The club's "Shower of Money" machine would allow players the opportunity to scoop up as much as $1,000.

The wall of money, an estimated 60,000 $1 bills, was pure Horseshoe.

"We've made arrangements for visitors to have free photographs taken in front of the money," Stupak said. "The pictures certainly will make an excellent souvenir for the folks back home."

He claimed his small club would have $1 million on display, something sure to draw gawking Midwesterners to the north side of Sahara Avenue and Las Vegas Boulevard, an area of the city no one ever called the Strip. He claimed his club would become no less than "the finest repository of gaming history in the world" and separate tourists from a few dollars along the way.

Although as gaudy as anything on the Strip, it was a humble operation with only 15 slot machines, a few antique green felt tables, casino chips, and wall-to-wall gimmicks. The Million

Dollar Historic Gambling Museum opened on March 31, 1974, as a dolled-up slot joint, but it immediately fell victim to its mediocre location. His total overhead: $397 a day.

And it was a good thing. The museum's parking lot was much fuller when it was a car lot.

Not that Stupak didn't try.

Once he realized his $250,000 jackpot had failed to capture the imagination of wayward visitors, he decided to up the ante. If $250,000 on a dollar machine wouldn't work, surely a $50,000 jackpot on a nickel machine would do the trick. Although such lucrative payoffs would become common two decades later, not even the biggest casino bosses offered such impressive jackpots in 1974. The upstart Stupak began touting his magical Million-to-One machine.

"We believe that this slot machine will be in use 24 hours a day," he boasted. "Where else can the average guy get a chance to end his financial worries for only a nickel?"

It was a good question. Not even Stupak knew how he would pay off a couple of lucky winners—most of his savings was dumped into renovating the building—but that minor detail wasn't as important as improving his bottom line and attracting a few customers through the door.

The curious came to gawk at the faux $100,000 bill and try their luck at the behemoth slot machine, but more tourists were interested in the nearby massage parlor, the topless bar to the north, and the string of prostitute-infested motels that still grace the strand of Las Vegas Boulevard between Sahara Avenue and Fremont Street.

With his slot joint struggling, Stupak kept hustling. He set his sights on the Sinabar Lounge on Ogden Avenue, a grimy operation that was zoned for table games. If he moved quickly, Stupak might be able to expand his low-rent empire with the Sinabar.

As always, Stupak's best game was self-promotion. In an era when some Las Vegas casino operators were afraid to be quoted by the press, Stupak courted the media and managed to get a

guest spot on the popular television show of the era, "To Tell
The Truth." Only Peggy Cass guessed that the baby-faced young
man in the powder-blue leisure suit was the upstart owner of
the Million Dollar Historic Gambling Museum.

To generate a little publicity, Stupak posed for a promotional
photograph lighting his cigar with a dollar bill. The picture
wound up being published by the *National Enquirer*. The tabloid, normally filled with sensational celebrity stories and wild
predictions from starry-eyed clairvoyants, featured the photo
above a caption: "Bob Stupak has money to burn."

They might have blown their predictions of the outcome of
the presidential race, movie-star marital breakups, or UFO
sightings, but the *Enquirer* prognosticators were right on the
money where Stupak was concerned.

At 7:40 p.m. on May 21, 1974, tourists on the sidewalk across
from the Million Dollar Historic Gambling Museum noticed
smoke rising from the back of the building. Witnesses would
give conflicting statements regarding what happened next. Some
saw smoke also begin to pour forth from the front of the building.

Within minutes, black smoke had billowed high into the
balmy evening. Suddenly, everyone in Las Vegas was noticing
Bob Stupak's first casino.

Nine units from the Las Vegas Fire Department converged
on the scene. A hook-and-ladder truck unfolded and firefighters
blasted the blaze from above as well as from ground level. Police blocked traffic along Las Vegas Boulevard and Sahara, and
automobiles backed up for miles. In minutes more than 1,000
people stood outside to watch Stupak's dream disintegrate.

Stupak appeared hysterical at the scene. His big chance at
Vegas stardom was going up in smoke with hundreds of people
watching. There were tears in his eyes.

Reporters immediately sought him out.

"How did you get the money you invested in the Museum?" one asked, alluding to the rumor that Stupak had been bankrolled by his dice-dealer father and his friends.

"I busted my ass to get it," he said.

As if to inadvertently illustrate how poor business was going, the joint's assistant manager, Dave Strawser, told a reporter that no customers and only five employees were in the place when the fire broke out. Strawser was quick to offer his opinion that the fire had started in the museum's attic air-conditioning unit.

The blaze was ruled suspicious even before the last flame was snuffed.

Damage estimates ranged from $500,000 to $2 million. Smoke and water damage ruined the first floor. The second floor, where the fire had broken out, was gutted.

The fire destroyed the bogus $100,000 bill. Firefighters concentrated on keeping the flames from burning up the genuine bucks. They rescued large sections of the greenback wallpaper and piled the plastic-encased cash on the hood of a car. Stupak cried over the soggy wallpaper, the lost revenue, and the lost potential. The historical museum was itself history, and Bob Stupak had some tough questions to answer.

The next morning, Stupak, who had worked so hard to attract the media, woke to this *Las Vegas Sun* banner headline:

STRIP CASINO MUSEUM
DESTROYED BY BLAZE

The *Las Vegas Review-Journal* was more cynical:

ARSON PROBE BEGUN
IN CASINO BLAZE HERE

Las Vegas Fire Chief Jerry Miller said his department had tried to get Stupak to install fire walls in the place to avoid the sort of rapid spread that occurred, but the casino owner had balked. Within a week, Miller's crew of investigators had failed to determine the precise cause of the blaze.

"A lot of unaccountable things have been given to us by witnesses," Miller said. "One individual said he saw the fire start simultaneously in the front and in the rear of the building and another said there was a person in the attic area 15 minutes before the fire started.

"I've never had a fire as crazy as this one in all my life. The owner said he had no insurance on the building the night of the fire, but we checked and found that he was fully insured."

The chief's confusion was understandable. First, authorities had allowed Stupak to open despite a long list of fire-code violations. Inspectors recommended fire walls be installed in key areas and ordered the removal of extension cords and shoddy wiring leading to slot machines. The recommendation was not followed by the Las Vegas City Commission, and Stupak was allowed to operate while he made a good-faith effort to correct the problems. Second, the best witnesses couldn't agree on the source of the smoke. Third, although it's true Stupak was insured, the policies barely covered his financial investment at the tiny casino.

What few workers remained were kept busy attempting to separate the $1 bills from plastic wallpaper. Although the salvage job drew inquiring press photographers, Stupak was unable to take advantage of the moment. He had nothing left to promote.

The summer of 1974 was as scorched as the museum, and Stupak struggled to remain in the game. In September, he filed insurance claims for $200,000 in losses on the building, $76,700 for equipment, and another $20,000 for cash and office furnishings. It seemed little enough, but the insurance company wasn't buying.

By Thanksgiving, he had decided to resurrect the Million Dollar Historic Gambling Museum & Casino, but he also was busy cleaning up the care-worn Sinabar Lounge after purchasing it from John A. "Slim" Ewing." The location near Fremont Street's Glitter Gulch was no worse than the Las Vegas Boule-

vard site, but with arson rumors circulating, Stupak found few
friends on the Nevada Gaming Commission.

"Your track record is not too great," Commissioner Clair
Haycock told Stupak.

Although he was already licensed, his rumored problems in
Australia briefly became the focus of the commission's attention.

"He had a partnership situation there that caused questions
with taxes," Control Board Chairman Phil Hannifan explained.

Commissioner Peter Echeverria added, "You were cooperative in our investigation and based on that I will go along. But if
anything happens, you are in trouble."

It would not be the last time those words would echo through
a gaming hearing involving Bob Stupak.

The atmosphere at the Sinabar was shadowy. It became a
favorite hangout for downtown dealers and wiseguy gamblers.
Although he had his mind set on returning to Las Vegas Boulevard, Stupak was at home in the cozy lounge with its slots and
four table games. The Sinabar would be Stupak's laboratory. It
was there he began to experiment with blackjack variations that
would pay big dividends in years to come.

"I had three '21' tables, one crap table, half a dozen slot machines, and a bar," Stupak recalled later. "It was directly across
the street from the California Hotel.

"It was a difficult time because it was a very small casino,
and it was very hard to generate business. One time I got a bright
idea—I used to get a lot of dealers that worked at the Fremont
Hotel. At 6 o'clock they used to come into this small place and
have a few drinks before going home. I wanted to generate some
business. So I decided to deal both cards face up—regular blackjack, no rule changes—just both cards face up. I put a sign in the
break room of the Fremont Hotel announcing that we are going
to be showing both cards from 6 to 6:30. At 6:01, all three games
were filled with Fremont dealers. So I instantly brought business in. It went for a half hour and when the clock rang, the
dealers started dealing normally; everybody got up and cashed

in their chips. I went from three full games to none. I wound up losing about six hundred dollars on bets ranging from two to ten dollars.

"But my philosophy was, since they played and got up when the alarm clock went off, we'll just keep playing. I tried it again the next day with basically the same results. And that was the end of that experiment. It was over. I just forgot about it."

Stupak was again learning his lesson in the power of possessing the right location, since the Sinabar, like the Million-Dollar Museum, sat in a mediocre spot. It also suffered from another malady—the lack of a kitchen. Dealers wanted to eat as well as drink when they got off work, but Stupak's lounge had no room to expand. So, he did the next best thing. He ordered out.

Stupak collected menus from neighboring restaurants and provided his customers with arguably the most eclectic variety of entrees available in the city. The fact he had to dispatch an employee to retrieve the meals was not mentioned to his satisfied customers, who must have wondered about the Sinabar's magical chef.

"When somebody wanted something to eat, he'd run next door," a friend recalled. "He'd get Chinese food from a Chinese place. There were always rumors that Bob was carrying in the food."

In July, Stupak found what he believed was a much improved spot for his gambling museum at 735 Las Vegas Boulevard South on the site of an Orange Julius stand. It was still a few blocks north of the previous location, but at least he would be back on the playing field—even if he was requesting only six slot machines in the whole place. This time, officials weren't about to let him open without full approval of fire-safety and building inspectors.

But Stupak had more pressing problems. Fireman's Fund

rejected his $297,000 claim, and he rejected the company's $158,000 settlement offer. Having reached an impasse, the insurance company in March 1975 attempted to resolve the dispute in federal court through an umpire. The mediation was to take place later that year.

"There was a big hurrah in town over whether Bob had actually torched the place," Stupak's longtime friend, Klondike casino owner John Woodrum, said. "The fire department ruled it arson. The insurance company didn't want to pay. But Bob got smart and hired the attorney Ralph Denton. It was quite a hassle. There were all kinds of rumors floating around town, but you never knew what was real and unreal."

In June, the tempo of the game changed. The insurance company filed a lawsuit in U.S. District Court alleging Stupak set fire to his casino, then grossly overstated his losses. He was being openly accused of arson.

"The company believes...prior to such fire, the defendant willfully and with intent to injure, prejudice, and damage the company entered into a conspiracy with other persons to defraud the company," the suit alleged.

Stupak responded with a counterclaim seeking in excess of $1.5 million in damages. He attacked not only the insurance company, but also City Attorney Carl Lovell and Assistant City Attorney Peter Burleigh, both of whom represented the interests of Las Vegas as well as Fireman's Fund. The suit alleged that the attorneys, "acted in concert...to stall and delay the ordinary and good-faith settlement of his claim, and that they acted intentionally and in bad faith for the sole purpose of depriving Stupak of the benefits of the policies of insurance issued by the company."

The potential conflict was clear:

The insurance company retained the attorneys knowing they "were City Attorney for the City of Las Vegas and Assistant City Attorney for Las Vegas and were legal advisors and consultants, therefore, to the fire department and, particularly, the individual investigators of the fire department and were likewise attorneys for the building department of Las Vegas and were, therefore, in a position to influence, and did influence, determinations and decisions of such fire department and building department."

By Stupak's estimation, the alleged "outrageous bad faith" was worth $500,000 for economic detriment, $500,000 punitive damages, and $500,000 for severe emotional distress and special damages. Lovell and Burleigh denied any conflict, but the body blows had been struck.

In the end, Stupak prevailed: the case was resolved outside the courtroom. Stupak failed to cash in on his $1.5 million request, but his $300,000 claim finally was paid. Still, the rumors of arson at the Million Dollar Historic Gambling Museum & Casino would circulate for the next two decades.

Hustling coupon books in Pennsylvania and Australia was child's play compared to turning a dollar as a casino operator in Las Vegas. The market was deeply deceptive. While it appeared to outsiders that experienced gambling bosses such as Benny Binion of Binion's Horseshoe Club simply threw open the doors and ushered willing suckers inside their casinos, the game was far more complex.

If his early efforts at operating casinos were failures, Stupak's Dine Out Las Vegas coupon program proved a resounding success. With hundreds of restaurants and bars vying for tourist and local dollars, business owners were more than willing to allow Stupak to add their names to his list of clients.

"He'd go around to various places and convince people that he was going to bring them a lot of business if they'd let him put a two-for-one coupon in the book," John Woodrum said. "He sold a lot of them. In those days, I think he got about seventeen or eighteen bucks for each book."

To counteract his lack of credibility in the wake of the casino fire, Stupak hired local television personality Gus Giuffre. Giuffre was among the city's most popular celebrities. His was one of the most likable faces on television and voices on radio. He hosted matinée movies and cut commercials for local businesses. In hiring the television personality, Stupak borrowed Giuffre's name and face recognition, and more importantly, his credibility with locals.

"Gus was like a father to a lot of people," Woodrum said. "He was a sweet and gentle guy, just a wonderful guy. Everyone loved him. Bob used him as a front for the Dine Out Club. Gus would go on TV and sell his Dine Out thing. Gus was a tremendous asset to Bob."

Bob Stupak purchased the lease on a Fremont Street hole-in-the-wall called the Glitter Gulch from Ray Snichter for $100,000 with an option to buy the property from owners Jackie Gaughan and Mel Exber for $800,000. At the time the home of topless bar, the joint was renamed Bob Stupak's Glitter Gulch. When it reopened, the tawdry slot arcade was designed for rubes only. It was distinguished by Stupak's Vegas Vicky, a flashing sign shaped like a cowgirl meant to complement the Pioneer Club's famous Vegas Vic across the street. When Stupak sold the Glitter Gulch years later to Herb Pastor, he sold Vegas Vicky separately, and at a profit, to the Young Electric Sign Company.

Stupak wasn't going to get rich with a slot parlor, but he was smart enough to appreciate the value of the land beneath the building on Fremont Street. In two years, he sold the place for $2.2 million, an enormous markup for such a thin slice of land. The deal helped bankroll his future Las Vegas investments.

"At the time I bought it, it was the highest-priced square footage in Nevada," Stupak said years later. "I moved it up from there."

By August 1975, Stupak had sold the old Sinabar, which he had renamed the Vault, and sought to have the burned-out hulk of his first casino rezoned as a used-car lot.

But it would take every beat of Bob Stupak's hustler's heart to prevent his big Vegas dream from landing in the city's vast neon graveyard.

THREE

Only at Vegas World

With the arson rumors still smoldering at the edge of his reputation, in the late 1970s Bob Stupak found his career precariously positioned. With a minor downtown slot operation and a piece of real estate on the wrong side of Sahara Avenue, he remained a small-stakes player who possessed visions of glory and more confidence than was warranted. But like his father, Stupak was nothing if not tenacious.

He strained to gain access to the bankers and businessmen who made Las Vegas run. While he had difficulty blending in at the Las Vegas Country Club, his prospects improved greatly when his work ethic came to the attention of Valley Bank founder E. Parry Thomas, perhaps the most important player in the city's history. Thomas's bank was responsible for servicing millions in loans from the Teamsters Central States Pension Fund, dollars that were used to develop not only casinos on the Strip, but also the city's first private hospital and its first large-scale shopping mall. More than the trusted shepherd of the Teamsters fund, Thomas and his partner, Ken Sullivan, were community leaders who left their mark across the valley in places such as the University of Nevada at Las Vegas and numerous housing developments. Thomas was largely responsible for guiding the career of casino mogul Steve Wynn, who met Thomas in the late 1960s and went on to become the head of the casino corporation now known as Mirage Resorts. When Stupak needed seed money and the break of a lifetime, he received both, thanks to Thomas and Sullivan.

"I came into Kenny Sullivan's office every few weeks with an idea," Stupak recalled. "I think he got tired of seeing me."

Although Bob Stupak wasn't deeply connected to the city's power base, no one could deny his relentless striving. Sullivan and Thomas finally took Stupak seriously and agreed to work with him. In June 1978, Stupak's dream manifested in the groundbreaking of Bob Stupak's Vegas World, the first hotel-casino built close to the corner of Sahara Avenue and Las Vegas Boulevard since the Sahara opened in 1952. In more recent times, the only casino to open in close proximity was the Jolley Trolley, a tacky mob bustout joint that has long since been replaced by a department store-sized souvenir shop.

Vegas World was completed 13 months later at an advertised cost of more than $7 million. In reality, it cost a little more than $3 million. The dollar difference was simple.

"I lied about it," Stupak said in an interview. "I lied about it like everybody else does."

Valley Bank considered lending Stupak up to $1.5 million for his Vegas World idea—but only if he managed to raise the rest of the money from other sources. He took the bank's consideration as confirmation and hit up Home Savings for a loan. After all, if Valley Bank was willing to back the deal for $1.5 million, couldn't a smaller institution such as Home Savings throw in a measly few hundred thousand?

"They thought I already had the loan, and I didn't tell them otherwise," Stupak said.

The pitch worked at Home Savings and at Nevada State Bank, where experienced lenders knew Valley Bank seldom made a mistake. With a fourth loan from a Reno bank, Stupak's hustle was complete.

Before Vegas World opened, Stupak would return for $700,000 more from the bank that Parry Thomas built. Although they knew Stupak never had been responsible for building much more than his name, the cost overruns still irritated the bankers.

"When I ran out of money to finish it, they were hot," Stupak recalled years later. "They didn't talk to me for three months, until after it was all over and the thing was built."

Glorious, Vegas World was not. It hardly qualified as a major Las Vegas property. When completed, it boasted all of 102 rooms with vague plans to add another 500. Even in those years, major Strip properties commonly had more than 1,000 rooms and the Las Vegas Hilton and MGM Grand (later renamed Bally's) were among the largest resorts in the world. Still, Vegas World was a testament to Stupak's perseverance.

The original hotel and casino sat on the three-acre site of the gambling museum, and Stupak worked overtime to sell his gaudy paradise in the middle of no-man's land. His most outrageous pitch was the idea that the presence of Vegas World broke down an invisible barrier and extended the Strip north of Sahara Avenue. Not surprisingly, the Las Vegas media picked up on the story and joined Stupak in the cheer.

"I think the location is great," he gushed to a reporter. "You can see it from all over town and people walk down from the Sahara. I'm trying to create my own market."

In reality, while other hotels along Las Vegas Boulevard enjoyed a Strip address, Vegas World would forever risk being known as the gateway to Naked City, one of the town's roughest neighborhoods. Gushing television reporters might herald Vegas World as the city of Las Vegas's first resort on the Strip (the city ended at Sahara Avenue; the Strip proper was in Clark County), but locals were less impressed.

Naked City, a downtown neighborhood bordered by Las Vegas Boulevard, Industrial Road, Wyoming Avenue, and Sahara Avenue, is said to have received its name as a tribute to the showgirls who once occupied its art deco apartments and sunbathed in the nude. Its streets were named for America's major cities, but when Vegas World opened its residents for the most part were not from this country. Located just a block from the Strip, it was a million miles from the booming prosperity gambling provided the rest of the city.

Naked City became the first neighborhood for southern Nevada's ever-changing immigrant population. Whether Mexican, Cuban, or Vietnamese, it was a source of inexpensive housing for the newcomers who eagerly filled the thousands of service jobs generated by the casino resorts.

By the late 1970s, Naked City was changing once more.

In the wake of the Mariel boat lift months into the new decade, which brought thousands of Cuban immigrants—many of them hardened criminals—to the United States, Naked City had emerged as a Little Havana. Upward of 2,000 Cuban immigrants moved to Las Vegas. Most were lawful and hard-working. The ones who weren't made banner headlines for their drug dealing and extreme violence.

Criminal activity wasn't limited to a single ethnic group. Drug dealing was rampant and prostitutes walked the strand lined with cut-rate motels along Las Vegas Boulevard. As in poor neighborhoods across the country, much of the drugs were sold to residents from cleaner, wealthier parts of Las Vegas who visited Naked City to score their dope. Shootings occurred regularly and Metro dispatched a special task force of narcotics detectives to knock down the trafficking and gunplay.

Stupak wisely attempted to work with city officials to clean up the ramshackle apartments and matchbox houses that bordered Vegas World. He also purchased some of the slums at a steep discount. City building inspectors descended on the neighborhood and began citing landlords for electrical violations and structural deficiencies. Junk cars were towed and garbage was collected.

The Metropolitan Police Department parted with local custom and dispatched officers to walk a foot patrol through the neighborhood in an attempt to get the law-abiding citizens, who seldom walked the streets at night, to begin reporting criminal activity.

"You put too many rats in a box and they start killing each other," Metro's Undersheriff Don Denison said after investigating 10 homicides in 16 months in a four-block area. "People are the same way."

Dressed in a wild sport shirt with an open collar, Bob Stupak was flanked by Dallas Cowboys cheerleaders and fawned over by local TV personality Gus Giuffre and then-City Commissioner Ron Lurie for the Friday, July 13, 1979, opening of Vegas World. Touted as the newest hotel on the Strip, it stood eight stories high and just on the wrong side of Sahara Avenue. In a town teeming with casino competition, its location was suspect from the start. But where others would have been circumspect, Stupak began immediate expansion plans. In short order, his eight-story hotel was headed toward the 20-story mark.

"The basic policy in the building of the new Vegas World was to please the home folks, the residents of this county," he said.

It wasn't all ribbon-cutting and press conferences.

Stupak's bankroll was as slender as any showgirl on the Strip. State gaming regulations demanded sufficient money on deposit in the cage to cover large payoffs, and an early hit from a high roller would devastate him. More than that, it would expose his shoestring operation for what it was.

Stories of Stupak's desperate attempts to remain financially solvent are legion in Las Vegas. Some friends recall him borrowing from downtown casino men for quick turnaround loans to keep enough cash on hand. Others remember him coming precariously close to losing the deed on Vegas World in high-stakes card games.

John Woodrum remembers yet another story that separated Bob Stupak's stock image as a high roller from the reality of his financial predicament. In the early months at Vegas World, there were many nights the tables hosted more action than the house could cover.

"Bob didn't start out with pockets lined with gold," Woodrum said. "When Bob opened up there he had a Rolls-Royce, of course, and a big five-carat diamond ring he was wearing, but no bankroll. Gaming Control requires that you have enough cash to open these places. So he went downtown to one of the guys in the pawnshop business down there. He pawned his ring. Bob pawned his ring and I think his car, too, to open up Vegas World.

"That's always been his act. In later years he told me he did that. I didn't know he did it back then, and I'm sure Gaming Control didn't know it, either. Had they known what Bob had done, I'm sure he never would have had a chance to open up. He's a very slick manipulator, and that ain't all bad in this industry. Bob is a little bit of a throwback in this industry. God knows he took a spot in a terrible location and made it work."

Stupak's relationship with the Hotel Employees & Restaurant Employees International Union, more commonly known as the Culinary, was stormy from the start. Stupak might have made suspect business transactions in Pittsburgh, Melbourne, and at the Sinabar, but on his wildest day he couldn't match the Culinary Union for notoriety. The Las Vegas local of the nationwide service employees group had maintained a close relationship with the Chicago Outfit for two generations and was not above negotiating through intimidation. Al Bramlet, the union's hard-nosed and highly regarded leader, had been murdered. His replacement, Ben Schmoutey, was an intimate associate of organized crime figures linked to Chicago and New York mob families and rarely traveled without at least one tough guy at his side.

With an anemic bankroll and few friends in the Las Vegas casino establishment, Stupak figured to be an easy mark for Culinary organizers. With a little pressure out on the sidewalk and a barrage of tough talk, he was bound to buckle.

Illegal pickets showed up outside Vegas World three months after it opened. Union organizers knew it would take weeks for a judge to force them to leave, and by then the Vegas World contract was sure to be sewn up. Even before the hotel was finished Stupak was approached by union organizers, who attempted not only to force him to hire dues-paying waiters, chefs, cocktail waitresses, and housekeepers, but also to slip them a little something extra to ensure labor peace. Although Stupak had welcomed the Teamsters' presence at the hotel—the truckers' union had organized the front-desk workers and parking lot attendants—he balked at the tactics of the Culinary Union. No one was going to strong-arm him without a fight.

By November 1979, the war was raging. Pickets posted on the sidewalk 24 hours a day were beginning to have some impact. Trucks hauling food, linen, and other supplies to Vegas World were delayed by the marchers.

Adding to a previous unfair-labor-practices complaint, in late November the Joint Executive Board of the Culinary and Bartenders unions filed a lengthy list of charges against Stupak and Vegas World with the National Labor Relations Board. Stupak and his executives were accused of all manner of nefarious anti-labor activity, from firing workers for daring to organize to bribing a coffee-shop manager to prevent union members from obtaining jobs.

The organizers, including a few underworld types, were mistaken in their estimation of Stupak as a sucker. Stupak's street sense was strong. And he not only refused to pay protection, but he also fought the union's use of illegal pickets outside his door. And he did so in the sort of unorthodox manner that was becoming his trademark.

"Al Bramlet's interest was to organize Stupak's place," John Woodrum recalled. "After Bramlet got killed, Ben Schmoutey became the head of the Culinary Union, and they had a big push on. They were going to organize the workers in there. Well, the union men would come into the coffee shop and glare at old Bob. When they'd meet him across a table they were always giving him the eye. Real tough guy stuff. And Bob would jump up on top of the table in the meetings and start screaming, 'This is un-American! You can't do this to me!' And these tough guys would come in with their shirt sleeves rolled up, and Bob would roll up his shirt sleeves and his tattoos would show. Bob is skinny as can be, but he's as cocky as a four-headed billy goat.

"They put a picket line up at Vegas World, and I'll never forget it as long as I live. Their signs said, 'Bob Stupak and Vegas World—Unfair Labor Practices.' So Bob takes his own workers from Vegas World and uses them to put up a picket line around the union picketers. They're carrying signs saying, 'Unfair Union Practices.' It was the most comical thing in town. I'd just park and sit there and laugh because none of us would ever have thought of doing something like that. We knew we couldn't win with that kind of bullshit. So there was no sense in fighting City Hall and the union. And it wasn't in our best interests. But with Bob it was the principle of the thing."

Stupak, who already knew a thing or two about being a laughing stock, was making a joke out of the union. He continued his crusade against Schmoutey, going so far as to hoodwink the union boss into playing a "game of chance" for the contract. In the early days at Vegas World, Stupak employed a carnival-trained rooster to play tic-tac-toe against customers for money. In fact, Stupak's so-called Polish rooster was undefeated at Vegas World before gaming regulators persuaded the owner to put his best gambler out to pasture.

"This is strictly out of the carnival," Woodrum said. "You aren't going to beat the rooster because the rooster always gets the first pick. When the rooster gets the first pick, you can't win no matter how you push the buttons. After a long negotiation Stupak says, 'I'll make you a deal. I'll sign the union contract if Ben Schmoutey will go out there and play against my Polish Rooster. If he beats the rooster at tic-tac-toe, I'll sign the contract. If he loses the tic-tac-toe game, then you guys go away and leave me alone.' At this point the union organizers started telling him what a goddamn idiot he was. Didn't he know who he was dealing with? Schmoutey says, 'You ignorant SOB, I've got 20,000 members and I'm going to play tic-tac-toe against a goddamn rooster?' But that was the straw that broke the union's back. They walked out and the place stayed a nonunion house."

In January 1980, the National Labor Relations Board ordered that the illegal pickets be removed from the sidewalk.

"We have written assurances from the Joint Executive Board that they will not engage in unlawful picketing," NLRB resident agent Ken Rose said.

Stupak was viewed as anti-labor and as a certifiable nut after word circulated that he not only had challenged Schmoutey, but also had negotiated with the union men from behind the bar at Vegas World singing, "Look for the union label," while he served his adversaries free whiskey and beer.

After all his antics, Bob Stupak had won a small victory.

They would prove hard to come by in the future.

Stupak was obsessed with building a reputation as a man who, like Horseshoe patriarch Benny Binion, was willing to accept wagers that would make today's corporate casino bosses stammer. Stupak constantly dropped Binion's name and sought him out at the Horseshoe coffee shop almost daily.

Stupak ordered signs for his casino with "The Sky's the Limit" emblazoned in lights and neon. Hours after he opened Vegas World, he raised the table stakes from $50 to $100 and soon allowed up to $2,000 bets. At the time, Caesars Palace allowed half as much.

"Don't come to the big place with the small bankroll," his sales pitch shouted. "Come to the small place with the big bankroll."

Problem was, his bankroll was still suspect. He was, after all, the man who later confided to friends that he had opened Vegas World without enough nickels and quarters to fill all the slot machines in the place and had to hock his car and diamond ring to cover his action.

Fortunately for Stupak, his relationship with Benny Binion and his eldest son, Jack, transcended sage advice and a cup of coffee. When Vegas World's cage ran short of money, like many operators Stupak took advantage of Binion's ready cash loans.

One night, a gambler appeared at a Vegas World crap table and began a run that depleted the casino's reserves and threw a genuine scare into Stupak. A few more passes and the stranger would be in a position to own a large piece of the building, which Stupak was rapidly paying off. If the player were an acquaintance of management, it would have been acceptable to pull him aside and explain the predicament. But with a stranger, that was not possible—and it was too late to close the game.

"He had more money on the fucking crap table than I had in the fucking cage," Stupak recalled. "There was nothing I could do but let him play and get on the phone to Jack Binion."

It was after midnight when Binion answered the phone. The request neither shocked nor dismayed the casino veteran, who had broken into the business before he was old enough to vote. Stupak needed $300,000.

"Go to the cage," Binion said. "It'll be waiting for you when you get there."

Stupak returned to Vegas World an hour later with a small fortune in cash in brown sacks, and weathered the storm. Instead of losing Vegas World to a single high roller, Stupak later bragged that he paid off his bank loans in a year.

"There was a time here when a man's word was his bond," Stupak recalled years later. "Men like Benny Binion, Jackie Gaughan, Mel Exber. Their word was good and they knew the business. It takes years to learn the business, and they probably knew more than anybody."

Stupak sought their advice often. He would need all the insight he could gather to make a success out of his Naked City experiment.

Not long after Vegas World opened, Bob Stupak met David Sklansky, the man who would become Vegas World's gaming guru. The son of a college professor, Sklansky was a published author who had turned his formidable knowledge of numbers into a successful career as a professional poker player and all-around gambler.

"Bob walked into the Horseshoe tournament and decided he wanted to learn how to play poker," Sklansky said. "I'd just written a couple of books. I told him I knew more about gambling than anybody alive, and that I thought he'd want to meet me. He threw out the crapless craps game to me. He wanted to know about the house edge. I got him the answer in a few minutes, and he realized I probably knew what I was talking about."

True to Stupak's flamboyant nature, Sklansky's business cards would read "Resident Wizard." Stupak and Sklansky for years were spotted having lunch at different casinos. They bounced their gaming strategies off the competition almost daily.

"We were always trying to figure out what made people tick, what made people want to gamble, what made people want to stay at a place," Sklansky said. "I believe we had good ideas. The sad part is, we never had a really nice place to use them."

With a casino set smack on the edge of a rough neighborhood along a section of Las Vegas Boulevard that no one but Stupak called the Strip, the vicar of Vegas World was forced to constantly promote his place, face, and games. He touted himself as a gutsy gambling innovator. Early advertisements for Vegas World showed a caricature of Stupak shouting the incredible gambling deals available only at his casino. The ads called attention to his sense of humor as well as his hustler's heart.

INTRODUCING POLISH ROULETTE!
WE LOSE MONEY ON EVERY SPIN,
BUT WE HOPE TO MAKE IT UP IN VOLUME.
NO ZEROS

Las Vegas casinos have seldom let the truth get in the way of a good sales pitch, and Stupak's strategy was part of the great tradition.

BLACKJACK AS YOU'VE NEVER PLAYED IT BEFORE!
SEE THE DEALER'S HOLE CARD
PLAY DOUBLE EXPOSURE "21"
BOTH DEALER'S CARDS DEALT FACE UP!

Stupak's newfangled blackjack seemed so easy to play, it was hard to imagine how anyone could lose.

"How often have you wished you knew the dealer's hole card?" the ad asked. "How often have you had a 13, 14, or 15 and hit and busted when the dealer had a 10-count card turned up? Then the dealer turned over a 5 or 6, hit it, and busted too. You could have won if you had known his hole card.

"Now, for the first time you can play 21 and see both of the dealer's cards. Both dealer's cards are dealt face up. You know exactly what the dealer has before you decide what to do yourself. Stand, hit, double, split, etc. It's all new! It's fun, and it's only at Vegas World!"

The newspaper ad was marred by some graffiti next to Stupak's image that read, "He's Polish." Someone in the newspaper ad department had attempted to play a practical joke on Stupak, who initially was peeved but quickly grew to incorporate it into the act.

"I said, 'Well, geez, this is great. It looks like it just ties in with the game, given its personalized Stupak way, you know.' So from that time on, for the next few years, everything I ever did had Bob Stupak with little black hearts saying: 'He's Polish,' with the 's' backwards.

"And I was always considered a maverick with these special games, so one day somebody wrote something in the paper and they referred to me as the Polish Maverick, putting the two things together. I sort of liked that handle, too. And I used that for a few years.

"Double Exposure was an immediate success. Every day broke a record from the previous days. Then I started advertising on billboards, in the in-flight magazines—in every place that I could legally advertise the game. After two years, I just had an absolute marvelous run. No other major casinos put it in."

The advertisement, of course, failed to mention that the trade-off for viewing the dealer's hole card was that pushes, or ties, went to the house instead of the usual return of the wager to the player, but that was a minor detail the player would accept after he had placed his bets and taken his chances. In addition, a player's natural two-card 21 won even money, instead of the industry-wide 3-to-2, and players were not allowed to double down or split cards. Double Exposure 21 played as it was at Vegas World gave the house a .5-percent edge—which was about the same as the usual advantage cooked into the game through regular house rules—but only if the player played Double Exposure basic strategy flawlessly. A player with a looser strategy faced even steeper odds, and almost everyone who tried this new game made mistakes. Despite the obvious disadvantages, blackjack fans flocked to Vegas World for the opportunity to look at the dealer's cards.

Double Exposure lured the players through the door and the wonders of Vegas World did the rest.

Stupak's Experto 21 game, in which a single deck was dealt down to the last card, gave Vegas World a 2.3 percent advantage over basic-strategy players, but the ploy was successful in attracting card counters as well as the curious.

By counting the cards, or keeping a weighted average of the ratio of high cards to low cards that have been dealt, the skilled player improves his odds of beating the house as the deck diminishes. The tradeoff in Experto: a blackjack, which normally pays 3-to-2, pays even money.

Experto 21 was an honest game, if not exactly a square deal for the average player. The uninitiated would be attracted to a single deck dealt all the way through and might not realize that the even-money adjustment for blackjack put even the experienced basic-strategy player at a minimum 2.3 percent disadvantage. Standard single-deck 21 deals to a nearly flat house advantage.

It's something California card counter Alan Brown was thinking about as he took a seat at the Experto table and began working the deck. Brown, a U.S. Department of Defense engineer, had been making weekend runs to Las Vegas as a serious blackjack player for a little more than a year when he stumbled upon Stupak's intriguing proposition.

Playing with an uninterrupted deck is every counter's dream, but he proceeded cautiously. Even after only a year of visiting Las Vegas, Brown was well aware of Bob Stupak's reputation.

He approached the floorman, who explained that the game had only been open a few days. Most players, a superstitious lot, were spooked by it.

Brown's hesitancy was based on math, not mysticism; he was well aware of the impact of the even-money payoffs on naturals. The lone player at the table, he began playing $25 a hand. As the deck diminished, and the situation warranted, he bumped his bets up to $100.

"That doesn't seem like a lot of money today, but back then playing $100 a hand was serious money," Brown recalled. "As a card counter, you always want to get deep in the deck. That's where you get your advantage. The impression I had of Stupak was that he often did this kind of gimmicky stuff to attract customers. Jumping into a game where you're right off the bat losing 2.3 percent, you've got to make it up somewhere."

So he counted down the deck until he was certain of the make-up of the final cards, then spread his wagers to the maximum allowed—and began to win.

"The next thing I know, I look over and Bob is sitting right next to me," Brown said. "He said, 'Hi, I'm Bob Stupak.'

"We shook hands. He had the softest hands I've ever felt, like he'd never done a day's work in his life."

Stupak was intrigued by the counter, who had begun piling up chips.

"He sat there with me all day. He left the table occasionally to go to his office or take a phone call, but he came back and watched me play. He was just fascinated by the game."

After Brown had accumulated approximately $3,000,

Stupak's curiosity turned to playful inquiry. It wasn't the money that bothered him; it was the mechanics of the game he was attempting to straighten out.

"Do you think you can beat this game?" Stupak asked.

"I'm not sure, Bob," Brown answered. "But I think so."

"He was trying to find out how good I was, but more than that he was trying to find out about the game. Because of all the conversation and interest, I assumed I was the first good player to come in and try it. It's unusual for a casino owner to come down and sit for that length of time with a player. He was really very cordial, not intimidating at all."

He also implored Brown to return the next day. When Brown returned, he jumped back in and gradually lost more than $2,000 back to the house. He walked with $800, and Stupak eventually reduced the betting spread to a 3-to-1 ratio.

The prevalence of players of Brown's skill level led Stupak to print cards of another kind for counters. The cards read:

Dear Card Counter:
Your play is welcome, but due to severe losses, we have to restrict your wagers from 1 to 7 units. Your cooperation will be appreciated.

Professional card counter Howard Grossman took his Vegas World experience one step further. In the early 1980s, Grossman came to Stupak's attention while he was playing and beating Double Exposure and Experto. Before long, Grossman received a call from Stupak who, of course, had a wild proposition: a $50,000 single-deck match. Head to head, no gimmicks. Grossman rushed to Vegas World.

"I really don't want to play against you," Stupak told him. "I just wanted to get you down here."

Stupak went on to tap Grossman's knowledge of Experto. Like Brown, Grossman was asked whether he was certain he could beat the game. Challenged again to a match, Grossman agreed to play Experto for high stakes. But Stupak was merely testing him.

"I really want you to work for me," Stupak told him.

And he did. Over the next two years, Howard Grossman trained dealers, occasionally ran a shift on the casino floor, and served as a jack-of-all-trades consultant for Stupak. Grossman learned more about human nature than the casino business. He also learned a few things about his flamboyant boss.

"Stupak was a character. He's a clever man," Grossman said. "He didn't always have a lot of knowledge about the games, but he would gain his knowledge by taking a gamble. Where most operators obtain their information beforehand, he would gamble first. We changed his casino around and we beat just about everybody.

"He wasn't that respectful of people; his employees, he didn't treat them that well. He was nice to his customers, though. He went out of his way to be nice to them. He was a clever gambler and always tried to get the best of it. As long as he had the best of it, he would take the gamble."

Unlike many executives of multimillion-dollar businesses, Stupak rarely conducted the day's affairs in his office. Instead, he staked out a table in the Vegas World coffee shop, read the newspaper, drank coffee, and chain smoked from just after breakfast until shortly before dinner. Through the day, he entertained a constant stream of customers, friends, con artists, restaurant suppliers, casino men, card sharks, would-be comedians, and newspaper reporters.

"People would come in and try to sell him anything," Grossman said. "He taught me about negotiations. My impression of him has always been that he's very driven to success, as if he's trying to prove something, to gain someone's respect."

Gambling consultant and author David Sklansky defends Experto and all of Vegas World's gimmick games, most of which he had a hand in developing.

"Experto was always a great game for Vegas World,"

Sklansky said. "It remained a great game for Vegas World. I predict it will one day become *the* great game to be played in Las Vegas casinos."

Crapless craps proved to be one of Vegas World's best come-ons. It wasn't the game itself that the average player couldn't resist; it was the idea of playing longer and getting something for nothing that so many found irresistible. In an age in which fewer gamblers pitched dice, Stupak concocted a variation with a built-in 5.4 percent house advantage—far higher than the 1.4 percent best bet players of the standard game enjoyed. A shift in the rules changed the odds. For example, although a player could not crap out on the usual 2, 3, or 12 rolls, don't pass and don't come bets were disallowed. Other rule changes helped sway the odds in the house's favor. Players threw dice longer, but they won less.

Stupak also raised the limits at Vegas World to rival, and in many instances exceed, the action accepted at the Strip hotels. In 1979, Stupak's $1,500 limits attracted high rollers from the poshest suites on the boulevard. They might have slept elsewhere, but they were willing to go slumming at Vegas World.

"When I went to the highest limits," he recalled years later, "I started to get serious company. My first taste came with a visit from Adnan Kashoggi. He came in on the first weekend and dropped a hundred and ten thousand. That was my biggest score at the time in the casino business. That particular night gave me a real taste for money. I knew I could never go back to being worried about nickels and dimes. I wanted to start dealing to high rollers. I did everything I could to develop a reputation as a gambler, and I tried to convey the image of a loose-cannon type. I took up poker and splashed as much money around as I could. Sometimes I made foolish bets intentionally. And sometimes I made bad propositions with twenty-one players just to get the word out there that here's a guy who'll take a risk—and you never can tell how he feels that day or what proposition he may or may not get on."

Stupak's willingness to entertain all propositions generated much-needed publicity for Vegas World, but it also attracted card counters, wiseguy gamblers from across the country, and in at least one case, from as far away as Great Britain.

It was there that Kenneth Speakman was born and raised, but it was in the casinos of Las Vegas that he plied his trade as a blackjack card counter.

Card counting is not illegal in Nevada casinos, but the technique is frowned upon by management. In most instances, a person suspected of counting is notified by floor personnel that his action is no longer welcome at the casino. But Stupak publicly welcomed card counters. Where others treated them like Soviet spies, Stupak kept the action flowing.

Speakman strolled into Vegas World in August 1980 and began playing. He'd won approximately $3,200 when the dealer and casino manager thought they had spotted something. It was then that casino manager Chuck Wenner stepped in and halted play, which is the club's prerogative.

Wenner detained Speakman. The first call the counter made was not to his lawyer, but to the police. Speakman was eventually charged with cheating, but his quickly placed call complicated matters.

Thus began a legal action that resulted in a lawsuit and the awarding of a far larger pot to Speakman. Speakman claimed that Vegas World had violated his rights and had falsely imprisoned him. He feared for his safety, a lawyer would claim more than three years later when the case went to trial before a jury in U.S. District Court. The jury awarded Speakman $25,000 in compensatory damages and $23,000 in punitive damages.

"I'd known Ken Speakman for some time," Howard Grossman said. "He swore to me he didn't do anything. Chuck swore the cards were bent and Ken swore he didn't bend them."

Through it all Speakman did not blame Stupak for his troubles. After all, the Polish Maverick was a self-proclaimed friend of blackjack players.

But not all card players. While the Vegas World blackjack pit had become a refuge for counters accomplished and amateur, the poker room had begun to take on a distinctly more dangerous appearance. Stupak's own reputation as a high-stakes gambler attracted some of the best players in the city, but, like many poker parlors in Las Vegas, it also attracted an underworld element.

Associates of the Chicago mob's Las Vegas enforcer Anthony Spilotro made Stupak's card room a satellite office for suspected extortion and loansharking activities. Spilotro was a suspect in two dozen murders, but was never convicted of a felony during his lifetime. His lifetime ended abruptly; in June 1986, the bodies of Spilotro and his brother, Michael, were unearthed from an Indiana cornfield.

But in the early 1980s, Spilotro and his street gang of burglars and strong-arm extortionists struck fear in illegal bookmakers, poker players, and many a Las Vegas casino boss. Metropolitan Police Department Intelligence detectives and local FBI agents, who had been obsessed for years with Spilotro, noticed tough Tony's people frequenting Vegas World and were instantly intrigued. Surveillance teams regularly spotted Spilotro's brothers, John and Victor, in the poker room.

Were the boys planning to strong-arm their way into Vegas World? Had they already done so and were they now watching after their interests?

The detectives and agents couldn't find out quickly without help from the inside, the sort of assistance only Stupak could provide. But Stupak, raised on the streets of Pittsburgh and schooled in poker rooms from the South Side to Sydney, was no stool pigeon. Members of the gambling industry have quietly cooperated with federal investigators for decades, but it was bad for business to let word circulate that a casino boss was providing an extra pair of eyes for law enforcement, especially when so many good customers had nefarious reputations.

Then along came Betty Carey, and the cops found a way to get inside Vegas World.

Carey was a self-professed world-class poker player in her early twenties with friends on both sides of the table. She made regular appearances in high-stakes tournaments and was the youngest woman operating in the male-dominated rooms. Like many other skilled players, Betty Carey gravitated toward the heavy action in Vegas World's poker room in 1980.

It was there, she later claimed, that she was cheated out of approximately $250,000 and perhaps as much as $415,000 by house mechanics, cheaters who operate with the approval of the boss. Bob Stupak surely would have some explaining to do to state Gaming Control Board investigators. If the allegation was confirmed, he would lose his license and be banished from the industry.

Carey accused Stupak of using suspected card cheaters Clifford Isbell and John Deems to take her for the money she had won at poker and blackjack. Isbell was a valued informant for Metro Intelligence's Lt. Kent Clifford, whose men watched Spilotro day and night. Clifford had played an integral role in shattering the Chicago mob's influence in Las Vegas casinos. It was through Isbell that Clifford attempted to turn Stupak into an informant. The tradeoff: silence in the Carey cheating accusation.

"John Spilotro was hanging out in his hotel," Clifford said later. "I saw him (Stupak) as an avenue, as an informant against organized crime.

"I had a meeting with him and that's what I told him I wanted from him—information on organized crime. He was allowed to continue operating his business down there (in the poker room) in return for giving me information."

Stupak's dilemma was growing increasingly complex. First, he swore he hadn't sanctioned the alleged activity of Isbell and Deems. Second, he suspected Carey was being used to extort money from him under the threat of being exposed as some sort of cheater. Third, Metro's finest were using the Carey allegation as a pressure point to force him into cooperating against people whose close proximity put his business in jeopardy.

Stupak had little choice but to pacify the police. He met privately with Clifford in August 1980 and agreed to help when he could. Then he shrugged and went back to work.

Years later, Clifford admitted that Stupak made a terrible informant. For all the time the Polish Maverick spent in his casino, he rarely seemed to notice anything.

"Occasionally he would give me something, but very little," Clifford said.

Placating Betty Carey would not be as easy.

Carey failed to file suit until December 1984 and gaming regulators didn't investigate Carey's allegation until several years later. The delays proved a great help to Stupak's case.

By then, Isbell and Deems had become Carey's best witnesses. But Stupak's attorney, Frank Schreck, also provided witness statements that contradicted Isbell's testimony.

"Isbell told me that he orchestrated the entire incident...in order to get even with Stupak and to make money in the process," one affiant recalled. "'If I can't get the money one way, I'll get it the other way,'" Isbell was alleged to have said.

For his part, Stupak was supremely confident he would prevail.

"If anybody ever comes up with any evidence that shows I ever cheated anyone, I'll jump off my building, and I won't use an airbag," Stupak crowed to a reporter. "Betty Carey never lost an amount of money anywhere near $415,000. That figure is completely ridiculous. As a gambler, there's nothing worse that I could possibly be accused of than these allegations. I'd rather be accused of murder. I welcome any investigation. I don't have any trouble sleeping at night."

The Control Board investigation found no credible evidence that Stupak had cheated Carey. Stupak was cleared of the cheating allegation in 1986. Carey's civil racketeering suit against Stupak was thrown out that same year on the grounds that the three-year statute of limitations had expired. She later unsuccessfully appealed the dismissal to the state Supreme Court.

Carey also lobbied U.S. attorney's offices in California and Nevada in a desperate attempt to prod federal authorities into taking the cheating case. They also passed.

Through it all, Stupak maintained his reputation as a standup guy who managed to tell the police what they wanted to hear without revealing what he knew. Not that he was enamored of the mob. Far from it.

Stupak would later recall being approached by organized crime figures angling for a piece of his action. He was wise to the traditional mob move: he knew if he relented in the slightest, if he granted a single concession, he would be opening a door he would never be able to close. By standing up to the illegal Culinary pickets on the sidewalk outside his club, he had rebuffed their first move. He knew the only strategy they'd have left would be to sit down and attempt to persuade him that it was in his best interests to take on some partners.

They met in the hotel coffee shop, and Stupak put on quite a show. He went bug-eyed, and it spooked them into thinking he was unstable.

"You don't go to bed with the boys. Once you get into bed, you never get out," Stupak said. "I handled the Outfit by being absolutely nuts. They let me know what was going on, said I was going to be with them, and I got all excited.

"'When is the meeting?' I said. 'Do I get to carry a gun? I can't wait. Do I get a kiss? Am I a made guy?' I was outrageous, but it was nothing they could ever wake up to. Pretty soon the word went around: 'That Stupak, he's too nuts.' They thought I was completely nuts. Nobody ever reacted that way to them."

It wasn't the first and wouldn't be the last time that people surmised that Stupak's mental deck lacked the proper number of cards, but the temporary insanity had the desired effect. The Chicago boys went away.

In late February 1981, Stupak announced on the "Merv Griffin Show" that Vegas World would be home to the largest jackpot on Earth. Dressed in a loud sport shirt with an open collar, Stupak said it came to him in a dream.

Four slot machines were grouped in the casino with a flashy

sign touting the possibilities. The payoff was $1 million and could be hit only with the maximum $3 bet. Some of the smaller pay-offs on the machines could be hit by lining up S-T-U-P-A-K. Never mind that aligning five straight 7s would require more than a little luck. It was sure to attract tourists to his place and attention to himself.

The last time he had attempted a similar pitch, his promotion was interrupted by the fire at the Million Dollar Historic Gambling Museum. And that was only a $250,000 jackpot.

"I want to offer people more than they can get at other places," he said. "It's a bit of a risk, but I'm willing to take it.

"This will give me world prominence."

Or at least *National Enquirer* celebrity. The $1 million jackpot was touted in national tabloids. Stupak's sense of promotion had landed him on the front page again with an idea that would catch fire in every casino in Nevada a decade later. He admitted that he wasn't sure how people would react to it. If they didn't bite, he would work another angle.

As part of Vegas World's development, Stupak added a 340-seat showroom. The keno and poker parlors were expanded, the coffee shop cleaned up, and the casino enlarged from 16,000 to 27,000 square feet. Never one for understatement, Stupak had five chandeliers installed, and new oak paneling gave the place a touch of Binion's Horseshoe. The eight-story hotel still had only 106 rooms and just four suites, but Stupak was on a roll.

Vegas World employees gave away faux $5 bills with Stupak's face on them for use in select slot machines.

He announced Push-Over 21, in which ties above 21 would count as a push, returning a player's wager. The fact such a co-incidence rarely happened was beside the point. If it enticed a few more tourists into Stupak Country, it eventually would pay off.

Then four weeks before Christmas 1981, a fire broke out on the third floor of the hotel. Black smoke began to pour through the halls. A pile of linen had caught fire. Las Vegas firefighters were dispatched to the scene.

With skeptics still remembering the suspicious Million Dollar Historic Gambling Museum blaze, the last thing Bob Stupak needed was another fire. Even though he had collected money from the insurance company and no wrongdoing was ever proved, Stupak still faced suspicion. People were sure to suspect he was some kind of part-time torch. City inspectors wasted no time lending their opinions about the fire's origin only hours after it was extinguished.

"We are calling it a suspicious fire at this time. It's very likely that it is arson but we don't know that for a fact," fire inspector Paul Keeton told a reporter. "Someone could have flicked a lighted cigarette into the stack, and it eventually ignited. But the question is, what was the pile doing in the hallway in the first place? There were no maid carts around to indicate that employees were working in the area."

The theory had a million holes in it, but that didn't prevent it from making print. The suspicious fire eventually was ruled an accident, not arson, by local fire officials.

Stupak continued to pour his small but steady profits back into his garish operation. Neighbors complained of increasing numbers of robberies taking place in the Vegas World parking lot, but their voices were drowned out by the promise of expansion. In July 1982, he won approval for a 24-story, 339-room tower at a time Las Vegas was in the throes of one of the most serious slumps in its history. The expansion would give Vegas World a total of 441 rooms.

While some of the other casinos suffered during the slump, Stupak didn't wait for customers to find his place; he all but dragged them out of their homes in the Midwest by offering special vacation packages that they couldn't refuse. While other casinos were cutting back their complimentary privileges and tightening their belts, Stupak was training telephone sales crews and making mass mailings touting his vacations.

In the early years at Vegas World, it was rumored that the

generosity of Stupak's slot machines varied dramatically almost from day to day. There was a reason for it. He loosened them during the week, when Vegas World had trouble attracting players, and tightened them on the weekends, when his vacation-package marks hit town. The figures varied, but casino man John Woodrum recalled Stupak telling him his tightest machines held 25 percent—approximately five times the industry average.

When the bus customers hit the casino with their cups of quarters, Stupak just grinned.

"Here at Vegas World I have the B and B program—Bust them Buses," Stupak told Woodrum.

Stupak was schooled in the fine art of the hustle, not in customer service, but soon after he opened Vegas World he realized his high rollers expected more than a wide-open game. One time Stupak was entertaining a wealthy player from Chicago, who was good for a $50,000 loss each time he visited Vegas World. This particular night, the player was in really deep. He was down $200,000 and requested a glass of fresh-squeezed orange juice. Not juice from the bar. Not juice from concentrate, but fresh-squeezed. The cocktail waitress tried to explain that the player was at Vegas World, not Caesars Palace, but Stupak quickly intervened. If he wanted fresh juice, he would get fresh juice.

Stupak quickly rounded up a bag of oranges and headed to the kitchen. With the player growing impatient, the boss started squeezing. The gambler not only got his glass of juice, but he came away with the knowledge that the owner had squeezed it himself.

"All of a sudden, after my fourth or fifth orange, it hit me like a ton of bricks," Stupak said. "I paused a moment, put the knife down, and asked myself, 'Who's the sucker here, that Chicago businessman out there losing two hundred thousand, or me in here frantically cutting and squeezing oranges?'"

At that moment Stupak had something of an epiphany. He decided that he would like to be as big a sucker as the Chicago businessman one day. He would like to be so wealthy that he wouldn't think twice about spending $200,000 and receiving a glass of orange juice for his effort.

"So I made up my mind what my true ambition in life really was—I wanted to be the world's biggest sucker with the ability to afford it," Stupak said.

A man with millions can afford to be a sucker, Stupak figured. He became so enamored of his pet philosophy that he had a gold bracelet made with diamonds spelling the word "SUCKER."

It was the kind of twist his father, Chester, could appreciate. After all, Chester Stupak had become an extremely prosperous "sucker" on the South Side by treating his good customers with high regard.

When in Las Vegas, Chester would go on dice runners at Vegas World. But after a few hours, Florence Stupak could always find her husband downtown at Binion's Horseshoe, where he liked the tables and the characters of Benny Binion and his son, Jack.

"We were both very proud of Bob, and we used to go three or four times a year to his club," Florence said. "One time when we went to Bob's place we played and we won. Then we went to the Horseshoe and we lost. I'll never forget him saying to us, 'Why don't you go there and win and come here and lose?'"

Chester Stupak remained his son's hero even after his death in 1991 following a long illness. Feisty Florence Stupak continues to make her home in Pittsburgh.

Out on the sidewalk, Stupak faced more problems from organized labor. He had formed a construction company called High Rollers Inc. to serve as general contractor for the expansion, and he refused to hire union workers. Stupak had become a favorite target of the Southern Nevada Building Trades Council, whose members passed out handbills just beyond the Vegas World property line. With his tenuous reputation, the union bosses might have argued any number of safety issues associated with one of his buildings.

By September, while the AFL-CIO's 26th annual national convention was meeting in Las Vegas, Nevada's organized-labor leaders announced a boycott of Vegas World (along with the Imperial Palace and Bingo Palace) due to its non-union status.

Stupak's stubbornness not only infuriated local labor leaders; it also served as something of a precedent on Las Vegas Boulevard. Prior to his expansion, Strip resorts were built almost exclusively with union labor, as were the majority of other commercial and industrial buildings in southern Nevada.

Stupak had made an enemy for life.

The expansion created other problems as well. Vegas World's star entertainment policy rarely shined brightly, but it reached its low point after construction began on the new hotel building. The temporary facility featured folding chairs, cinder block walls painted black, and a tiny stage with a stage door that opened onto an alley. Performers would enter from the alley and exit through the showroom and the casino. The showroom was torn up and Vegas World became known as the Bermuda Triangle of entertainment.

Stupak's $1 "Construction Special" attracted tourists and locals who were curious to find out whether they would get their buck's worth. From singing trios to a combination magician and ventriloquist, the joint offered a little bit of everything, none of it worth a standing ovation.

Stupak's showroom also was home to *Jahna Reis and the Boob Tube Review*, a $4.95 variety show that emphasized jiggle over talent. At Vegas World, encountering oddity in the showroom was half the fun. Where else could a patron watch Jerry Lee Lewis and busty strippers in the same week?

Perhaps the oddest program ever to headline at the hotel was *Outrageous Vegas*, a vulgar drag-queen show that nonetheless proved popular with locals and, surprisingly, vacation-package buyers.

Stupak, a Vegas history buff, in years to come would advertise his desire to befriend Frank Sinatra, but the acts at Vegas World never approached Rat Pack level.

In the early 1980s, Vegas World testimonials began appearing in national newspapers and magazine advertisements. Stupak hawked Vegas VIP Vacation packages and shouted nonstop about the action available at his casino.

His hotel and casino grew wilder by the day. Its interior design was a cross between early brothel and the set of *2001: A Space Odyssey*. The walls were lined with mirrors—ensuring that first-time visitors would have difficulty finding the restrooms and the exit—and an astronaut and spaceship hung from the ceiling. The Starship Enterprise-sized big six wheel took an electric motor to spin.

Outside, Stupak commissioned a mural that covered the entire east wall of his hotel. The image: cards falling through space with the Earth in the background. Stupak immediately dubbed it the largest mural on the planet.

In time, Stupak would bolt a giant astronaut to the side of the hotel. The marquee would be shaped like a rocket ship, in stark contrast to the ancient entertainers it often announced.

Stupak's willingness to improvise and operate his business by the seat of his pants was evident when he opened Vegas World's sports book and immediately began accepting wagers that would have sent corporate handicappers into cardiac arrest. During the 1982 college football season, for example, betting was hugely lopsided on the Peach Bowl, which opened with Florida State as a seven-point favorite over West Virginia. It was one of the few bowl games that year in which the favorite appeared all but assured of victory and the line climbed accordingly. Florida State became a whopping 15-point favorite at every sports book in Las Vegas—except Vegas World.

Stupak locked in his line at 7 1/2 and wrote $1 million worth of action. The sharpest sports bettors in Las Vegas rushed to Vegas World to take advantage of Stupak the sap, who stood to lose more than $400,000 if Florida State won by more than a touchdown. If West Virginia somehow covered the point spread, Vegas World would be $600,000 richer.

West Virginia not only covered, but beat Florida State outright, 28-6. Stupak's reputation was growing.

"Where most people want to balance the books, Bob wanted to gamble. All the wiseguys came into Vegas World to bet against Stupak," Howard Grossman said. "Stupak got lucky and beat them. He loved that."

Stupak was rapidly building a reputation as a gambler and never passed up an opportunity to remind skeptics of it. His boasts resulted in officials at "Ripley's Believe It or Not" labeling him "The man who will bet on anything." At the Vegas World pool, Stupak once bet a friend $5,000 on who could hold his breath longer. Despite being a chronic cigarette smoker, Stupak prevailed. It made great grist for reporters and television producers.

Stupak once bet writer Roger Dionne he could beat him in a game of Ms. Pac-Man. Stupak won. Dionne recounted the tale years later in an entertaining feature in *Gambling Times* magazine:

"Since he finds it unnatural to do anything unless there's money in it, we played a game for $50. I thought it would be the easiest $50 I ever made, since I played Ms. Pac-Man quite a lot while Stupak didn't. Going first, I racked up something like 82,000 points. A lock, I figured.

"But Stupak's final score was 86,000.

"As I reached disconsolately into my pocket for the $50,

Stupak laughed. 'You know,' he confessed, 'I've never come anywhere close to scoring that many points.' But there was a match on—it didn't matter whether it was for $50, $5,000, or $50,000—and Stupak did what he had to do to win. I may have had more skill playing Ms. Pac-Man, but he had more determination, more of that special quality which backgammon champion Paul Magriel calls 'an insane desire to win.'"

Nowhere is Stupak's reputation as a gambler more manufactured than in the game of poker. Although he was raised shooting dice and learned in a hurry about blackjack and sports betting, until early 1980 he had never played a hand of poker.

He would eventually become known as a high-stakes poker player and would win several championship tournaments, but he was a laughably bad player when he took up the game. And the high-stakes tables of Las Vegas are the last place on the planet a person should attempt to school himself in the sport of kings and queens. A few months after Vegas World opened, Stupak decided to learn the game. As usual, he did so with a fistful of cash and a mouthful of bravado.

Champion poker player Puggy Pearson taught him a few basics, and Las Vegas poker aficionado Eric Drache gave him numerous tips, but Stupak was anxious to scoop up the glory to be had at the high-stakes tables. He succeeded in part by forcing his will on other players with withering raises and a dangerous energy.

Although he was a daydreamer as a schoolboy, Stupak had to be a quick study in the Binion's Horseshoe poker room or he might have wound up penniless. One night, he shocked a crew of sharpies with a string of kamikaze head-to-head hold 'em matches for $5,000 apiece. He numbered keno tickets from one to eight and passed them out to challengers like tickets to the circus. Surely, the professionals figured, they had a bona fide clown in their midst.

He dispatched Number 1 in short order and followed beating Numbers 2 and 3. His luck was running strong.

Then he lost to Number 4. Instead of allowing the winner who beat him a chance to collect his winnings, Stupak doubled the stakes and beat Number 4 in a $10,000 game. After two no-shows, Number 7 joined the list of losers. When Number 8 took a powder, Stupak's class had ended. He figured he could take on the world.

"Here's a sucker sitting here and nobody wants to play him," Stupak puffed.

Stupak quickly became known as an insanely aggressive poker player capable of busting out a table at breakneck speed. He made sure to buy into the annual World Series of Poker, if only to improve his name recognition, and it was across a poker table that he met professional player and Minneapolis leather-goods company-owner Lyle Berman, who would later become his partner in the biggest bet of Stupak's life.

In the early 1980s, Stupak became hooked on poker, and he clearly saw his newfound forte as a way to promote himself and his casino. In 1983, he played host to the America's Cup Poker Tournament. Not only did he promise the winner a Rolls-Royce Silver Shadow, but he also challenged all comers to play head-to-head for stakes ranging from $5,000 to $1 million.

A year later, with cameras from the "Ripley's" television show recording the match, Stupak took on ORAC, a poker-playing computer, for $500,000. The computer was programmed by professional player and author Mike Caro. Downtown casino owner Jackie Gaughan staked the computer, and the world was introduced to the wondrous poker skills of Bob Stupak—who had played his first hand just four years earlier. Stupak beat the artificial brains out of ORAC.

That same year, he placed third in the deuce-to-seven draw competition at the World Series of Poker at Binion's Horseshoe. The finish was good for $31,500, but Stupak commonly played for even larger pots in cutthroat side games at Binion's.

_____

...never enough action for Stupak. He constantly ...d the players at the table into making side bets. Nothing was off limits. From the bra size of a cocktail waitress to pitching coins against a wall, the propositions never ceased. His patter not only distracted some opponents, but it increased his image.

Of course, he was unable to pull off every stunt. One night in Binion's poker room, he tossed out a wild proposition: For a few thousand dollars, he would drive blindfolded down Fremont Street and around downtown, returning safely to Binion's. If he hit anything, he would lose the bet.

Word circulated through the casino quickly. So quickly, in fact, that security was notified, Metro was called out, and police were positioned on the street. They had no intention of letting Stupak endanger lives for the sake of a stunt. The bet was called off.

Another night at Binion's, Stupak was growing bored with a high-stakes game against top poker players, including Puggy Pearson, so he amused himself with an old barroom con. He bet anyone willing to flash some cash that he could perform between "two and three hundred" pushups without resting. In a finger snap, he had action.

On the carpet in the poker room, he assumed the horizontal position and reeled off three pushups before collapsing dramatically.

His challengers figured they'd beat the wimp from the Steel City, but he laughed and explained their dilemma. They had bet that he would do somewhere between two and three hundred pushups, not between two hundred and three hundred, like they'd assumed. He did more then two, and they coughed up the cash.

Another time, Puggy Pearson fell victim to an even older trick when Stupak bet the gambling wild man that, without being touched in any way, Pearson could not stand on top of a chair for a three-count. Pearson took the bet.

He stood atop the chair and Stupak counted, "One."

Moving toward the door, Stupak said, "Two."

Waving goodbye to his friend Puggy, who'd become the focal point in the crowded room, Stupak left the building. Outside, he laughed until tears filled his eyes as Pearson looked around for assistance. When he got the punchline, he stepped down from the chair and handed over the cash. Stupak never told him precisely when he would say "Three."

It was at Binion's that Stupak encountered Eddie Baranski, the Joliet, Ill., poker player who became his fast friend and never ceased to marvel at the Pittsburgh native's sense of humor and gambling audacity.

Outside the poker parlor, Baranski and Stupak were often together. Baranski, who had fought a weight problem for many years, realized he had found a true friend in Stupak when he heard the huckster's latest proposition: Could Baranski lose 60 pounds with a few thousand bucks riding on the line?

For that kind of money, he could certainly try. After a few days, he began to get unexpected help. Stupak hired a dietician and sent his pudgy pal through a weight-loss program.

Baranski won the bet, and although he gained some of the weight back, he knew he had found a friend.

"That's the kind of guy Bob is," Baranski said. "I hang around Bob for one reason. I never know what's going to happen next."

As a player, Stupak was the classic steamroller. He lacked patience for drawn-out strategy and had difficulty sitting through tournaments. In nightly games, it was no-limit or nothing at all.

"Was he a great poker player? Not really," one nationally recognized Las Vegas player said, choosing to remain anonymous. "Not in the true sense of knowing the game inside and out.

"But he was excellent at getting the money. In that regard, he's probably in the top one percent of all poker players. He knew the value of sticking to situations that gave him his best shot. That meant he played no limit. You have to understand that no limit is a whole other ballgame. When you play for big stakes, everything is different. The pressure is enormous."

Every player seeks an edge, and Stupak's was obvious.

"He used to like to play guys who were short on money. He knew they had to win for financial reasons, and he didn't care about the money. It was winning that mattered. That was his edge.

"Bob constantly runs mind games when he plays. He infuriates some players because of it, but that's Bob. You'd play him for huge amounts of money and he'd be coming up with all kinds of side bets. Some had nothing to do with the game. People liked to say that it wasn't worth playing Stupak even when you won because of the aggravation."

Although he tried at every turn to make a sucker out of his competition and customers, Stupak was himself a sucker for fancy automobiles. He collected Rolls-Royces as a status symbol and for their investment potential, and at one point called Imperial Palace owner Ralph Engelstad—owner of one of the world's largest classic car collections—to inquire about a model's worth. When Engelstad explained that the particular model was worth approximately $50,000, Stupak thanked him and hung up.

Weeks later, Engelstad discovered Stupak had paid three times the car's worth.

Stupak was more at home in the casino. He even managed to turn some of his losses into wins. After dropping $10,000 to two-time World Series of Poker champ Stu Ungar in a Texas hold'em freeze-out at Vegas World, Stupak challenged him to a simple game of chip lagging. The closest to the wall would win the bet, in this case $100 and later $500 per throw. Stupak gradually won back the money he had lost in the poker game.

Without an intergalactic advertising budget, Stupak set out to generate name recognition for Vegas World any way he could short of standing on the sidewalk in a sandwich board. And what better way to do that than run for elected office?

Traditionally, casino operators didn't run for office—not even for mayor, which every four years attracts an eccentric collection of candidate characters worthy of Robert L. Ripley. From late-show vampires to retired prostitutes, freaks of every stripe are drawn to the office like moths to neon. With so few sober choices, the race for the job of chief ribbon-cutter in a city built on atomic doses of hype rarely is hotly contested. In the previous three decades, Las Vegas had changed mayors about once a generation. Oran Gragson, a charming furniture-store owner who overcame a heavy stammer to become the city's top public leader, served as mayor for 16 years. His successor, Bill Briare, held the post eight years. With most of their competition coming from candidates with hand-painted signs, Oran Gragson and Bill Briare merely kept smiling, cutting ribbons, and winning.

Rather than put themselves out front, the state's gambling bosses instead generally adhered to a simple credo: Why be one when you can lease one? They had money to make, and couldn't be bothered worrying about neighborhood zoning or the latest citizen complaint. They let their campaign contributions and their all-pervasive influence determine the outcome of elections. And they rarely had difficulty communicating their wishes to those they had helped elect.

If the people were to draft a gambler for the job, Stupak would not have been their first choice. There were several more popular options. Horseshoe Club patriarch Benny Binion enjoyed his role as the wily sage and grandfather of Glitter Gulch. Sure, he had obliged a few men whom he believed needed killing during his wilder days, but a little gunplay never hurt a fellow's reputation in Las Vegas. Then there was Jackie Gaughan, the former Omaha gambler who, with Brooklyn-born partner Mel Exber, turned a downtown grubstake into a formidable casino empire. Gaughan and Exber would have made a good team, but they were too busy taking care of business.

Flamingo developer and mob representative Benjamin Siegel captured the political philosophy of the old Las Vegas gambler when he took to task his assistant and boyhood friend, Moe Sedway, a little fellow who smoked long cigars and dreamed of legitimacy. Sedway's entree into Las Vegas society in the early 1940s was so successful that he wanted to run for office; he temporarily forgot he was an outlaw's assistant. Siegel reminded him.

"We don't run for office," Siegel sneered. "We own the politicians."

His political aspirations dashed, Sedway hid from the maniacal Bugsy Siegel for weeks.

In a similar vein, Flamingo frontman Gus Greenbaum, who took over the place after Siegel was murdered in 1947 in Beverly Hills, sometimes was known as the Mayor of Paradise. Mayor Greenbaum and his wife, Bess, had their throats cut in 1958 in Phoenix.

Even if Greenbaum's title was ceremonial and the cause of the homicide not politically motivated, perhaps Stupak should have taken it as a sign.

Gamblers' resumes had improved measurably since the days of Siegel and Greenbaum, but the credo remained the same.

In March 1983, Bob Stupak quietly moved from his residence in the county into Vegas World with its city address. The move made him eligible to run for an office in Las Vegas. When filing opened for the spring election, Stupak picked the post with the highest profile: mayor. To reach his goal, he would have to unseat well-liked Bill Briare. While casino bosses had long dictated policy in Nevada, daily governmental operations in Las Vegas were run by staff and the city manager. Although the mayor sat on the City Council, his duties were largely ceremonial. The job paid little, but Stupak wasn't in it for the money.

"I've met Mayor Briare on several occasions and he is, without a doubt, a fine man and a dedicated mayor," Stupak said, already sounding very much like a seasoned politician. "However, eight years is long enough for any man in such a demanding job. Today we need someone with a fresh outlook and a different point of view, a man who is visible and willing to make changes. If nothing else, I assure you I'll make the heart of this city beat as fast and as vibrantly as it ever has in the past."

Stupak promised not to accept campaign contributions larger than $50, but he was far from the people's candidate. He immediately began flooding local newspapers and radio and television stations with advertisements stating his goal of restoring a "winning attitude to Las Vegas." Most of his ideas were ringing clichés, but he appeared to be having a good time. Although his outlay topped $100,000 for the campaign, it put his name and mug in every home in southern Nevada and generated publicity outside the community as well.

Not all of his ideas were crafted as sound bites. Although the office is nonpartisan, Stupak began talking like a well-meaning socialist. If elected, in the first 30 days he promised to create a program that would give senior citizens discounts on medical and dental care. He later expanded the theme to include discounts on clothing and entertainment. As if they didn't know, senior citizens were welcome at Vegas World day or night, too.

On Election Day, Briare prevailed with 61.5 percent of the vote, but Stupak ran second. His 33.1 percent placed him well ahead of a topless bar proprietor, a retired motel operator, a sporting-goods store owner, and a gaggle of others. Although Stupak hadn't come close to winning, he had developed a dangerous infatuation with politics, one that would return to embarrass him years later.

But in 1983, Stupak was nonchalant about his second-place finish. He knew he had enjoyed his 15 minutes of political fame and more; the campaign cash was money well spent.

"That's the way it goes," he said. "I was looking for a miracle. So many miracles have happened to me since I've been in Las Vegas, I was starting to get used to them."

Less than a year later, Stupak hit upon a way to attract attention to his casino that not even the city's legendary promoters had considered: he would hire a guy to jump off the building.

He found his man in Dan Koko, a divorced father of three from North Carolina who specialized in high-altitude stunts. Dressed like a pilot without an airplane, on May 19, 1984, Koko stepped out of a window on the 20th floor. Arms wide, he dropped 250 feet and landed atop a giant airbag.

The fact Koko had dropped more than 80 yards and lived barely caused a ripple in the Las Vegas media. Local newspaper editors were so used to Stupakian stunts that they played the photograph, which depicted Koko falling off the Earth, on page 10 of the local section.

Three months later, Stupak upped the stakes and drew national attention: he promised to pay Dan Koko $1 million if he would free-fall 326 feet from a scaffolding atop the hotel. The record for such madness was 311 feet.

Koko accepted and stepped into thin air outside Vegas World on August 30. This time, Stupak made certain the press was watching. Photographers from the *National Enquirer* and *People* magazine and cameramen from "Entertainment Tonight" were there to capture every second. Stupak again had seized the moment. For a short time, the gambling world was looking his direction on the Strip.

Koko landed safely and the feat was memorialized from coast to coast.

"I feel pretty good, just a little shaky," Koko said, after the jump.

His emotional state soon grew noticeably shakier. According to Stupak, while he was playing high-stakes poker in Ireland, Koko concocted a contract in order to secure the huge safety airbag he used for his jumps. The bag's manufacturer believed Koko was cutting him in on 25 percent of a million-dollar payday. Stupak discovered the problem when he returned to Las Vegas and found Koko and company waiting to be paid.

The fallout from the jump held all the promise of a public-relations fiasco, so Stupak devised a plan he thought would make everyone happy. He announced that he had charged Koko a $975,000 landing fee for the million-dollar jump. Reporters laughed it off as yet another Stupak caper. Koko was ready to take his money and run. Only the duped airbag manufacturer was displeased. So much so, in fact, that he sued Stupak for breach of contract.

But in those days, Stupak seldom entered into an agreement without getting the best of the deal. After a three-day trial, a jury found in Stupak's favor. Koko, meanwhile, went into hiding.

All in all, it was just another day at Vegas World for a man becoming known as the biggest promoter in a huckster's paradise.

FOUR

The Huckster in Paradise

Bob Stupak worked long hours to make a name for himself as a fearless high-stakes gambler, but casino industry observers were beginning to realize that self-promotion was Stupak's greatest strength.

The image of Stupak as a marketing expert was bolstered by the growing success of Vegas World despite its inferior size and location. But if he were ever to rival the success of Atlantic City casino mogul Donald Trump or Las Vegas casino legends Benny Binion and Jackie Gaughan, he would have to sell more than his rooms and games. He would have to sell himself to a public that viewed him with growing skepticism.

"The guy is such a marketing genius," casino owner John Woodrum later said. "You're not talking about the average marketing person here. With Bob, everything's got a little curve on it. Everything Bob's ever done, you've got to read the small print because what you see ain't what you get. He's always been one of those guys who carried a two-headed nickel. When Bob said, 'I'll take heads, double or nothing,' he had you. Both sides of that nickel were heads."

Gaming consultant Howard Grossman recalled, "He knew how to gamble and he had the mentality of a gambler. There was no reason to come to Vegas World. It certainly wasn't a nice place. Even when he fixed it up it still wasn't anything to talk about. But it was full of people.

"He knew how to bring in people. With his vacation offers, he gave away the rooms. Customers basically stayed for free, but he made sure you were gambling at his casino. So the people had no other place to go when they got there. Vegas World wasn't close to anywhere. Other places would be empty, and we used to have almost all the business. He knew how to get people in and he knew about gambling."

How strong were the vacation offers?

Grossman recalled the time Stupak took a map of the Midwest, spun it on a table, closed his eyes, and pointed to a spot.

"Send a mailer out to this place," Stupak told one of his people.

"It was amazing," Grossman said. "He had a tremendous response to it."

In various forms, values, and prices, Vegas World's Vegas VIP Vacation packages allowed Stupak to successfully overcome his lousy location and other limitations. Where resorts in the heart of the Strip relied not only on their marketing but also on a percentage of walk-in customers, only transients and "funbook Freddies" were likely to stumble into Stupak's place. The vacation packages helped even the score.

They also set him at odds with state attorneys general and Nevada gaming regulators for years to come.

The basic package was promoted through direct-mail marketing and national newspaper and magazine advertisements. The prices and perquisites varied—many offers cost as little as $398 per couple—but it took a coupon-clipping bargain shopper to get the most out of Vegas World's "virtually free" promotion. One of the better values included two nights at Vegas World, $200 in cash, $200 more in table action, $400 in slot action (good only at special machines that paid off as often as the Chicago Cubs won the World Series), tickets to Vegas World's showroom, unlimited cocktails, a load of other gambling paraphernalia, and a sapphire-and-diamond pendant liberally valued at $270.

Many other similarly worded advertisements lacked the $200 cash kicker, and Stupak's special slots were notoriously stingy, but the packages packed Vegas World as never before. His annual revenues jumped from $7 million when he opened in 1979 to nearly $100 million in 1986.

The ads left no doubt as to the owner's motivations.

"When asked how he could possibly give so much for so little, Stupak explains:

"'Even though you are under no obligation to play with your own money, many people will. And a few high rollers will gamble enough to cover the cost of your entire vacation—with all the benefits.'

"All winners are paid in cash. Players keep what they win. There are no additional charges of any kind."

A national consumer magazine cut through the hype on both sides of the issue and captured the essence of the $398 VIP Vacation.

"It doesn't appear to be a scam, but it's not much of a deal, either. The only real money in the 'bankroll' is $200 in cash; the other $1,000 is 'action' credit for some long-odds casino play. In effect, what you're buying is two days of lodging, dinner, and some modest extras for $198, about par for downtown Las Vegas."

"The real truth of the matter is that the people who bought a vacation club in essence were getting their rooms for about free," David Sklansky said. "The principle behind why this deal worked, especially in the beginning, is that a casino can afford to give away rooms for free if, in return, they know people have $400 in their pocket.

"Bob's location turned from a negative into a positive because, since it wasn't really within walking distance, people were less likely to leave."

Another curve was Stupak's advertised "Free $50 Casino Bankroll in Vegas." It wasn't a bad value even if it was divided into $20 in table chips and $30 in slot action at Vegas World's suspect machines. For a $2 registration fee, how could a person go wrong?

The hook was in the fine print. Participants received the $50 value over the course of nearly three hours. It left them plenty of time not only to spend the so-called free money, but a little of their own cash as well. It was precisely the sort of pitch that ensured Vegas World's survival, but it did not impress the Strip's well-heeled operators. Stupak was almost as good at annoying his peers as he was at attracting customers.

To assist in his customers' decision making, he produced a 1985 book titled, *Stupak on Craps*. Ghost written by Roger Dionne, the book was a collection of tips on playing casino games. On the cover, *Stupak on Craps* was touted as the book of the year by something called the American Gaming Association. In all, Stupak himself wrote eight pages of the text.

"Craps is basically one of the easiest games in the casino, even though it looks like the most complicated," Stupak wrote. "I'm going to explain craps to you as simply as possible, and after you've read the next few pages, you should know as much about the game as anybody at the table."

The book was dedicated "To all the crapshooters in the world, especially to my father, Chester Stupak, and Eric Drache."

Stupak groomed his image as a high-stakes hustler in Las Vegas, and by 1986 his gambling philosophy was well developed. Casinos weren't for every jurisdiction, just as cards and dice weren't for every person. Over the years, he had seen scores of friends and customers go from lighthearted bettors to degenerate players. He loved the image of the gambler and, indeed, the element of chance coursed through his veins, but he was decidedly opposed to legalized casinos in Melbourne, where he had built his personal fortune and met his two wives. In light of future events within the industry and the eventual expansion of various forms of wagering to 48 states and throughout the world, his candor caught Australian reporters by surprise during a business vacation.

"If the Premier rang and begged me to corrupt this city with a casino, then I'd be willing to accommodate him," he said in Melbourne. "But what does a casino give to people? It's not culturally enriching and it's certainly not socially good.

"I've seen what casinos have done to my own country. Atlantic City was a dying city and now with 11 casinos it's become a bigger slum and is full of degenerates."

A staunch prohibitionist couldn't have said it more clearly, and Stupak was anything but that. But neither was he a hypocrite. He knew that a casino, no matter its size or number of hotel rooms, was "still just a gambling joint." And Melbourne didn't need a casino disguised as a resort on the Yarra River.

His comments would not sit well with his casino colleagues in Las Vegas, where powerful operators such as Steve Wynn had long since taken to using Stupak and his gaudy operation as the butt of their jokes.

"The idea you have to have a casino to be in the big time is nonsense—New York, Los Angeles, and Tokyo don't have them and Melbourne's up there too," Stupak told the press.

"What do you want? To ruin your kids and make 10 percent of your population degenerates? It would be okay in Alice Springs or some place in the middle of the desert like Las Vegas. I lived here as a young man for a few years. I was twenty-one years old and working in the advertising industry. Melbourne is a very gracious city. Why would you want to ruin it?

"Places like Vegas, well, people make an effort to go there. If you had a casino here you could pop in every couple of hours for a bet and it would get compulsive. If people want to join the big league, they should join the big league of cities that don't have casinos. It's places like Monte Carlo and Egypt that have them and then they ban the local people from going in. Australia is a free society so you couldn't ban the locals. You're better off without. I've been lucky with gambling and at the moment I reckon I'm 6-to-1 to go upstairs when I die. I hope to earn a few extra points by keeping gambling out of Victoria."

The Aussie reporters knew too well that Stupak's behavior ran contrary to his warning to the general public.

"I know the risks, but no way am I compulsive," he said. "I am a professional. I need all the information before I bet. That's the difference."

After nearly two decades away from Melbourne, Stupak still managed to attract attention wherever he went. While dining at the posh Lazar's restaurant, his table for 14 grew into a party of 23.

"We fitted them in somehow," said a general manager. "Bob said his guests could have anything they liked—and one ordered zambaglione for dessert containing two nips of Louis 13th cognac.

"It cost $80."

Back home, Stupak returned to his world of operating his own casino and wagering a fortune from Binion's Horseshoe to Caesars Palace. Although he owned a half dozen Rolls-Royce automobiles, he had taken to driving up and down the Strip in his Vegas World "rocket car," a cramped coupe with his casino logo emblazoned on the side. He was easy to spot in traffic. The speedy racer rarely reached speeds topping 35 miles-per-hour in Strip traffic.

Not everyone appreciated his sense of style, or his parking skill for that matter. When the Frontier Hotel sponsored the Jack Strauss Poker Tournament, Stupak couldn't wait to test his talent against the best players in the world, including his contemporaries Puggy Pearson and Bobby Baldwin. So he drove the rocket car south on the Strip and pulled into the middle of the Frontier portico. He untangled himself from the James Bondmobile, entered the casino, and took his seat amid a veritable hall of fame of poker.

In a few minutes, Frontier Executive Vice President Richard Schuetz approached the table and quietly mentioned that Stupak's rocket vehicle was blocking the hotel driveway.

"I'll move it in a few minutes," Stupak said.

A few minutes later, Schuetz returned to remind him.

"I said I'd get to it in a few minutes," Stupak said.

After another few minutes, Schuetz returned once more.

"If you don't move your vehicle, I'll have it towed," he said.

Stupak balked again even after being told that the unassuming Schuetz was not a valet attendant but a casino executive. By the time he got out to the portico, the rocket car had been towed to the back of the property.

"He was quite rude, I thought," Schuetz recalled years later. "Bob's attitude was, 'I don't give a fuck.'"

Approximately a decade later, Richard Schuetz would take over as president of Stratosphere in the wake of mountainous operational problems and attempt to bail out the property. The rocket car was last seen parked with a flat tire outside Gene Maday's Little Caesar's casino.

Stupak's nights were filled with forays into enemy territory, where his reputation as a high-stakes player with a kamikaze style preceded him. On a hot night, he made more money in a few hours than Vegas World did all week. When he went cold, he nosedived down to his last nickel.

It was on just such a night that John Woodrum encountered Stupak dining at Caesars Palace's Ah'So Japanese restaurant. Woodrum was there with his wife on their anniversary. Before their meal arrived, Stupak called him over to his table, where he proceeded to explain how the night's action had gone from bad to worse.

"I blew my bankroll," Stupak said. Worse, his dinner date had stood him up. But, Woodrum noticed, Stupak was seated with another man.

"Aren't you going to introduce me to your friend, Bob?" Woodrum asked.

Stupak turned to his dinner guest.

"What the hell is your name, anyway?" he asked.

Stupak, who had a complimentary dinner for two, met the stranger at the bar and, not wanting to waste the freebie, invited him to dinner. Then Stupak's real motivation for signaling Woodrum became clear.

"John," he said quietly, "I'm busted."

"Totally busted?"

"Totally busted," Stupak replied. "I need a couple hundred to cover the tip. That's why I hollered at you."

Woodrum loaned his fellow casino owner $200. Stupak over-tipped as usual; he didn't want to be considered a stiff—especially with John Woodrum's money.

Like many of the Las Vegas casino operators who had come before him, including Ben Siegel and the reigning king of Las Vegas, Steve Wynn, Bob Stupak had long been infatuated with Hollywood. Siegel flunked his screen test but still maintained a friendship with film-gangster George Raft, while Wynn starred in his own commercials with Frank Sinatra and Whoopi Goldberg and made a cameo appearance in the hour-long made-for-TV infomercial, "Treasure Island: The Adventure Begins." Stupak was even more aggressive in courting speaking roles in television series and big-budget films.

By his count, Stupak has appeared in eight movies and television series. Few of the movies were memorable—*Fever Pitch* and *Night Tracker* were not exactly art cinema—and his roles were mostly limited to playing the quintessential Vegas gambling boss with the loud sports coat and louder mouth. Some would call it typecasting.

Perhaps the pinnacle of his acting avocation was a role as Pete Bauer in the popular 1980s television cop show, "Crime Story." Set in the mobbed-up Las Vegas of the 1960s, "Crime Story" starred Dennis Farina as a tough-talking mob-buster. Stupak debuted February 28, 1987.

He played an independent gambling boss out to make the

Lucky Star casino the most profitable joint in Las Vegas. But, in the TV show, Bauer finds himself the victim of a classic mob bustout and takeover.

First, the cash reserves disappear.

"We ain't got no money left in the cage," one of the feckless insiders informs him. "You got to go to the bank."

"Hey, look," Bauer snarls. "You go tell the blackjack dealers to turn both their cards up to the players. All righty. Single decks. Get the card counters in here at three hundred dollar minimum bets. Now go."

The scriptwriter had taken a page out of Stupak's own Vegas World casino strategy.

Then the news gets worse.

"Don't nobody ever lose in this joint?" he asks his shifty accountants. "We ought to have an advertisement. You know, 'Everybody wins at Pete Bauer's Gaming Emporium.'

"You're going belly up, Mr. Bauer," the no-good accountant says.

In the next scene, Bauer appears on stage in the crowded Lucky Star showroom before his employees.

"This means everybody has to work seven days. No overtime," he says as the hired help grouses.

"Listen, listen. We're going downhill and we're going downhill fast.

"You blackjack dealers, you hear me? From now on, when you bust and the customer busts, the customer don't lose no more—it's even.

"That's the kind of thinking Pete Bauer's going to bring into this place. You know, we get the players in here, we can roll in the money.

"And remember, our customers are the best people on Earth. So when they come in here you treat them like a friend, like your family.

"And then beat them out of everything they got. You understand? Now get out of here—and win!"

First, hoods planted inside Bauer's casino skim the daily

count and create all sorts of havoc. Then, when he can't pay his mortgage, Bauer is informed that he no longer is the owner of record. The mob is.

"With three mortgage payments in arrears, we thought it time to step in and kind of shore things up," the Outfit business-man says.

"You mean you were the guys who stepped in and bought up my paper?"

"This will give you time to rethink your financial situation. Think of us as taking over the casino on your behalf. We still want you to stay with our organization."

"You know, I could have paid you back."

"It doesn't work that way, Pete."

"What'd you do this to me for?" Pete Bauer asks, wiping his eyes.

"Paulie, get him out of here."

Longtime locals who watched the show recognized Stupak's casino philosophy. A few also would have laughed at the irony of the gaudily dressed gambling man falling prey to the mob. Stupak had been suspected of his own unsavory associations and had fended off advances from street hoods for years. And his father had such a long history of dodging organized crime figures in Pittsburgh that he easily might have served as a "Crime Story" adviser.

With Los Angeles crime figure Mike Rizzitello on his way to prison for attempting to extort money from venerable gaming figures Benny Binion and Moe Dalitz, much of the television series' plot was based in fact.

Stupak clearly reveled in the celebrity. In early 1987, he took out advertisements in industry magazines promoting himself and his role. Surely producers would knock themselves out pursuing Bob Stupak, "The World's Greatest Gamblin' Man":

"Now Available For Acting Roles and Gambling Consultation For the Motion Picture and Television Industry."

His list of credits included appearances on "60 Minutes," "Merv Griffin," and "Ripley's Believe It or Not." He boasted of being "the man who beat a computer at poker for half a million dollars in front of 25 million people; the man who owns the world's largest non-corporate hotel-casino: Vegas World; the man who bets and accepts the world's largest wagers; the man who challenged anyone to play tic-tac-toe with a chicken for thousands in his casino; and the man who changed the face of Vegas gambling."

So what if the Imperial Palace actually was the largest non-corporate hotel-casino in the country? Few people would know the facts. Although it's unclear how a chicken tic-tac-toe challenge might tickle the fancy of a finicky casting director, Stupak was anything but shy. With Michael Mann (producer of "Miami Vice," starring Don Johnson) acting as his personal agent, Stupak appeared ready to embark on an acting career. Of course, his critics at the Gaming Control Board for years had claimed his casino-boss routine was little more than over-the-top role playing.

Scott Higginson, a future Las Vegas City Councilman who in 1987 was an executive with R&R Advertising, designed the strategy for Stupak's Hollywood coming-out. Higginson recalled Stupak wanting to parlay his small television role into a higher profile—and not strictly for personal aggrandizement. Stupak knew the popular television show would be good for his casino business. But even Higginson scratched his head over the use of the chicken reference.

Fact checkers from one magazine's ad department were confused by the side-by-side photos of Stupak and Bauer. Higginson was called.

"They figured, 'That must be the character,'" Higginson recalled. "I said, 'This one is the character, Pete Bauer. This is Bob Stupak.' They couldn't tell the difference."

Stupak's act didn't stop with a bit part on television. In fact, in the spring of 1987 his Las Vegas detractors figured he had switched from drama to comedy when he announced his second mayoral candidacy. Laughter erupted in every corner of the Las Vegas Valley. There he goes again, cynics cackled, promoting himself and that Naked City eyesore. Stupak was supremely shameless in a city without shame. When would he ever learn?

Like most Las Vegans, Scott Higginson had difficulty taking Stupak seriously. When Stupak asked Higginson to become his campaign manager, the advertising man laughed out loud. He did, after all, plan to live in Las Vegas and had no interest in joining Stupak as a community laughing stock.

"I thought it was another one of his publicity stunts," Higginson said. "I liked Bob, but come on, there was no way he was going to be taken seriously."

Higginson wasn't Stupak's first choice, of course. Stupak preferred to hire nationally recognized political consultant Sig Rogich, whose credits included Ronald Reagan's successful presidential campaigns. But Rogich knew better than to link arms with the Vegas World owner. That fact did not, however, preclude Stupak from hiring Rogich as a consultant as a way of preventing him from joining the opposition.

Still, Higginson was considered one of the brightest young minds in the southern Nevada image business, and Stupak was persistent. His offers became increasingly generous, and at one point he offered Higginson a large consulting fee and a classic 1958 Corvette.

"Take the job and the car's yours," Stupak said.

Only in Las Vegas would a candidate make such an offer. Higginson nearly blushed at all the attention from his political suitor, but still declined to officially manage Stupak's campaign. He did agree to render his honest opinion of Candidate Stupak. When Higginson went to see Stupak at Vegas World, he asked an employee for directions to the boss's office. The employee laughed.

"He doesn't have an office," she said. "His office is in the coffee shop."

In reality, Stupak's office was a dingy, little-used space on the third floor of Vegas World. When Higginson eventually saw it, he was stunned.

"It literally had dust on everything," he said. "He was never there."

When he sat down with Stupak, Higginson remembered the confusion over the advertising photographs and smiled. Stupak was more of a character than the TV character ever hoped to be. He wasn't mayoral material even by Las Vegas standards. With his 1,000-decibel sport coats and dress shirts opened to the Vegas minimum two buttons deep, Stupak was a ringing stereotype of the old-style operator as one part crap dealer, one part con man.

"Why won't you handle my campaign?" Stupak asked. "I want your honest opinion."

"Number one," Higginson replied, "you need a haircut. Number two, you need to get rid of the clothes...You don't look like a mayor. You don't act like a mayor. You don't dress like a mayor."

By the time Higginson was finished unloading, Stupak's Vegas-guy image had been picked to pieces, from his too-slick hair to his pinkie ring. Stupak was, after all, a man prone to wearing sunglasses at night in his casino. Higginson left the meeting feeling bad about the way he had treated Stupak. The ad man was certain it was impossible for Stupak to change his gaudy spots.

"The next week I got a call from Bob," Higginson said. "He wanted me to come down to Vegas World and talk to him again."

Higginson reluctantly agreed.

He had difficulty believing his eyes. Pete Bauer had vanished. The diamond pinky ring was gone, as were the tinted shades. The technicolor sport coat was history, and Stupak's hair was styled and blow-dried. He was dressed in the standard power outfit favored by congressmen. Stupak wore a dark blue suit, pressed white shirt, and red tie.

"I'm standing there thinking, he's got a haircut. He's got a suit on. He looks like a businessman," he recalled. "I was pretty impressed. I wasn't sure what kind of candidate he would make, but at least he was dressing the part."

But in 1987 not many Las Vegans cared whether Bob Stupak ran for mayor or moved to Boise. His relentless self-promotion had managed to irritate even the most jaded residents, and he was fast becoming the butt of jokes by radio disc jockeys, newspaper columnists and, far more importantly, his fellow casino operators.

In early March 1987, a strange thing began to happen. A petition began to circulate the city. Something called the Committee to Draft Bob Stupak Mayor was attempting to pull the Vegas World owner into the race. Stupak claimed to have no knowledge of such a movement; why, he never had considered such a thing, he said. In short order, more than 1,000 names were collected, including those of prominent physician Elias Ghanem and popular television host Gus Giuffre.

What groundswell of broad-based public support was this?

Did Las Vegans secretly love Bob Stupak?

Not exactly.

The petition was the bright idea of Stupak's portly pal Chris Karamanos, a caterer and university regent who owned a restaurant at Vegas World. Karamanos was the city's godfather of cocktail franks, who had gained access to inner circles in large part by providing hors d'oeuvres to the hoi polloi. He took the petition and produced a newspaper advertisement that made it appear Stupak was the people's choice.

"Chris is a good friend of Bob's and he collected the signatures," a Vegas World spokesman said. "It sounded like a good idea."

So much for political intrigue.

It was later revealed that some of the signatures were forged. Not that it mattered. The petitions were mere advertising props.

Although many of the signatures belonged to Vegas World employees, it was clear that the irrepressible Stupak had the mayor's race in mind. But by late March, three perfectly acceptable candidates—Councilman Ron Lurie, Clark County Commissioner Thalia Dondero, and Republican Party stalwart Tom

Wiesner—had filed for the office. With his background in retail sales, pro-business Lurie fit the city's mayoral tradition. The voters had three safe choices, so the tradition of nice-guy ribbon-cutter was sure to be secure.

Stupak announced his candidacy April 3rd and immediately refused to answer reporters' questions. He went out of his way to skip an opportunity to debate his adversaries, who were running for a job that paid $33,500 a year.

Instead, he began pumping money, much of it his own, into his campaign. By mid-April, he had dumped $130,000—$65,000 out of his own pocket—into a variety of advertisements. In response to the threat, downtown casino operators—Stupak's own brothers in arms—began filling up Lurie's campaign warchest.

While other candidates squabbled over the issues, Stupak's name filled television screens night after night. He would be a 24-hour mayor for a 24-hour town.

Not that it kept him from contributing to his opponents. Stupak, ever the savvy gambler, hedged his political bet by contributing $10,000 to Lurie's campaign through the Leeman Corporation.

"That $10,000 I gave Lurie I could use now for the campaign," Stupak cracked to a reporter.

With a reported net worth of $54 million, he could afford to be generous, but the Lurie donation raised the issue of whether he was merely interested in promoting his name or truly serious about winning the office. While other candidates scrambled to scrape up enough cash to pay for yard signs and radio advertisements, Candidate Stupak donated freely to other candidates.

He also courted registered voters with gifts. In the days leading up to the May primary, Stupak's political team delivered hundreds of fruit baskets and clock radios. He twice issued promotional shares of stock in Vegas World. In all, he spent an estimated $300,000 in the five weeks leading up to Election Day. His opponents howled in protest, but for once Las Vegans were being entertained during the normally sedate mayor's race.

He didn't just hand out loot. His irreverent television commercials endeared him to many Las Vegans who had considered him little more than a casino freak. Stupak's ex-wife, Sandy, and father, Chester, appeared in the commercials, and at one point the casino candidate threatened to sue "Saturday Night Live," which vilified Las Vegas in one of its late-night skits. He even offered to bet Lurie $1,000 at 50-to-1 odds—which would yield the councilman $50,000 if he prevailed—that the two would square off in the general election. Lurie wouldn't take the bet.

By early May, Stupak had thrown a considerable scare into the local political establishment. He appeared to be attempting to buy the election. And he had sellers.

On May 5, the voters went to the polls—and the media went to its battle stations. The primary was competitive, but Stupak grabbed the early lead and held it. By the end of the night, Lurie was thankful he didn't take that bet. He would have lost his money.

Stupak garnered 33.4 percent of the vote, Lurie 26.1 percent, Dondero 21.2 percent, and Wiesner 16.4 percent.

The morning's headlines reflected the surprise on the part of the press and the pundits. The traditionally staid *Review-Journal*, which had not taken Stupak's candidacy at all seriously, declared on Page 1:

STUPAK CAPTURES PRIMARY

The *Las Vegas Sun*, rarely one for understatement, splashed the news across the front page:

STUPAK WINS PRIMARY? YOU BET!

"The voters of Las Vegas sent a message that they're tired of politicians," Stupak told reporters. "They want fresh blood, something new. I'm it."

Ron Lurie, the machine favorite, struggled to put the best spin possible on playing second banana to Bob Stupak.

"I'm not disappointed I finished second because I wanted to

get in the runoff," he said. "We're going to take the issues out and discuss them with the people...What he's done is very questionable and I think the voters will see through it.

"Bob Stupak hid behind the television this campaign and failed to appear at any event to discuss the issues. As critical as things are in this city, he can't afford not to discuss the issues with the public any longer."

Lamented Wiesner, "I'm disappointed because I have a high regard for the electorate and they got conned. I feel bad that the voters of Las Vegas are that susceptible. The media let them get conned. They made a joke out of it, but he's there."

Dondero said, "This shows you that you can buy an election."

The also-rans immediately threw their support behind Lurie.

And so, the mayor's race suddenly turned into one of the most significant political struggles in Las Vegas history. The elderly and working class were getting a kick out of Stupak, but the establishment immediately began panicking. Clearly, the paranoid political power structure in Las Vegas saw Stupak's primary victory not as a joke, but as a threat to its security and the image of the city. After all, Las Vegas had a difficult enough time earning respect from the nation without electing the wacky wizard of Vegas World as its most visible representative.

The political establishment came out in force on behalf of the soft-spoken Lurie. Governor Richard Bryan, later a U.S. Senator, took time out from his duties to endorse Lurie, as did Clark County Sheriff John T. Moran, at the time the most popular elected official in the community. Party bosses from both sides lauded Lurie in an obvious attempt to slow Stupak's momentum.

But Stupak couldn't exactly go fishing until election day if he planned to win skeptical hearts and convince the citizenry that he was a viable candidate. And a sober one. Rumors of his persistent drug use had become a campaign issue.

In a campaign forum at the Senior Center a few days before the general election, an odd request was shouted from the crowd.

Would the candidates submit to drug testing?

Stupak couldn't blame everyone in the offending crowd for thinking what so many others were thinking: that the casino candidate couldn't pass a drug analysis. Rather than claim that his privacy was being violated or that his integrity was being questioned, Stupak agreed to be tested. Lurie also said yes.

Had Lurie's advisers scored a death blow?

Hardly. Rumors to the contrary, Stupak's test was negative. He wasn't going away that easily.

As the general election approached, Lurie's image as the safe choice for mayor was beginning to sink in with Las Vegans. They might have had more laughs with Stupak, but they figured they were better off with Lurie.

On election night, Stupak's confidants were giving him the bad news. Their exit polls and the early official returns gave Lurie what appeared to be a small but stable lead. A disconsolate Stupak lost control.

He drove to Lurie's headquarters and attempted to meet with his opponent. In the process, he dumped over a table of deli food and acted like a man possessed. His physical aversion to losing was showing through at the worst possible moment.

With reporters gathering around, he attempted to concede. But he was glassy eyed and emotional. At one point, a young reporter asked him if he was on drugs.

Instead of laughing or even yelling at the reporter, Stupak lightly slapped his face. Thousands of southern Nevadans watched his open-handed battery.

"I hated to see Bob the way he was that night," Higginson said. "People didn't realize how badly he wanted to win. He was just that close to gaining the respect of the community and his own colleagues, none of whom could say they had been mayor of Las Vegas. He was so close. When he knew he was going to lose, he just couldn't handle it."

John Woodrum added, "He never could handle losing. You're talking about one competitive son of a gun."

When the votes were counted, Lurie defeated Stupak, 18,013

to 15,451, in the most expensive campaign in the city's history. Combined, they spent $1.3 million. Stupak's camp spent $839,407—nearly $800,000 out of the candidate's own pocket—in what even for him was one of the more expensive poker games of his life.

In the wake of the election defeat, Stupak vowed never again to run for public office and to get out of politics for good. The sighs of relief coming from the Chamber of Commerce and casino executive offices were almost audible. But it was a vow he would not keep.

Stupak had long since become a favorite target of local columnists, who couldn't resist doubting his acumen and lampooning his every move. Rebuffed by the local newspapers for his dubious games of chance and his celebration of all that was gaudy about Las Vegas, Stupak in late 1987 decided to channel his ranting into a loud-mouthed weekly newspaper called the *Bullet*. Its motto: "Taking AIM with the TRUTH!"

With a small staff tucked into one of Stupak's Naked City buildings at 300 W. Boston Street three blocks from Vegas World, the *Bullet* fired its first shot on February 3, 1988, with an exposé of street-corner preacher John 3:16 Cook. It wasn't exactly Pulitzer material, and Cook's antics with the city's homeless were well known and hardly sinister, but the effort managed to attract the attention of southern Nevada's two dailies, both of which ran articles on the *Bullet's* first issue.

Local reporters quickly labeled the *Bullet* a rag unworthy of reading, but the sensational scandal sheet, which featured a weekly exposé, along with columns by the publisher and upstart Las Vegas City Councilman Steve Miller, gained a small but loyal following of outcasts, gadflies, casino employees, and southern Nevadans who recognized the danger of a traditional Las Vegas press that had long since grown too cozy with the casino industry and the political powerbrokers.

"'I think the public needs to know a lot more than they're getting,' Stupak told his own reporter in the paper's premier issue. "Stupak sees the two daily newspapers in Las Vegas, the *Review-Journal* and the *Sun*, as having become afflicted with 'tunnel vision over the last couple of years. When the *Valley Times* was alive, it came up with controversial stories. I don't think anybody ever filled that gap. The *Review-Journal* and *Sun* report the same things.'

"'...Some people may think I'm doing this for vindictive reasons, but nothing could be further from the truth. I thought some people might be interested in my opinions.

"'The paper will be hot, controversial, factual and never boring or dull...The success of any newspaper is determined by its bottom line, and I expect to put up with losses. We are not going to let an advertising dollar interfere with the editorial content. I just want it to be factual.'

"'It can bring a message I want to make. If there's some point that I want to make with the politicians, the establishment, the citizens of Las Vegas, I have a vehicle to do it."

Stupak's "As I See It" column lacked the fire of *Las Vegas Sun* publisher Hank Greenspun's "Where I Stand" essays, but it enabled the *Bullet* publisher to punish his enemies, laud his friends, and hold forth on a number of topics. And, he might snicker, how many high-school dropouts in America had their own newspaper?

Miller's column, "Inside City Hall," managed not only to infuriate his political colleagues, but also get him sued for libel after he accused a local businessman of skimming. Several years later, Miller's insurance company settled the case out of court for a six-figure settlement.

Although it took aim often in its 18 months in circulation, in the end the *Bullet* fell victim to the caliber of its character and to the changing interests of its publisher.

Aside from the *Bullet* and a stint as a monthly columnist for *Gambling Times* magazine, Stupak's interest in journalism was limited to seeing his name in headlines. In January 1989, he made a huge score, not only monetarily but in the form of newsprint as well.

The occasion was Super Bowl XXIII on January 22, 1989, the most watched television event of the year and Las Vegas's biggest betting day. Stupak was determined to cash in on the moment.

But how?

Casinos weren't allowed to advertise on television, and besides, 30-second spots were going for more than $250,000.

Stupak would do what he did best: go head to head against someone with an outrageous bet—say, $1 million. Anything less wouldn't guarantee press coverage. Anything more and he might break into an uncontrollable sweat. Stupak found his man in Little Caesar's casino and sports book owner, Gene Maday.

Sure enough, he received several times that amount in press coverage for himself and Vegas World. The bet focused international attention, even when it became suspected that Stupak had arranged the wager as a publicity stunt. Maday grudgingly went along with the idea.

Stupak called the bet a reaction to a problem he was having with a girlfriend.

"The Super Bowl bet wasn't actually designed for publicity, but it got me in the world-wide spotlight immediately," he told journalist/author James Rutherford. "I was on TV in Australia, I was on the front page of Japanese and Chinese daily newspapers, I was everywhere. It was 1989. I liked Cincinnati over San Francisco. The night before, I had had an argument with a girlfriend. And when we woke up, the beef was still there. Now some guys, when they have a problem with their girlfriend, go out and drink too much. Me, I bet too much. So I went up and down the Strip, to Caesars and the Barbary Coast, figuring I'd bet a few hundred thousand, looking for the right place—but no one wanted to mess with the big bet. So I ended up at Little Caesar's, and he asked me to bet a million. I asked him why. Gene wanted to get himself even. He gave me a break on the juice. I was only going to bet three hundred thousand, but he said that if I wanted to bet a million I'd only pay half the juice. I got a fifty-thousand-dollar discount on a million-dollar bet. Then I went home and took a nap. When I woke up, the game already started."

San Francisco was a seven-point favorite to defeat the Cincinnati Bengals. Stupak took the underdog Bengals and the points. When the final score fell, San Francisco 20, Cincinnati 16, Stupak was $1 million richer.

With the cameras capturing the moment, Stupak exited Little Caesar's carrying a box and a McDonald's sack supposedly filled with cash from the bet. Television stations across North America showed the scene, and Stupak never let on that the box was empty and the bag full of paper.

Afterward, Gene Maday rarely discussed the bet, and casino bosses on the Strip scoffed at the notion of its authenticity. Maday died in 1995. His wife, Gerry Maday, recalled her husband's sometimes frustrating relationship with Stupak, who gave Gene Maday a miniature rocket car as a gift after the Super Bowl win. The car sat in the Little Caesar's parking lot for several years.

Stupak gave Maday much more in the form of big bets.

"Gene used to say Bob was a bad gambler, especially when it came to betting football," Gerry recalled. "Gene didn't want to take the Super Bowl bet. Bob insisted. Gene knew it was for publicity reasons, and Bob ran to the newspapers with the story."

Far from taking a massive hit at Little Caesar's, Maday simply balanced out his betting action on the game by laying off wagers on the other side. He not only didn't lose money, but he gained a steady customer in Stupak. And Stupak's Super Bowl luck didn't last the year. He spent plenty of money at Little

Caesar's.

For months afterward Stupak would be hit with speculation that he had faked the bet by wagering on both sides. The Gaming Control Board inquired into the validity of the wager and found no compelling reason to doubt Stupak. But for Stupak, it was just another example of how he was treated differently than other casino operators by the state regulators.

"Even if I did [bet both sides], what is that to investigate?" Stupak asked. "It wasn't the publicity. It was just a fucking bet. I could always get publicity. Publicity is overrated. Everybody made a big deal out of it. Everybody always made a big deal out of everything. It stopped bothering me years ago.

"Bob liked to be around Gene, but Gene didn't always like to be around Bob," Gerry Maday said. It was bad for her husband's image.

Like the time the Madays were out socializing at the Las Vegas Country Club and Stupak followed them around like a puppy. Gene Maday tried to avoid Stupak, who at the time was on the outs with most of the gambling establishment. When that didn't work, he sniped at Stupak.

"I told him, 'Gene, that was rude,'" Gerry Maday recalled. "He said, 'Rude? The guy gets on my nerves after a while.'"

Maday was not alone, but Stupak remembered the relationship differently. "Gene was a friend," he said. "Me and him were buddy-buddy."

In the late 1980s, Atlantic City casino mogul Donald Trump easily was the most visible figure in the gaming industry. When America thought about legalized gambling, it saw Trump's baby face and gawked at his ostentatious lifestyle. For a huckster like Bob Stupak, the image of the silver spoon-sucking rich casino magnate was too much to resist. Whenever possible, he derided Trump as an empty suit. Stupak's motivation for harassing the Donald became clear in early 1989 when word leaked out that

Stupak was part of an investment group bent on building a casino in Atlantic City. Like many of Stupak's expansion plans, the deal failed to materialize, but that didn't keep him from selling himself to willing reporters.

"Well, the first time I went to Atlantic City is when Resorts opened up. That was quite a while ago," Stupak said in an interview. "I remember what it was like then. And then when I went back, there were two casinos—I believe it was Caesars and Resorts—and the lines were still there. You had to line up to play a slot machine. You still had to line up to play a 21 game.

"Those lines now have dispersed. They have to start marketing new merchandise to get people in there, but their numbers are still phenomenal. And they're continuing to show signs of growth…

"I think my best asset is myself. Because, as an example, customers at Caesars Palace never get to meet Caesar. I've never seen Aladdin running around the Aladdin Hotel. They are corporations—they're large companies. In my particular case, I get to know most of my major customers—and not-so major customers. I think it's important when a person knows who they are losing their money to. Or who they are winning their money from. I try to have a direct response or contact with the customer. I use my personality. I'm very visible in this casino. If I were in Atlantic City, I think I would be very visible there. When people come in, they could expect to see me. You know, I spend twelve to fourteen hours a day here. People aren't surprised to see me anymore like they used to be. I don't think that many people bump into Donald Trump."

Atlantic City was only one destination. Stupak also planned to see his name in lights in Reno. He was beginning to act like a corporate executive, but he made it clear that he had no intention of changing his vision of the casino business.

"I think the gambling industry is probably its own worst enemy," Stupak told an interviewer. "What they have done is legitimize this business too much over the years. Ten, fifteen years ago, this business had a mystique about it. When people came to Las Vegas they expected to find a gangster behind every tree; they felt that every third person was in the mob here; they envisioned people with black shirts and white ties. Every time they saw somebody carrying a violin case, they fantasized that there was probably a machine gun in it. Whether it was true or not, I believe that that image is what made Las Vegas what it is today. That's why Las Vegas became as popular as it is. It was exciting; it made your blood boil.

"But the gaming industry, which is now comprised primarily of public corporations, didn't like this image. I understand what it's like when I leave Las Vegas and go to New York and tell someone that I'm from Vegas; they step back about three feet and look at you like you're some stranger from another planet."

Stupak was adamant about ensuring that the gambling business remain respectable—but not too respectable. To Stupak, mainstreaming the gambling racket took much of the fun out of it and left little room for his carnival barker's personality.

"We always have promotions on the agenda," Stupak said. "The problem with this business is you're only as good as your last promotion, or should I call it my last trick? I just have to keep on coming up with different promotions, with different angles on a continuous basis. I used to think, five or six years ago, what happens if I don't have another…trick to promote—another deal to do? But every time I need them, they've been coming. People ask me where I get them from and I tell them I get them from God, because I really don't know where they come from. I guess they do come from Him. He hasn't let me down for the last ten years and I don't have any reason to believe that He's not going to keep on rolling with me."

For Stupak, God was Luck, a trinket to be squeezed, a benevolent uncle to be tapped in times of need. As a man living in a huckster's paradise, he delighted in his good fortune.

———————

It didn't hurt his image as a gambler to begin showing up at the final table in the high-profile games at Binion's Horseshoe's World Series of Poker. In 1989, Stupak turned a $5,000 buy-in in the deuce-to-seven draw competition into a $139,500 win and a world title. He placed 16th the following year in the no-limit Texas hold'em tournament and came in fourth in the 1991 deuce-to-seven draw game. By 1993, his career earnings at the World Series were $222,700, with an incalculable figure attached to the publicity his casino received.

"What poker is all about is moxey, guts, courage," Stupak once said. "That's what gambling is all about. Just remember, whatever your hand looks like, when you put a lot of chips out, everybody might fold behind you. And they'll fold more times than they'll accept. So what you've done is you've eliminated the value of money, and now the only thing you're doing is playing for points. That's the secret of poker."

Stupak had plenty of detractors, but he always had a friend in University Regent Chris Karamanos. The two were business partners and had known each other for years. They shared an interest in the Kelly & Cohen's restaurant at Vegas World and the Thunderbird Hotel a few blocks north on Las Vegas Boulevard. Stupak conducted his affairs from a coffee shop, but he knew almost nothing about running restaurants. Although his other business forays seldom proved successful, Karamanos appeared to have a keen understanding of the restaurant trade.

In late October 1988, they were something of a daring duo in helping to disrupt an armed robbery in progress at the Bottle Collector's Liquor Shop at 1328 Las Vegas Boulevard South. The two suspects were stopped by police after firing shots and waving a .45-caliber pistol at the portly Karamanos and the slender

Stupak.

It was that kind of friendship.

Karamanos had survived 1980 FBI and Clark County District Attorney's office inquiries into the propriety of his catering business, his intricate web of political, social, and Hollywood contacts, and the use of his position as a University Regent to further his catering-business interests. He had survived 42 lawsuits in 18 years. Karamanos, whose jet charter service once was accused of cocaine smuggling by the Colombian government, even survived his appearance as a character witness for Jimmy Chagra in a federal narcotics trafficking case. Chagra was later convicted of drug running and conspiring along with Charles Harrelson, father of "Cheers" actor Woody Harrelson, to kill a federal judge.

But Karamanos couldn't outrun his own reputation as a big-hearted but immensely sloppy businessman. Cocktail franks and party meatballs were his calling cards, and he never appeared to worry whether bills got paid. He had run up thousands of dollars in debts, borrowed heavily, and was in the process of seeing his catering business go bankrupt in 1989 when the FBI again began to inquire into his friendships and associations.

Karamanos, who had thrived on his ability to make friends, influence people, and cater parties, died alone. His body was found June 9, 1989, in a Mesquite hotel room. His death was attributed to an overdose of sleeping pills. It was a suicide.

Influential members of Las Vegas society, who had relied heavily on the generosity of Karamanos, expressed shock and sadness at learning of their dear friend's demise. Beyond their grief, they would have to find someone else to supply food for their soirees.

Before the funeral service, which was attended by dozens of the people Karamanos had befriended, Stupak was inconsolable.

"My best friend," he said, sobbing openly before a reporter. "I love him. I just love him."

John Woodrum never will forget what he saw as he sat near Stupak at the funeral. When the time came for the congregation to pay its last respects, Stupak joined the procession and approached the casket. As he reached the body of his old friend, he removed some slips of paper from his pocket and transferred them to the pocket of the deceased.

"I know Chris owed Bob quite a bit of money," Woodrum said. "He ran the restaurants for years at Vegas World and he borrowed a lot from Bob. At the funeral, Bob takes out of his pocket some papers and stuffs them in Chris's pocket.

"Bob said, 'He may get lucky and send me back some money some day.'

"Chris was a close second to Bob in everything when it came to running a business," Woodrum said. "Chris would give away the whole store, then turn around and rob the next three guys without a gun. But Chris was a good friend, and Bob loved him."

So of course Bob Stupak forgave the dead man's debts.

Most of his casino colleagues were less forgiving. Stupak had long since begun to wear out his welcome with gaming regulators and corporate gaming bosses. Take Steve Wynn, for instance. Although Stupak would recall many instances in which he and Wynn had "partied together, hung out together," by the mid-1980s Wynn was embarking on a personal mission to remake the Strip in his own image. That image had no place for tacky Vegas World and its uncultured owner.

If Wynn thought Stupak déclassé, then someone as image-paranoid as Donald Trump wouldn't even acknowledge his existence. Trump had emerged as easily the most recognizable face in the gaming industry in the 1980s. In the decade when greed was good, Trump was the flashiest entrepreneur in the casino business. His Atlantic City hotels and New York towers dominated their respective skylines as he dominated the headlines. Although his billionaire status was largely structured out of heavily leveraged cardboard and he would fall victim to his own arrogance by the close of the decade, Trump remained a media darling. From producing bestsellers to purchasing professional football franchises, he appeared to have his hands in everything.

When he announced on television the creation of "Trump, The Game," a board game that was sure to make America forget Monopoly, Bob Stupak must have been stunned. Surely Stupak believed the double-smooth Donald was encroaching on his action as the gaming-industry's No. 1 huckster.

Within days of the announcement, Stupak set to work to trump the Donald. He responded the only way he knew how: If Trump was serious, Stupak would beat him at his own game for $1 million. He communicated the proposition none-too-subtly in an advertisement in the *New York Post*.

With the sort of frat-brother arrogance that for some reason appealed to the nation at the time, Trump scoffed at Stupak's offer. After all, who was Bob Stupak?

The national media were bent on finding out, and again Stupak reveled in his instant celebrity over the $1 million wager—even if he hadn't yet set eyes on the game.

Still Trump wasn't biting.

Trump told the *New York Post*, "It's always possible to lose, even for someone who's used to winning."

Stupak later told an interviewer, "Several months ago on 'Entertainment Tonight,' they had a little press conference and he was talking about his new board game: 'Trump, The Game.' And I remember he said, 'This is the game that will tell you if you have it or not. But if you don't have it, don't worry, you can always enjoy the wife and kids.' That stuck in my mind. I don't know, I just kept thinking about it and I decided to offer him a challenge. I was going to beat Trump at his own game. How many people get to beat Trump at his own game?"

In some regards, Stupak's entire business life had been an exercise in finding out whether he "had it" or not. But the Trump challenge was more than a personal grudge; Stupak also incorporated it into his Vegas World marketing plan. And that wasn't all. He accepted wagers from a few friends, who bet that the Donald would be smart enough to ignore the Nevada nuisance.

"They told me Trump would not respond to the ad—that he would ignore it—that he would lessen his credibility by responding. I had one guy who placed 2-to-1. And the rest was gravy, because I felt that he had no choice but to respond because it wasn't going to be me pushing the issue—it was going to be the media pushing the issue. In fact, this did take place.

"It just seemed like a good thing to do. The challenge was supposed to go into the *New York Times*, not the *Post*. But the *Times* refused to take the ad. So did the *Wall Street Journal*. So I ran it in the *Post* and the Atlantic City paper, just for full coverage. Never saw the game. Friends in New York were scrambling around trying to get their hands on it. It went back and forth in the press. Trump had a lot of bullshit to say to the press, like the money should go to charity. I came back with, 'The hell with this talk about charity, I wanna walk with your money.' I would have found an edge. I've got a lot of experts around me. You know, I'd have had the basic strategy of the game down. Also, I can play. I play games of chance fairly well. So I would have had the edge, I'd have been the favorite. So anyway, two weeks later, I finally saw the game. It's an interesting game. Any number of people from three to eight can play it."

Three to eight, but not man to man.

"You couldn't even play with two," Stupak said. "Trump never even said so."

No one ever accused Stupak of quitting on an idea, especially if it generated publicity, and in May 1990 he returned with another challenge for Trump. If Trump's game was unsuitable for two, then Stupak would produce his own board game.

In national advertisements the Polish Maverick introduced "Stupak, the Game" and issued an open challenge to Trump, this time for charity. Stupak promised to split $250,000 between Las Vegas charities, namely Goodwill Industries and Opportunity Village, and Trump could pick any charity he wished—at Stupak's expense. For his part, Trump was struggling to keep his financial empire from collapsing into the Atlantic Ocean. The point was not lost on a chiding Stupak.

"I read that things are a bit tight at your place so I'll put up all the money," Stupak bragged. "Surely you can spare a few hours away from your lawyers for a friendly game when your favorite charity (or mine) will be the big winner."

The advertisement was, to say the least, pointed: "Now Bob Stupak has thrown down another challenge…one that is going to be tough for the Donald to dodge. Trump can't lose a penny, but the winner's charity could benefit a cool quarter-million dollars!"

Trump again nixed the notion. Officials at Opportunity Village, a work-training center for mentally challenged southern Nevadans, even sent a telegram to Trump.

Stupak, miffed at the snub, said, "Donald says he wants to come to Las Vegas. If he does, then he should come out and get involved in the community. I hope he accepts the challenge this time, because it's for a worthwhile cause."

Not that Stupak wasn't sincerely interested in whipping a billionaire head to head.

In the end, Trump declined again, but Stupak had found yet another way to promote himself and his casino.

Reflecting on the Trump Challenge and his 1989 Super Bowl bet, Stupak was candid with a reporter: "I wound up with two major national stories that hit the wire services. It seems like a barrier you break down. After the Super Bowl bet was picked up by so much media, the Trump bet was picked up again.

"I've never disappointed [reporters] on anything frivolous, it's always been sort of something bona fide and newsworthy. I think the same criteria has happened with the national media now.

"Everything I do is more or less to promote Vegas World. I can't stop growing, I can never be satisfied. I sort of have a motor in my stomach that keeps on turning and I couldn't turn it off even if I wanted to.

"Always having a project, always having things to do, you know, I guess it avoids the boredom. I have so many different projects, it keeps the mind, I think, you know, healthy."

———————

Vegas World was now generating in excess of $100 million per year in gross casino revenues, but Stupak dreamed of bigger things. His huckster's heart appeared to warm considerably when it came to booking acts for Vegas World's surrealistic Galaxy Showroom. Magazine writers and pop culture critics might savage Stupak's taste in bringing in such ancient acts as Tony Martin, Allen & Rossi, and the latest Elvis or Sinatra impersonator, but the Vegas World vacation-package set went wild. For $6, crowds were treated to Marty Allen's trademark "Hello dere," the consummate straight man Steve Rossi, and the talented singer and pianist, Katie Blackwell.

Stupak booked the act after learning that his friend, Rossi, was working again. What began as a favor quickly became a favorite with tourists and Las Vegans on an endless cruise for neon kitsch.

"We signed what Stupak calls a 'lifetime contract,'" Allen told a reporter. "Then I threw out the line, 'My lifetime or yours?'"

For Tony Martin, who had played Las Vegas when Ben Siegel was still running the Flamingo and had held the 1950s captive with his hits "La Vie en Rose" and "To Each His Own," returning to the stage was an opportunity to remind people that he was neither retired nor dead. He was playing Vegas again—Vegas World.

Then there was the amazing stripper who went by the moniker Platinum Peaks for obvious reasons. When she performed to packed houses in Vegas World's Galaxy Showroom, the hotel marquee read, "88-DDDDDDD."

"She did a midnight show," Stupak said. "The show was an hour and a half. She only did the last five to six minutes, and that's all they came for. And she couldn't do any more than that. But it was worth it."

When asked if there was a time when he dated Platinum Peaks, Stupak demurred.

"Oh God, I dated a lot of things," he said, laughing.

While the Las Vegas press never misses the annual shareholders meetings for corporate gaming giants such as Mirage Resorts, Circus Circus Enterprises, Hilton, and MGM Grand, they rarely bothered to observe Stupak's rendering of such stodgy affairs. And they missed a treat.

Stupak's May 1990 so-called shareholders meeting lasted 19 minutes, and the traditional formalities were rapidly dispatched. As if to spoof the corporate bosses whose megaresorts were leaving Vegas World in the past, Stupak made no mention of his company's finances. But he did take time to remind the more than 400 friends and followers who packed the hotel's showroom that his movie, *Bloody Mary*, which had been shot on location at Vegas World, would be coming soon to a theater near them. Stupak was entertaining, if not terribly informative. The crowd erupted in laughter and adulation.

It was the most praise the happy huckster would receive for a while.

FIVE

The Big Idea

Years after leaving Melbourne, Bob Stupak occasionally made trips to Australia to visit his daughter, Nicole, who attended school there. Australia held fond memories for him, and nearly two years after he had warned Melbourne news readers of the problems with legalized casinos, he was back Down Under. This time he was in Sydney with Nicole.

On the way to lunch, Bob Stupak noticed something that would change his life forever.

"What's that?" he asked.

"It's the Sydney Tower," his daughter replied.

They would eat lunch there, he decided. The Sydney Tower, tallest structure in the country, dominated the skyline and held an enormous fascination for Bob Stupak. As they approached the tower, he noticed something else, something that always made him tremble with excitement.

A crowd. A grand tangle of humanity snaked outside the entrance to the tower. What were they doing? Were they actually waiting in line to ride an elevator to the top?

They were, indeed. And they were paying $5 a head for the privilege. Lunch could wait. Stupak had to see for himself. So he stood in line nearly an hour and took in the view from the top.

His plans for building the tallest sign in Las Vegas were scrapped half a world from Vegas World.

The big idea was born.

If thousands of Aussies converged on the Sydney Tower, what might the millions of tourists who visit Las Vegas each year do at a tower and casino?

When he returned to Las Vegas, he set to work learning all he could about the economics and engineering of towers.

His was not the first big idea in Las Vegas history. As early as 1961, Kansas City developer Frank Carroll decided to build a 14-story tower and casino in the shape of the Seattle Space Needle, which was gaining national attention as the centerpiece of the World's Fair. Carroll quickly decided to raise his Landmark tower to 17 stories, which would make it the tallest building in Las Vegas, a full three floors higher than downtown's Mint.

Carroll, also known as Frank Caracciolo, had difficulty funding his big idea, but by 1966 managed to coax a $5.5 million loan from the mobbed-up Teamsters Central States Pension Fund for the Landmark, which by then had grown to 31 stories. The Landmark featured a revolving restaurant on the 31st floor and a spectacular view of the valley. Edward Hendricks of Los Angeles was the architect.

By then, it had become obvious that Carroll's contacts with organized crime were more than casual, and he was denied a gaming license.

Thanks in part to the maneuvering of Howard Hughes aide Robert Maheu, the Landmark was sold to Hughes in 1968 for a whopping $17.3 million. Like other Las Vegas casino acquisitions by the eccentric billionaire, it proved a monumental waste of capital.

Maheu would recall in his memoir, *Next to Hughes*, that his elusive boss couldn't even decide when to unlock the place and whom to invite to the grand opening.

"The opening of the Landmark was planned as the most glamorous event to hit Las Vegas in years," Maheu recalled. "...Although Howard wanted desperately to have a grand party, he didn't want it to be overshadowed by the opening of the International [now the Las Vegas Hilton, across the street from the Landmark], scheduled for the following day. For weeks, we argued over the opening date, and for weeks we could not agree.

"The absurdity of trying to organize a major event without knowing the date didn't seem to make any impact on Hughes' mind."

Neither did the fact that he paid millions more than the property and building were worth. The 500-room tower opened in July 1969 and struggled from the start. It continued to change hands after Hughes' Summa Corporation sold it for $12.5 million in 1978. The Landmark lingered in and out of bankruptcy for the next 15 years before the Las Vegas Convention and Visitors Authority purchased it in 1993 for $15.1 million—still less than Hughes' original price 25 years earlier. On November 17, 1995, the Landmark was imploded to make way for a parking lot.

Stupak planned to avoid the fate of Frank Carroll and the curse of the Landmark. His research would be thorough. He was known as a huckster, a formidable liability in the straight financial world, and anything less than a precise prospectus would doom his plan to failure. There were plenty of precedents to draw from.

Tall buildings had been a part of the American psyche for more than 150 years. They had awed the masses and challenged their builders for generations.

Take the Washington National Monument, for instance. In an attempt to erect a monument worthy of the first president of the United States, the Washington National Monument Society was formed in the mid-1800s. The society hoped to raise $1 million by selling public subscriptions to the tower project for $1 apiece. Americans loved George Washington, but after four years the society had managed to scrounge up just $25,000.

The Washington Monument languished as an embarrassing stump in the nation's capital until 1876, when it was completed in time for the centennial of the American Revolution. At 555 feet, it was the world's tallest hunk of masonry.

Surely the Eiffel Tower, built for the Universal Exhibition in Paris in 1889 to celebrate the centennial of the French Revolution, was the most famous tower of the 19th century. It remains one of the most recognized structures in the world and is one of the few great towers named for its designer, Alexandre-Gustave Eiffel, who also designed the Statue of Liberty.

The 984-foot structure, which was built at a cost of $500,000 and designed to be dismantled at the end of the exhibition, was immediately condemned by French artists and intellectuals as a monstrosity, too mechanical looking to be classified as great architecture.

It was all too grotesque to be French, its detractors shouted. Among the most vocal critics were novelists Alexandre Dumas Jr. and Guy de Maupassant, the latter of whom was so disgusted by La Tour Eiffel that he ate lunch at its restaurant as often as possible for the pure pleasure of not being forced to look at it on the horizon.

But the people loved it, and no one dared touch a rivet to harm it.

"If La Tour was an insult to the representatives of the 'effete class,' it was love at first sight for the people," Mario Salvadori wrote in *What Makes Buildings Stand Up: The Strength of Architecture.* "Two million of them flocked to visit it during its first year. More than half of them reached its top. Thousands climbed the 1,671 steps before the elevators were open to the public. The crowds increased even long after the exhibition closed and, slowly but surely, their visits acquired new meanings. They went to look at the Tower as much as to look from it, to look inside, at its filigree of steel, as much as to point out the other monuments of their city. It became the symbol of Paris, the Mecca of all travelers, visited by far more people than Notre Dame or Sacre Coeur. And then it became, somehow, the symbol of France."

Could Bob Stupak with his eighth-grade education and questionable reputation be the man who changed the way Americans looked at Las Vegas by building a tower?

The Eiffel Tower also opened a new chapter in structural engineering. It was made by a mere 250 workers from 7,000 tons of wrought iron and 12,000 prefabricated pieces, and held together with 2.5 million rivets. Its cross-braced lattice structure gave it maximum wind resistance; it moved just nine inches in hurricane-force winds. So geometrically sound was the structure that it applied no more pressure on the ground than that of a person sitting on a chair, Salvadori wrote. It was a financial steal at a half million dollars and was completed in a little more than two years without the loss of a single life.

It also attracted visitors from around the world and was the source of countless news articles whenever someone attempted to climb it or fly an airplane through its arched legs.

Bob Stupak was beginning to dream big. And as he continued his research, he grew even more excited.

New York City has been the proving ground for America's tallest structures. It is the place where the skyscraper got its name. Manhattan's first impressively tall building was not a behemoth office giant, but the 350-foot Latting Observatory. Constructed of wood, it was completed in 1853.

In 1902, the Fuller Building, at 300 feet, became the world's tallest inhabitable building. It was soon forgotten after William Van Alen designed what would become known as the Chrysler Building. Heavily influenced by the Jazz Age, and the first building taller than the Eiffel Tower, the Chrysler stood 1,048 feet high and was completed in 1928.

The Empire State Building was more than a skyscraper. It emerged as a symbol of the strength of the American spirit during the Great Depression. The 85-story building, designed by Shreve, Lamb and Harmon, was constructed of 200,000 cubic feet of Indiana limestone at a cost of $52 million. In all, 57 tons of steel went into the building, which, including its 200-foot spire, stands 1,250 feet. It took less than one year to build.

The Empire State Building was designed and constructed as a mountainous office complex, but when it opened in May 1931 its developers made a killing off its impressive size. According to John Tauranac's *The Empire State Building: The Making of a Landmark*, "The gate for the ordinary, everyday view would have pleased a Scrooge. By the middle of November, the observatories were averaging 2,200 visitors a day, and had brought in $698,554. In the first year, a total of 775,000 visitors provided a gross income of $875,000 for the observatories, including the profits from ticket sales and the sales of souvenirs and refreshments to visitors. At that rate, the building was grossing about two percent of the building's construction costs every year."

Whether in the form of the 1,350-foot World Trade Center in New York or the 1,454-foot Sears Tower in Chicago, modern cities of any importance have a skyline to match their ambition. Towers appeal to the societal ego of modern Western civilization, and a Las Vegas tower was beginning to appeal to Stupak's sense of hyperbole.

"Las Vegas and Versailles are the only two architecturally uniform cities in Western History," Tom Wolfe wrote in 1965 in *The Kandy-Kolored Tangerine Flake Streamline Baby*.

"Las Vegas was the only city of its kind to be seen on this scale of thoroughness," Alan Hess wrote in *Viva Vegas: After-Hours Architecture*. "To call it untraditional would be an understatement; it was generally considered an urban freak, in thrall to the gigantic and the garish."

And what could be more freakish, fun, and financially feasible than a Las Vegas tower?

Toronto's 1,815-foot CN Tower, the world's tallest self-supporting structure, was completed in April 1975 after a little more than two years of construction. Built at a cost of $63 million, the 143,000-ton structure was made of reinforced post-tensioned concrete and included a revolving restaurant at the 1,150 mark.

Not only is the CN Tower a tourist attraction, but it helped spur an impressive development in the area. Today, a major league baseball stadium has sprung up nearby, and it continues to serve as a marketing and development centerpiece of Toronto and eastern Canada.

But nowhere in North America has a tower made more of an

Vegas World. The sign on the left eventually evolved into the 1,149-foot Stratosphere Tower.

Bob Stupak in marathon no-limit poker games—before and after the motorcycle accident. (Larry Grossman)

Australian Sandy Wilkinson Stupak celebrates with her husband after winning a celebrity poker tournament.

from left: Summer, Bob, and Nevada Stupak

Phyllis McGuire lent some class to Stupak's later years.
(Jeff Scheid/*Las Vegas Review-Journal*)

Bob Stupak's lifelong
love affair with motor-
cycles nearly killed him.

Though Frank Sinatra befriended Stupak, he never appeared in Vegas World's Galaxy Showroom.

Who gets less respect—Bob Stupak or Rodney Dangerfield?

Bob Stupak with the banker who built Las Vegas, E. Parry Thomas (above),
Las Vegan Debbie Reynolds, and billionaire Kirk Kerkorian (below).

Nicole Stupak's performance in a pre-election debate with opponent Frank Hawkins proved her undoing in the 1991 City Council race. (Jim Laurie/*Las Vegas Review-Journal*)

Politics and publishing—Bob Stupak ran for mayor of Las Vegas twice and lost; his alternative weekly newspaper, *the Bullet*, lasted 18 months. (bottom: Wayne C. Kodey/*Las Vegas Review-Journal*)

Stupak promoted his out-of-the-way casino on "60 Minutes" with Harry Reasoner, and promoted himself with a full-page ad in *Variety* announcing his juicy cameo on "Crime Story."

Dan Koko leapt from the top of Vegas World into a protracted legal battle over jumping and landing fees. (Rene Germanier/*Las Vegas Review-Journal*)

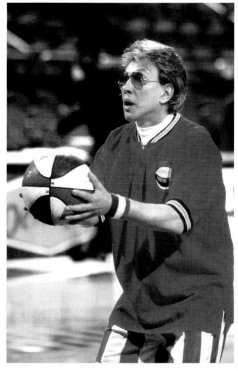

left: To fulfill a lifelong dream to appear with the Harlem Globetrotters on the floor of Madison Square Garden, Stupak donated $100,000 to the United Negro College Fund. Among his entourage was Las Vegas Mayor Jan Jones.

right: The derogatory moniker "Stupak's Stump" gave way to "Stupak's Roman Candle" during the brief but spectacular blaze at 510 feet. (Jeff Scheid/ *Las Vegas Review Journal*)

following page (top inset): Gilded statue of Bob Stupak in front of the Stratosphere "Wall of Fame." (Jeff Scheid/*Las Vegas Review Journal*)

(bottom inset): Grand Casino's Lyle Berman. (Larry Grossman)

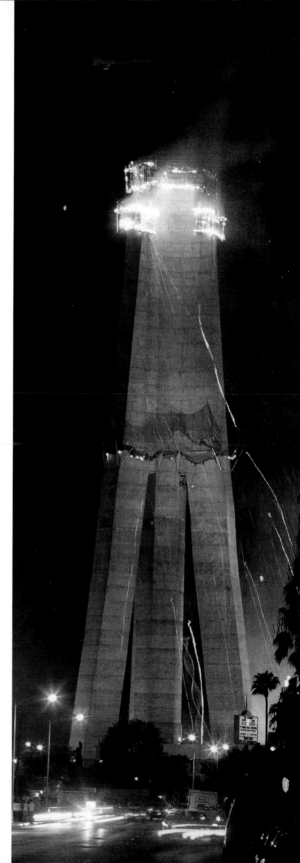

impact than in Seattle, where the Space Needle has long since become the central identifying image in the city's skyline.

Modern marketers have portrayed the Space Needle not as a restaurant or tourist attraction, but as a national landmark. Make that a national landmark generating millions in retail sales on everything from T-shirts to gourmet coffee. The national landmark attracts 3,000 people a day, or approximately 1.2 million per year, and has become a favorite location for New Year's Eve celebrations. Like a sports franchise or celebrated athlete, the Space Needle is so popular it collects fees for corporate sponsorships from Coca Cola, Mars, Eastman Kodak, and Boyd Coffee.

Beyond the symbol, the Space Needle's revolving restaurant is the 12th busiest eatery in America. To Stupak, the Space Needle embodied the powerful economic potential of observation towers.

Surely a Las Vegas tower would do at least as well. And with plenty of slot machines and table games strategically positioned at its base, there was no telling how much money Stupak's big idea might be able to generate.

The Seattle Space Needle had something else in common with Stupak's dream: a surprisingly similar location.

"Those working to rejuvenate downtown Seattle envisioned a compact, centrally located business district that would become both more built up and more attractive to pedestrians and shoppers," John M. Findlay wrote in *Magic Lands*. "Planners for downtown Seattle hoped to provide freeway access as well as plentiful parking and pedestrian landscaping. They also intended to attract new businesses and cultural activities that would help the downtown withstand the threat of suburban growth; to develop a public transit system that might forestall traffic congestion; to stimulate urban renewal in order to minimize blight."

Which is precisely what Las Vegas dreamers had been attempting to accomplish with their fortune-squandering downtown redevelopment projects, ill-conceived Fremont Street attractions, and heavy-handed use of eminent domain.

For the site of the tower, Seattle planners chose the Warren neighborhood. It was in several respects much like Naked City.

"Although hardly a slum, the Warren neighborhood had a higher crime rate than the rest of Seattle, more unemployment, fewer owner-occupied homes, a higher percentage of older, less valuable housing, more elderly residents, lower average incomes, and fewer families and school-age children," Findlay reported.

If the history of the Space Needle was any barometer, a downtown Las Vegas tower would affect a lot more than Stupak's business interests.

"The need for financial success weighed heavily on the businessmen who promoted the 1962 fair," Findlay wrote. "Yet proposals to import nude showgirls from Las Vegas and Paris, as well as to repeal local blue laws for the duration of the exposition, lent credence to the charge that fairs catered to the lowest common cultural denominator."

The fact that Stupak planned to build his tower as a hook to fleece the millions of tourists who sojourned to Las Vegas each year was beside the point.

It is important to note that venues for the performing arts and big-league sports grew out of the success of the Space Needle and the fair. The Space Needle quickly came to symbolize Seattle the way Disneyland defined Los Angeles.

A lot had changed since Stupak's original plan to build a 320-foot sign to advertise Vegas World. In October 1989, he announced his intention to build a 1,012-foot observation tower next to Vegas World.

"What I'm trying to do for Las Vegas is what the Eiffel Tower did for Paris, what the Empire State Building did for New York, what the Space Needle did for Seattle," Stupak said.

He asked the city Building and Safety Department to put on hold plans he'd submitted for a neon sign four times as tall as Vegas World. Then he quickly began redrawing his big idea to include an elevator and observation deck.

Stupak's detractors on the City Council immediately moved to block approval of the plans by passing an ordinance limiting the height of signs within the city limits, but the move was so painfully obvious that it died in committee. The so-called "Stupak Ordinance" faded rapidly.

In keeping with Vegas World's outer-space theme, Stupak would add laser lights to his tower, which now had a price tag, $30 million, and a tentative completion date, New Year's Eve 1990. That gave Stupak a little more than a year to bring it all together. If the Empire State Building could be constructed in a year, so could Stupak's tower.

"My daughter was living in Australia, and I went to visit her. We had lunch at the Sydney Tower. That's a 1,000-foot tower with a revolving restaurant on top. ... That gave me the spark of an idea. We're building this sign. Maybe I should put an observation deck at the top.

"Then we said, 'Well, maybe we can make it go a little higher.' Then we started fiddling with the tower and, after a while, forgot about the sign. And 1,000 feet high seemed like the right number. I made it 1,012 because it seemed like a more scientific number.

"The Eiffel Tower was 984 feet, and everybody was familiar with that, so I figured we had to be taller than the Eiffel Tower."

By 1990, gaming consultant Howard Grossman had left Stupak's employ, but he enjoyed dropping by Vegas World to listen to the city's foremost pitchman. That's where he first heard about the tower.

"I went into Vegas World one time to visit somebody there who was working for him and ran into Stupak," Grossman recalled. "I asked him about the tower. I figured it was another of his crazy ideas.

"He knew all about towers. He said every tower in the world makes money. He believed that he would have probably a couple million people a year coming through the tower. It would bring him business and I never doubted him."

As a last reality check before running headlong into the

project that was sure to make or break him, Stupak contracted with Arthur Andersen & Co., a national accounting firm, in an attempt to double-check his theory. Its numbers crunchers were impressed by what they saw.

"They came back with even bigger numbers, and I said, 'This is too good to be true,'" Stupak told a reporter. "I figured, 'To hell with casinos in Vegas, I'm going into the tower business all over the world.'

"I wanted it to be bigger than the Eiffel Tower in Paris, bigger than the Space Needle in Seattle. The CN Tower in Toronto is 1,815 feet tall, and I wanted it to be bigger than that."

And so the Stratosphere Tower was born.

At Vegas World, Stupak's motto always was "The Sky's the Limit." For all his shortcomings, he had gained a reputation as a man who, given the proper circumstances, would fade any bet. More than a slogan, it was his life's philosophy.

The financing and construction of his dream tower were about to test his philosophy to the breaking point.

SIX

The Huckster in Hell

In early October 1990, with the Stratosphere tower project only weeks from breaking ground, Stupak was hit with back-to-back complaints filed by the state Gaming Control Board. The first detailed alleged advertising transgressions by Stupak's Vacation Club, Inc., which touted its dirt-cheap trips to Vegas World in such widely read national publications as *Playboy*, the *Los Angeles Times*, and *USA Today*.

The second complaint held an equal potential to devastate Stupak. It outlined 29 private loans to Stupak by early Stratosphere investors that had gone unreported to state gaming regulators.

Although he faced a possible $2.9 million in fines for the unreported loans (ultimately the loan issue was decided in Stupak's favor), the advertising complaint figured to be the more embarrassing. The complaint's language may have been legalistic, but its message was clear: Stupak was labeled a con artist, one of the biggest in the history of the city.

In fact, several state agencies had received complaints from Vegas World customers who had taken advantage of the cheap vacation offers, but the Nevada Gaming Control Board and Gaming Commission were capable of putting Stupak out of business for good.

The Control Board had been receiving written complaints for years from participants in the vacation program. Although the numbers comprised a minute fraction of the vast crowds that took advantage of the packages, the complaints attracted the interest of consumer-affairs organizations and state attorneys general from across the country.

"These weren't just one-sentence letters," Chairman Bill Bible said. "They were rather lengthy and gave detailed explanations about what they didn't receive."

Stupak was charged under state gaming regulations with operating Vegas World in an unsuitable manner and undermining the public's confidence in the gaming industry with his advertising program.

Although the allegation might have sounded trivial in a state with a long history of scandal attached to its largest industry, Stupak faced the distinct possibility of losing his license. Despite keeping high-powered attorneys Frank Schreck and Jeff Silver, both former gaming regulators, on retainer, Stupak couldn't count on getting any breaks from the Control Board.

The reason was simple: Although his style of business had attracted international headlines throughout his career, it also at times had embarrassed the state's casino watchdogs.

Now it was all returning to haunt him.

The ads were not purely false, but they were deceptive. They promised that patrons would receive "$400 in dollar machine action good on dollar slot machines located throughout the casino."

Offers of $400 in slot "action" and $400 more in table "action" easily confused customers, who believed they would receive the equivalent of cash. Instead, "action" was limited to special slot machines and special chips at the tables.

The special slots were tightened so that they rarely paid off. Modifying the 12 gimmick machines without informing the Gaming Control Board itself was a violation of state regulation.

Then there were the "valuable free gifts" and their advertised value: from $189 to $1,500. Vacationers usually received costume jewelry or similar telemarketing premiums worth a fraction of the advertised price.

The Gaming Control Board recommended a $300,000 fine, and Stupak would not be able to pay it in vacation slot tokens. If approved by a vote of the Gaming Commission, the fine would be one of the highest in state history.

Critics of the vacation package also complained that Vegas World's entertainment policy and room quality were subpar for the price—even when participants saw the shows and received a two-night stay for as little as $22.82 after all the deal's angles were exploited.

"You know, I've got a live band, it's a big budget up there for those guys," Stupak said later. "I could do the same thing for 10 percent of the money. You know, I could have a Frank Sinatra impersonator and play the tapes. We try to make people happy.

"Where, for $22.82, do you get a room for three days and two nights, or if you come on the weekend a room for four days and three nights? Where do you get the gift, the souvenirs, the shows, the dining, the drinks, the champagne, the pictures, and all the other perks? Where do you get that for $22? Anywhere in this town? ... You know, I know that this is the best fucking deal in town. Bar none. Nobody can get that for $22.

"...Is the room worth $7 a day? When everything else is free? ...That's not the best deal in town? Where else can you get—for $22.82, where else can you get more? Tell me, because I want to go and get it, because I want to put it in my ad, for $22.82, don't come to Vegas World, go there!"

Stupak was proud of his direct-mail marketing skills, so much so that he boasted of his ability to attract customers from any point on the map.

"I send out 750,000 pieces in the mail each week. Hundreds of millions of pieces every year," he told a reporter. "I don't send out that much mail not knowing what the hell I'm doing."

Nearly 250,000 people visited Vegas World in 1990 alone, according to Stupak's count, and most by way of the vacation program. Obviously, the advertisements worked, but perhaps they worked too well.

After a series of negotiations in which he agreed to drastically alter his advertisements, in March 1991 Stupak agreed to pay a $125,000 fine and dramatically recraft his vacation packages. In return, gaming authorities dropped the allegations against him. For years to come he could say that he committed no offense greater than that of hyperbole.

But the trouble was only starting. Aside from the Vegas VIP Vacation, a probe of Stupak's early tower financing began to attract scrutiny from outside the state, especially from the aggressive Missouri Attorney General's office. Stupak's hell-bent salesmanship was catching up with him.

In front of the press, he didn't break a sweat.

"I felt I could learn something from Saddam Hussein. An early surrender was the best solution," he said. "Who gets the most business gets the most complaints. One Sears store gets more complaints in one week than we have ever received.

"Every complaint has been resolved. Fifty-nine out of one million customers isn't too bad...

"The ads were changed a long time ago. I've tried very hard to resolve this matter. I just wanted it settled."

Only the gullible believed Stupak when he insisted that he had sworn off politics for good after his loss to Ron Lurie in the 1989 mayor's race. For if there was anything the Las Vegas public should have learned by 1991, it was never to underestimate the street-corner sagacity of Bob Stupak. He studied politics the way handicappers size up horse flesh. Issues were secondary to the emotions with which voters responded to candidates. After all, his mayoral marketing test had almost resulted in his becoming mayor.

But what in the world was Stupak thinking when he entered his elder daughter, Nicole, in the race for City Council in Ward One in the spring of 1991? Was it another of his private bets? Was he using his daughter as a pawn in a local political game?

"It was basically my own decision," Nicole told a reporter in her lilting Aussie accent. "I asked him prior to going into it. He is supporting me, introducing me to people."

But in spring 1991, even non-skeptics would have found it hard to believe that the well-heeled Ms. Stupak even knew the boundaries of Council Ward One, which encompassed both the poorest and wealthiest neighborhoods in the city. In fact, up to the moment of her announcement, it had been rumored that her father was planning to take another run for the public office.

Nicole Stupak, who had spent much of her young life in Australia and had attended college in Switzerland, could not have known what she was getting into. She studied hotel management at UNLV and managed the food and beverage department at Vegas World. Her official home address, 1301 S. Sixth Street, also was Bob Stupak's home address.

"It's time to elect a new generation of leaders to the City Council," she told reporters. "Thirty percent of the people in my ward are under thirty-five years of age. I'm going to deal with people in my age group to see what they need."

Her opponent could not have felt less threatened by the soft-spoken 22 year old. Retired NFL fullback Frank Hawkins was expected to win the primary by a huge margin. Hawkins was a success story in the making with a seemingly limitless political future in Nevada. At 31, he was a black entrepreneur who owned a service station and minimarket, his own bar, and a construction company. He lived in a handsome home formerly owned by blues legend B.B. King on the edge of one of the most established neighborhoods in Las Vegas.

Hawkins was raised in the heart of Ward One's poorest neighborhood in the city's predominantly black West Side, had worked in city government, and appeared to be as committed to politics as he had been to football. In college he set rushing records at the University of Nevada in Reno (and earned a criminal justice degree). He later played fullback for the Los Angeles Raiders. He also had plenty of high-powered allies, including popular *Las Vegas Sun* columnist and executive editor Mike O'Callaghan, a two-term Nevada governor and easily one of the most popular politicians in the state's history, and Mirage Resorts Chairman Steve Wynn, whose interest in politics was only exceeded by his desire to make his casino-resorts the most successful in America.

Hawkins appeared destined to inherit the Ward One seat on his way to higher office.

Some pundits likened the primary to a display of Beauty and the Beast. The trouble was the Beast was well-versed on the issues and Beauty didn't appear to possess a clue about the city she intended to represent. Hawkins was one of the rising stars in the political community, while Nicole, whose campaign literature and yard signs splashed only her first name to reduce the connection to her father, spent most of her campaign time at carefully planned luncheons and afternoon teas in her ward's better neighborhoods.

By the primary election in early May, Nicole Stupak's campaign workers were busy reminding residents not to oversleep on Election Day—by handing out gifts of clock radios. If her campaign was independent of her father, which no one believed, it certainly was mimicking his style.

And it worked. Hawkins, the heavy favorite, failed to win a majority in the primary and settled for 36.1 percent of the vote. Nicole Stupak placed second with 31 percent.

None of the headlines hurt business at Vegas World. Within days Bob Stupak sent a letter to women in Ward One offering a two-carat diamond and sapphire pendant just for stopping by Vegas World. It never was made clear whether it generated any votes, but it certainly beat the turkeys Stupak once handed out to voters during his mayoral run.

She celebrated her surprise showing with a party that attracted thousands to her father's Sixth Street home. The celebration was as lavish as the parties marking some hotel grand openings. It came complete with food and drinks, as well a fiddler on the roof and an appearance by Zsa Zsa Gabor.

For his part, Hawkins tried not to act surprised by his opponent's second-place finish.

"Nicole had done a ton of yard signs without doing any walking, without doing any TV, without doing any campaign forums," Hawkins told a reporter. Despite Bob Stupak's reputation for guile, Hawkins was certain that the general election "won't be as dirty as the mayor's race because I won't let it be. But anytime you have Bob Stupak involved there will be fireworks."

Little did Hawkins know how soon those words would return to haunt him.

Business was slow at the Frank Hawkins Celebrity Sports Lounge. It was late. The owner and his sidekick were talking politics and drinking beer when the woman walked in. Her name was Nancy and she needed help with some pressing business concerns.

She was in the escort-service racket and had her sights set on the lucrative Las Vegas market. The Las Vegas Yellow Pages are jammed with advertisements for this trade, a thinly veiled front for prostitution. Nancy needed someone to help guide her business-license application through the proper administrative channels. Nancy's young friend, Shawna, needed help, too.

Shawna was an exotic dancer in California who considered Las Vegas the big time. And she would be willing to audition. Surely Hawkins had enough contacts to help Nancy and Shawna get started. Could he spare an evening with the ladies?

With days to go before the general election, the three met at an apartment not far from Hawkins' bar. Nancy did most of the talking. The dancer, Shawna Thorpe, did most of the smiling.

Introductions were made and the late-night meeting commenced. Thorpe was a 19-year-old blonde from Oxnard. She needed help circumventing local regulations that prohibit women under 21 from dancing nude where alcohol is served.

Acting as her agent, as well as a prospective escort-service operator, Nancy was attempting to purchase a little influence.

After all, it was obvious that Hawkins was the big favorite to win the City Council election. As such, he would be able to help Nancy's outcall service and gently usher Thorpe's work card through the process. He might even be able to get her a job dancing at one of the big topless clubs in town.

Meanwhile, Thorpe stripped to a G-string.

Hawkins suggested that the teenager try to find work at one of the alcohol-free strip joints, but neither woman appeared interested. They bantered about obtaining the proper counterfeit identification as the conversation dragged.

"So Frank," Nancy said, "if I got her the proper IDs, whatever, sheriff's card..."

"I'll get her the job," Hawkins finished.

"You would get her the job at the Palomino. Totally nude. Whatever?"

"Will they find out how old I am?" Thorpe asked.

"It depends if the ID is good," Hawkins said.

Nancy arranged for the delivery of a $2,000 cash contribution. During that meeting, Nancy continued to ask about Hawkins' willingness to assist in her escort service. Hawkins acknowledged he had a strong relationship with the sheriff, but declined to commit to acting as her advocate within the police department.

At the sight of the money, Hawkins finally got suspicious. After receiving the contribution, the whole set-up began to bother him. He called the FBI.

By then, of course, it was too late. Nancy Bugea, a former undercover narcotics detective-turned-private investigator, had done her job well. She had secretly recorded the conversations. And Hawkins, the ex-jock with mile-high political aspirations, had made her job easy.

Days later, a copy of the tape was delivered to *Las Vegas Review-Journal* Editor Sherman R. Frederick.

The courier: Bob Stupak.

"I gave you the information because I felt I was compelled to," Stupak said. "I don't want to get too corny, but I felt that people needed to know."

He denied direct involvement in the sting and Bugea declined to name her client.

"I did not agree to run women," Hawkins said, watching his bright political future begin to crumble. "They asked me if I could help her find fake ID and I said no. I never thought they would be that desperate."

For her part, Nicole appeared sincerely in the dark. But even she suspected her father.

"I had no idea whatsoever about this," she told a reporter. "We've had so many phone calls regarding rumors about Mr. Hawkins that are now being brought to light, things like escort services. I guess my father just took it a step further."

If Hawkins was going to salvage his campaign, he needed to act quickly. It was time for Nicole Stupak to be tested, if ever so slightly. She had to show that she was more than a straw candidate for her father, and a debate was the only way to accomplish that. Days before the election, the two candidates agreed to meet for one hour on an AM radio station.

Throughout the campaign, Nicole had avoided meeting Hawkins in a public forum. But what could one hour hurt?

Trouble was, Nicole Stupak wasn't overly familiar with Ward One. Hawkins quizzed her on her knowledge of the area and the issues. Hawkins was used to pressure; Ms. Stupak was not. At one point, she had difficulty defining organized labor. The young woman was clearly intimidated.

In keeping with local custom, the city's two daily newspapers split on the Hawkins taping issue. The *Las Vegas Sun* expressed outrage at the underhanded tactics used to entrap the bright young candidate, Frank Hawkins. The *Review-Journal*, shunned by Hawkins and his campaign manager, Dan Hart, for publishing excerpts of the secret tapes, viewed the incident as a character issue. Hart would later work for Stupak, but he wasn't about to betray Hawkins.

During the campaign, Hart took a liking to Stupak and appreciated his sense of humor. First, Nicole's father sent him a case of aspirin for the headache Stupak had given him. Then he sent an oxygen tank to show he thought that Hawkins was on his last legs as a candidate. Prior to Election Day, Hart received a funeral wreath. The last gift, a set of Gucci luggage to help usher Hart out of town, was not sent. The reason would become obvious by Election Day. Hawkins figured to win handily.

As if Stupak's political meddling were upsetting the heavens, a summer storm bringing 80-mile-per-hour winds roared through Las Vegas late in the spring 1991 campaign season, toppling Vegas World's gaudy electronic sign and forcing the evacuation of 130 guests whose rooms ran the risk of being demolished by gigantic messages: Bob Stupak's Vegas World, Gambling at its Best, and The Sky's the Limit. The sign was never replaced.

Meanwhile, much of the city suspected Bob Stupak was behind the secret taping, and evidence surfaced when investigative reporter Cathy Hanson made the link in a series of newscasts. Tapping into a source capable of tracking telephone numbers, Hanson revealed that a cellular phone used by Bugea had been leased by Stupak.

Stupak's sting ended up backfiring with voters, who were sickened by the sordid affair. They might have been dismayed by Hawkins' behavior, but they had to consider the source of the trouble. Hawkins whipped Nicole Stupak by a nearly 2-to-1 margin, 5,988 to 3,238.

After his daughter's turbulent attempt to gain a seat on the City Council, Bob Stupak retreated from the political front line. The words of Ben Siegel to his lacky were ringing true once more, and Stupak finally appeared to hear the call.

"I'll never run for office again," he said. "I have no interest in that whatsoever."

The City Council campaign wasn't the only race that season. Stupak's longtime ally, Steve Miller, was challenging Jan Laverty Jones for the mayor's seat vacated by Ron Lurie. Miller had written columns for Stupak's *Bullet* tabloid and had been an extremely outspoken voice as a councilman, and now he was looking to become the image-setter for the city. Jones, meanwhile, was an attractive Stanford graduate who had gained name and face recognition through a series of television advertisements for her family's automobile dealerships and grocery store chains. Jones first met Stupak during the early stages of the race against Miller.

She received a message requesting her presence at a meeting with the Vegas World owner and immediately became suspicious. What devilry was Stupak up to? At last she agreed to meet him for lunch, but only on the condition that she bring a friend as a witness. At the end of the meal, Stupak offered Jones $11,000 as a campaign contribution.

"If you win," Stupak said, "come back and I'll give you more."

Thus began an odd but enduring friendship between the street-wise high school dropout and the lady with contacts throughout Las Vegas society.

"It was vintage Bob," Jones recalled years later. "He was hedging his bets. Bob can be a pain, but his word is gold. A lot of people in this town like to think their word is gold and it is— until you piss them off. But Bob's word is his bond. Once he's given it, I've never seen him break his word."

Jones defeated Miller handily and watched from the mayor's chair as Stupak fought to see his tower idea materialize.

After balking at the thought of taking on official business partners in his sure-fire winner and encountering early trouble from gaming regulators after failing to report a few personal loans, Stupak decided to raise money to build his tower the best way he knew how. Thus, the Stratosphere Club was born.

A letter to prospective investors was typically confident: "Vegas World is destined to become the very hub of Las Vegas. The Stratosphere Tower has a rendezvous with greatness. It will be the tallest tower in America and by far the grandest jewel in the Las Vegas skyline."

But jewels aren't cheap.

The Stratosphere Club come-on was vintage Stupak: Aggressive but sincere, hyperbolic without telling an outright lie.

In another letter, he wrote to his repeat Vegas World customers, who were targeted for Stratosphere Club membership:

"This is your chance to join the most exciting and unique venture in the history of Las Vegas.

"Your charter membership in the Stratosphere Club ensures you a special status at Vegas World. You'll be treated royally each and every visit.

"The world has never seen an offer like this. Only Vegas World gives you five free vacations and $2,500 cash to do with as you wish.

"Since this offer will never be made to the general public, it is important to act now. Membership in the Stratosphere Tower is extremely limited and is only being made to our previous valued guests. This offer must be accepted by October 16, 1991."

Stupak's "exclusive" once-in-a-lifetime offer to join the Stratosphere Club was mailed to tens of thousands of former guests. For $1,950, charter club members would receive five free vacations at Vegas World, $500 cash with each visit, unlimited free drinks, free show tickets, free entry to slot tournaments, preferred restaurant seating, four free keno plays per visit, their names etched in granite at the base of the tower, and a home casino kit including playing cards, a crap layout, and Stupak's book on gambling.

To make his case, Stupak used an impressive chart that clearly illustrated Vegas World visitor volume from 1979 to 1990. Vegas World attracted approximately 30,000 visitors in the last half of 1979, the year it opened, and about 550,000 in 1990. Stupak defied his critics by claiming that his controversial vacation programs brought millions of visitors to Las Vegas: everyone benefitted from Stupak's sales tactics, but he took all the heat.

Stupak's tactics worked at several levels. The value-driven player was sure to be impressed by the long-range savings. The greedy visitor would go for the promise of $500 in cash. Those craving inclusion and recognition would be thrilled to be members of an exclusive club, even if the club had a potential membership the size of the population of Omaha.

Another Stupak letter exploited the personal touch:

"History is about to happen...and you deserve to be a part of it. Construction of the Stratosphere Tower is underway right now at Vegas World.

"This dream could never have become reality if not for our loyal customers such as yourself. It was you who made the dream possible by coming to Vegas World. My success stems from your patronage, as does my enthusiasm for bigger things. Without you this dream could not come true.

"Call me sentimental if you will, but the offer I am about to make you is the best 'Thank You' I can think of for your valued past patronage. The special Charter Membership you are going to learn about is being offered only to customers who have helped me make Vegas World what it is today...friends who share my top-of-the-world vision of what this resort will be tomorrow.

"Charter Membership in the Stratosphere Club gives you special perks and privileges that you can start enjoying right now...and continue to use up to the 21st century! (Actually, many are lifetime benefits.) But I'm getting ahead of the story. There's so much to tell and I'm just bursting inside to tell you about our grand vision and destiny of building the tallest tower in America..."

Even Stupak's caveat emptor gushed with confidence.

"I know this offer sounds too good to be true. Isn't that what you thought when you first heard about our super-bargain vacations? But this is even more mind-bending and you have to be wondering how all this can possibly work. Well, it's possible for two reasons. Gambling and Human Nature. You see, I know from experience that just about everyone will spend and/or gamble some percentage of the cash they receive when they check in. After all, it's fun. And a certain percentage will play all of their check-in cash and dig deep for more. These people, coupled with the percentage who are high rollers (who traditionally pay the bills for 'the rest of us'), make this incredible offer possible. Remember one thing. In the casino business, the percentages are always with the house. If they weren't, there wouldn't be a Las Vegas. That's the nature of the gambling business. It has always happened this way and always will."

In an industry that at the time refused to acknowledge any societal problems associated with gambling, Stupak's honesty was refreshing. The pitch promised special access to the project's 400-seat revolving restaurant, split-level cocktail bar, and outside observation decks, as well as VIP status in the Stratosphere Club Lounge. The elevators would be fast, but the action would be faster for club members.

Stratosphere Club orders were accepted via phone 24 hours a day. Some of the packages offered were for as little as $1,985. Others ranged upward of $7,000. All promised plenty of rooms, spending cash, and value.

"The Stratosphere packages were just a way to generate money to build the tower," Stupak consultant David Sklansky said. But the offer almost made it sound as if those who purchased the package were somehow investing in the building itself. It mentioned nothing of the deal Stupak was crafting to generate up to $85 million from a public stock offering that would fund the tower project. Or the fact that, although they would be members of the exclusive Stratosphere Club, they wouldn't actually have a piece of the project in the traditional stockholder's sense.

To add to the credibility of the Stratosphere offer, Stupak included a letter of endorsement from his old nemesis, former Mayor Ron Lurie:

"As Mayor of Las Vegas, I had the great pleasure of presiding over the City Council when Bob Stupak presented his 1,012-foot Stratosphere Tower project. We unanimously approved this visionary and world-class tourist attraction and I am proud to say that it has the overwhelming support of the city.

"This super tower promises to become the very symbol of

Las Vegas itself. As America's tallest tower, it is destined to stand proudly among the great towers of the world.

"My special thanks to Bob Stupak and Vegas World for bringing literally hundreds of thousands of new visitors to Las Vegas. Since the '70s, the great growth and success of Vegas World has been truly remarkable. It has grown into one of our city's largest and most spectacular megaresorts...with no end in sight."

Problem was, Lurie didn't write the letter. Or sign it.

Stupak's people did.

When he learned of the forgery, Lurie just shrugged. He liked the tower idea and might have been persuaded to publicly endorse its construction, but he didn't write any letter. Instead of threatening a lawsuit, he told reporters to consider the source. But the letter was too much to forgive, even for those accustomed to Stupak's style.

"I told him he could use anything I said about the tower at a public meeting," Lurie told a reporter. "But I didn't feel like it was right to sign a letter like that."

In his zeal to see his dream come true, Stupak had failed to fully appreciate the scrutiny he was facing from the Gaming Control Board. Perhaps he believed that, since only previous Vegas World vacation package buyers were being solicited for the Stratosphere Club membership, customer complaints wouldn't surface. He was wrong.

An independent analysis by the *Las Vegas Advisor* of one of several manifestations of the Stratosphere Club offer confirmed the suspicions of investors and consumer advocates. It was a compelling come-on, but it was not a wise investment.

For a $6,250 front-end investment, participants received 70 nights at Vegas World over 10 years, $10,000 in table action chips over the same time, VIP treatment, and preferred seating at the Stratosphere's showroom. Affording a generous 50 percent approximate value for the gaming chips and $35 a night for the rooms, and assigning an estimated $1,400 value for the other benefits, the total return amounted to $8,600 over a decade.

That's more than the $6,250 investment, to be sure, but still less than simply placing the same amount of cash in a bank account earning 4 percent interest ($9,250). Using history as an indicator of return potential, the same $6,250 invested in the stock market over 10 years would be worth in excess of $18,000.

Who could say where Stupak would be in a decade?

Other Stratosphere Club direct-mail offers were less risky. They offered a positive return on investment in two years. These $1,950 packages included five three-night stays at Vegas World, $1,000 in table action, and other perquisites. The conservative value was $2,500 on the $1,950 investment. With a 14 percent return guaranteed, it was far superior to the other package and proved attractive to investors.

It also generated its share of complaints from consumers who paid less attention to the solid arithmetic involved and more to the personality making the pitch. Even when offering a superior deal, Stupak couldn't shake his image as the consummate Las Vegas snake-oil salesman. And for good reason.

"I'm selling them immortality," Stupak argued. "The only thing that's different about this is that I've included them in the excitement of the tower.

"The tower being built has nothing to do with their benefits. The tower is a sizzle, a nice little sizzle, something to talk about that gets us press from time to time, but with or without the tower, does it really make a difference? The tower stuff is a very small part of the package."

Very small, indeed. So small, in fact, that the offer set off alarms at the state Gaming Control Board and the Missouri Attorney General's office, which again was receiving complaints from Stupak's customers.

By the time the deadline for joining the Stratosphere Club rolled around, Stupak had taken out foundation and concrete permits for the tower. The two dates had less in common than club investors might have believed.

Two weeks before the groundbreaking of the Stratosphere Tower, Stupak began paying the price for his overstatement. State Gaming Control Board investigators again were up to their eyebrows in complaints from customers and inquiries from out-of-state regulators.

Some of the customer complaints involved vacationers who were promised placement at Vegas World, but instead wound up at Stupak's Thunderbird Motel up the street. Vegas World's rooms were nowhere near the plushest in the city, but they were adequate—and decidedly nicer than the accommodations at the Thunderbird. Trouble was, the packages were so successful that on the weekends hundreds of customers were walked to the spartan Thunderbird north of Vegas World on Las Vegas Boulevard. Although provisions for rooming at the motel were contained in the fine print, the dissatisfied customers were vocal. And Stupak wasn't about to catch a break from irritated state regulators.

"No one is forced to stay at the Thunderbird," Stupak said defensively during the second Vegas VIP Vacation investigation. "They can change their dates, they can have a refund, or they can stay at the Thunderbird. Anyone who plans far enough ahead will stay at Vegas World.

"The main reason people like the Thunderbird is because it's not a high-rise, you know, for people who are worried about safety."

Other customers complained that an artist's rendering of Vegas World made it appear to stand at the heart of the Strip instead of in the netherworld north of Sahara Avenue.

"What's more desirable if you're staying in Las Vegas?" Stupak asked an interviewer in 1992. "Staying at the Excalibur or staying here? ...Right now we're two miles away from the Mirage. But next year, we won't be two miles away from the Mirage. The Mirage will be two miles away from us. That's the way it's gonna be. We're gonna be the center point. Anytime anybody calls up and wants to know where a hotel's at, they're gonna ask where it is in relation to Vegas World."

Stupak wouldn't even agree with the authorities' customer complaint figures.

"The fact is that we bring $100 million a year into the Las Vegas economy," Stupak said. "And over a 10-year period of running the deals we've had 59 complaints. Over 10 years. Not hundreds like they say in the papers.

"None of [the package solicitations] go to the general public. If we're out in the mass market, we're fair game. But we only sell [them] to our own customers, in-house people, regulars. See? Now, what are the benefits of the club package? First of all, no long lines. You waltz right up to the front of it. Second, the VIP lounge—$350,000 it cost me. When they come in, they go there, then we come and tell them their room is ready. It's a big plus. They get a pin, membership card, line passes, preferred seating, it's making the little guy feel important. And that's what they're paying for. Now how do you put a value on that? These are things that are important to people. Another thing. All those benefits are transferable. You got a friend? You call up and say, 'Look, I'm sending so-and-so in for three days. They come in, they get all the benefits that you got. Except the cash.'"

If the rumors of pending investigations by the state Gaming Control Board and attorneys general from other states weighed heavily on Stupak's mind, he didn't show it November 5, 1991, when he went before the press sporting a new look to announce the project of his life: the 1,012-foot Vegas World Stratosphere Tower. Nattily attired in a gray business suit and expensive haircut, Stupak tried to appear confident in his project, as well as his ability to charm a 500-pound African lioness. The first part was easy. The second took some doing.

"I think it's just outrageous. It's wild. It's typical Las Vegas,"

Stupak said between glares by the jungle cat. The animal was present not only to impress timid reporters, but to announce an African lion habitat on the grounds of the tower project. Not only would the new Vegas World feature a 1,012-foot observation tower, but the truly courageous would be able to take a chairlift that would pass just above the 60,000-square-foot faux jungle with 40 very real animals. The first drunken tourist to take a spill out of the lift surely would make headlines across America. Stupak attributed the idea to one of his favorite movies, *Mighty Joe Young*, in which an urban nightclub featured a lion's den and giant gorilla show.

"I saw the movie when I was a kid and it always inspired me," Stupak said.

The national media received Stupak's grand announcement with a sizable amount of skepticism. Declared *Newsweek*: "It'll be taller than the Mirage's volcano and have a better view than the high rollers' suites at Caesars Palace. But the Stratosphere Tower of Bob Stupak's Vegas World casino could also be tackier than anything else in town: The $100 million, 1,012-foot needle will feature an indoor African lion park, four wedding chapels, a revolving restaurant, a glass-bottomed observation deck and a rocket-like thrill ride."

Newsweek failed to note that, in Las Vegas and especially at Vegas World, tackiness was not a vice. It was a virtue.

As was Stupak's decision to halt early construction by his in-house contractor, Leeman Corporation. Leeman relinquished its role as general contractor on November 5, 1991, and Perini Construction, one of the largest builders in America, took over the job the following February. Thanks to questionable job-site hiring practices, in which observers noticed transients being used as cement workers, the tower already had a slightly misshapen leg. Structural experts insisted the defect would have no effect on the tower's ability to support its load, and Perini officials had the expertise in general construction to keep the project climbing toward the 1,000-foot mark and beyond.

While Las Vegas casino titans Steve Wynn and Anthony

Marnell had gained national reputations as designers and build-ers, Stupak saw his modest talents at Leeman Construction in the proper light.

"I learned in a hurry. The company worked good back then," he said of his early days at Vegas World. "It didn't work so good with the tower. No, the tower wasn't too good."

In another setting, Stupak was more philosophical about the importance of his over-the-top sales pitches and the price he sometimes paid for them.

"Any time that negative stuff happened, it gave me more drive and desire to say, 'I'll show 'em,'" he told an interviewer. "Every time somebody said something or wrote something bad about me, I'd buy a Rolls-Royce. It got to the point where I had six of them, but it didn't stop the bad publicity.

"People talk about my promotions, but they helped me build Vegas World from 100 rooms to 1,000, from $15 million gross in 1979 to more than $100 million each of the last six years it was open. And I did it all from cash flow. I didn't borrow a dime.

"I had the first million-dollar jackpot. I had crapless craps. I had a $2,000 betting limit when Caesars Palace was at $1,000, the Flamingo at $500. The only place higher was the Horseshoe, and they had me outgunned. I wasn't going to fight with Benny Binion.

"The only thing we did wrong with the Missouri thing was to miss a registered letter," Stupak argued. "You know, states and various locales from time to time write to us about the pro-gram. Ten years ago we got a lot of those letters. When we first started doing this, a lot of people were checking us to see that there really was a hotel, that we really existed. You know, Better Business Bureaus, state governments, what have you.

"The Missouri thing was just a letter asking questions, you understand? It wasn't complaint generated. It was a guy, there's a guy there in Missouri who does nothing but read ads in papers. So he sent a letter asking for backup information, he sent it registered, and we didn't pick up the letter for some reason. So they got angry, thought we were stiffing them. But we got it straightened out."

It wasn't quite so simple.

In late March 1992, the Missouri Attorney General's office issued a lengthy complaint against Stupak and his vacation pitch.

"The attorney general has reason to believe that Vegas World hotel and casino has used deception, fraud or misrepresentation in connection with the sale or advertisement...of merchandise," the complaint read. Stupak's "almost-free" vacation was costing him plenty.

With help from his confidant and Vegas World Chief Operating Officer Andy Blumen, who tap danced in the March 1992 hearing at the Missouri Attorney General's, Stupak simply agreed to take his mass mailings and overstated come-ons elsewhere.

Having temporarily weathered yet another regulatory assault on his normal business practices, Stupak watched as his big idea began to hit its stride. But the number of people who believed he ever would get the damn thing built wouldn't have filled his Galaxy Showroom.

SEVEN

Selling The Tower

For Bob Stupak to take his roller-coaster career in a new direction, he would need a new image. The Polish Maverick and high-rolling gambler grabbed tabloid headlines and played well with his customers at Vegas World, but it wouldn't impress members of the mainstream financial community. Stupak knew the street, but he didn't know Wall Street. In remaking himself with a new hairstyle and, according to one report, a facelift, Stupak hoped to change the picture people had of him as a Vegas caricature. He discarded his Vegas-guy sports coats with the casino-carpeting fabric patterns for a more tasteful wardrobe.

Stupak wasn't the first casino boss to work overtime on image enhancement. As he drew closer to Wall Street, Mirage Resorts Chairman Steve Wynn transformed himself from a Las Vegas rebel into the man *Time* magazine called the Great Casino Salesman. In many ways, Stupak was following in the footsteps of many casino operators who had come to Las Vegas to shake off their past and don a respectable persona. Stupak and Wynn were very different, of course. Where Steve Wynn had attended an Ivy League university and gravitated toward the highest level of society, chain-smoking Bob Stupak had been content with poker rooms and coffee shops. Stupak had his work cut out for him.

It didn't hurt that local society writers began to take note of his public relationship with entertainer Phyllis McGuire, who was respected throughout Las Vegas society for her impeccable taste. McGuire exuded class and had the contacts to match. She knew the famous and infamous, threw a helluva party, and was one of the first people approached when a local charity needed help. She also had a colorful history. The McGuire Sisters' hits included "Sugartime," "Picnic," and "Goodnight, Sweetheart, Goodnight," and the trio had graced the cover of *Life* magazine in 1958, but such accomplishments were rarely the first topic of conversation where Phyllis was concerned. To the world, she was the McGuire who fell for Chicago mob boss Sam Giancana. No matter how many hit songs she had, she always would be linked with Giancana and his world of hit men.

"Bob was absolutely nutso in love with Phyllis," Scott Higginson remembered. "He was head-over-heels, falling-down-goofy. Bob doesn't do things in small ways, and he really fell for Phyllis."

Stupak later confided, "I guess Phyllis is my one big love affair since I've been in town. It's unexplainable. Things happen. I don't know how they happen. It was completely unexpected. I'd never been with someone who was an entity in themselves, and Phyllis definitely was an entity in herself."

The fascination was mutual.

"Bob is a three-ring circus," McGuire said. "The man's ingenuity is incredible. He always has something up his sleeve."

McGuire came along at the right time in Stupak's life and she obviously helped him with his new look and his quest for respectability.

Not long after meeting McGuire, Stupak attempted to impress her with his skills on a motorcycle. The couple took Stupak's big Harley up to the Mt. Charleston Lodge, 40 miles northwest of Las Vegas, for a morning ride before church. Lost in conversation, Phyllis and Bob lost track of the time and appeared to be destined to miss Sunday services. As Stupak raced down the mountain back toward the city, Phyllis said, "Can't you go any faster, Bob?"

Stupak glanced at the bike's speedometer and winced.

"I'm doing ninety-five now!" he shouted.

He increased his speed to 105 miles per hour, and got Phyllis to the church on time.

With his love life heating up, along with the level of scrutiny from the Gaming Control Board, for the first time in many years Stupak began contemplating his spiritual luck and decided to return to the street. For months, he regularly volunteered to hand out coffee and doughnuts to downtown's transients. In his mind, he was not being kind or pious, but was attempting to improve his spiritual odds. To him, God knew all about luck and sprinkled it sparingly to those who had their life's priorities out of order.

Until late 1992, Stupak believed that he might be able to build his dream tower out of cash flow at Vegas World. And he started to do just that. After all, the original tower plan was to create a structure that would include a Space Needle-like restaurant and observation deck. That and fresh paint and carpeting at Vegas World might run as high as $50 million, and his Vacation and Stratosphere Club programs generated twice that much.

As the project expanded in concept and cost, it began to consume Stupak's net worth, as well as his daily casino revenue. With the state Gaming Control Board watching his every move, he couldn't allow his casino cash reserves to slip, or he would risk being publicly embarrassed and fined by the regulatory authorities. And after the $125,000 fine he paid to settle the state's Vegas VIP Vacation inquiry and the outside investigations being conducted into his Stratosphere Club offers, it was clear that he couldn't continue to rely on his traditional methods of raising revenue.

A public stock offering was the only way Stupak could generate enough revenue without losing control of the project. He set out in January 1993 to create Stratosphere Corporation with the assistance of attorney Mark Moskowitz. He also met with a number of securities analysts and stockbrokers as he attempted to enter a world about which he knew little.

One of the securities specialists he met with was Tom Hantges of USA Capital, which had raised $17 million in the Rio Hotel's initial public offering and had a clear-eyed view of the gaming industry. With Moskowitz on Stupak's side, Hantges knew the casino man was serious about going public, but he was stunned when he looked at the Stratosphere package. It was a great deal for Stupak, but a sucker bet for investors.

Hantges turned Stupak down.

"The casino was not involved in the deal," Hantges said. "It was just the Stratosphere Tower. I said, 'We're not fooled, Bob. We're not going to own the tower and you own your casino. We'd have to have a piece of that deal if we're going to do it."

But Stupak wasn't interested. Having closely guarded his casino from the start, he had no intention of relinquishing control, no matter how little, to outsiders.

Still, there was little time to waste. Construction on the tower was crawling and his cash reserves were dwindling. Large securities firms wouldn't touch the deal because of Stupak's reputation. For Stupak's IPO to fly, it would have to be handled by a group of small securities dealers on a best-efforts basis.

In a standard offering, securities are purchased and guaranteed by the brokerage houses, which resell them in order to generate capital. In a best-efforts offer, the securities dealers act strictly as sales agents. The money generated goes into an escrow account until a set minimum is reached. Then the company goes public and the capital transfers into corporate coffers. A best-efforts offer is a crapshoot that relies on the zeal of the securities sellers, the public image of the project, and the stability of the financial climate. Although their money is protected, many investors are unwilling to buy into a best-efforts deal for the simple reason they don't want their assets frozen for several months while the securities sellers roll their dice.

To lead the best-efforts offer, Stupak hired Yaeger Securities of California and Union Equity Partners, a feisty brokerage firm looking to make a name for itself in southern Nevada.

at it without the personalities involved and understood the business of towers, we thought it was a tremendous idea. But we also knew there would be an enormous hurdle and challenge with Bob Stupak because of his reputation."

As chairman, Stupak topped the six-man board of directors. Former Howard Hughes aide Robert Maheu was named vice chairman; president and chief operating officer Gary Zahlen, along with Donald Peterson, Andrew Blumen, and gambling adviser David Sklansky, were named directors.

Stupak would tell friends he added Maheu because he was a colorful character, but in doing so he also stood near a man with historical connections to the CIA and the Chicago Outfit.

Of note were Zahlen's stock options. As a bonus, he would be allowed to purchase his 300,000 shares at a below-IPO price of $4.25. Combined with his $200,000 annual salary, Zahlen found himself in splendid financial shape. As a top executive, he would be in a position to see his personal fortunes grow along with the company.

Zahlen, then 50 years old, was a casino consultant with a vast portfolio of high-caliber clients, such as Mirage Resorts and MGM Grand. He also served in executive positions with Desert Inn, as well as with Genting International Resort and Casinos, which had properties in Malaysia, Australia, and the Bahamas. Before coming to Stratosphere, Zahlen had held positions with the Lucayan Beach Resort and Casino in the Bahamas, Harrah's Marina Hotel-Casino in Atlantic City, Knott's Berry Farm, Magic Mountain, and Disneyland.

Sklansky was Stupak's in-house gambling guru. He had made the self-styled Polish Maverick millions of dollars by adjusting the rules of Vegas World's popular gimmick games. The probability wizard was a respected author of gambling books and had been paid as a consultant up and down the Strip.

Peterson had worked closely with Stupak on previous projects and, as a former general partner at Montgomery Securities, was experienced in venture capital and securities issues.

Blumen was Stupak's confidant and had been the general

counsel at Vegas World since 1989. He had practiced law in Nevada since 1983 and was keenly aware of the legal and political ground on which Stupak stood. Blumen was a gambler with a special affection for sports betting and poker, and that attribute endeared him further to Stupak.

Of all the directors, Maheu held by far the most intriguing portfolio. His career had been linked to Las Vegas for more than 30 years. In that time, Maheu had mixed with mobsters and G-men, pimps and politicians, billionaires and foreign spies. His legend read like a Ludlum novel, only his exploits were the stuff of nonfiction.

Maheu was an FBI agent until 1947, when he went to work for the fledgling Central Intelligence Agency, which had grown out of the Office of Special Services, a collective of World War II spies and intelligence gatherers. Maheu had worked in counter-intelligence during the war and was on retainer to the CIA in the early 1950s when he was introduced through channels to oddball industrialist Howard Hughes.

In his role as aide-de-camp to Hughes, Maheu's duties were diverse: he dug up dirt on wives, recruited paramours, negotiated with Chicago mob man John Rosselli, and helped manage the paranoid billionaire's seven casinos—all without a face-to-face meeting with Hughes. In the many years Maheu worked for Hughes, the rough-and-tumble private investigator never met his boss in person. Instead, they corresponded through memos and spoke on the phone many times a day. Hughes became dependent on Maheu for everything from his taste in television movies to his choice of casino managers.

Fragmented tales of Maheu's exploits have been chronicled in many books. Linked to such varied activity as bugging the inner sanctum of Aristotle Onassis, fixing city council races, funneling campaign cash contributions to Richard Nixon, and procuring Miss Universe contestants as girlfriends for Hughes, Maheu was a man of no small ingenuity, and he was extremely well paid for his efforts.

In the summer of 1960, Maheu played an integral role in devising a plot to hire the mob to kill Cuban leader Fidel Castro and enlisted the assistance of his friends Rosselli and Sam Giancana to do the job.

In the end, Castro stayed healthy and the CIA-mob plot to kill him stayed officially buried for many years. When it finally surfaced, few who understood the symbiotic relationship between the underworld and the intelligence community were surprised to find Maheu's fingerprints on the project.

After Hughes made his mystery-shrouded move to Las Vegas in November 1966 and set up his empire on the ninth floor of the Desert Inn, Maheu emerged as the billionaire's mouthpiece. After years of using him as one of his only links to the outside world, Hughes fired Maheu, sending the operative back into the night. In a rare interview in June 1972, Hughes was asked why he had split with Maheu.

"Because he's a no-good, dishonest son of a bitch, and he stole me blind," Hughes replied. "The money's gone, and he's got it."

It was severe criticism, indeed, coming from one of the shadiest industrialists ever to draw a paranoid breath. Hughes had played footsie with the mob and the international intelligence community most of his life. He had reveled in spying on enemies and building a political power base that ruined careers and lives.

Anyone who knew Maheu's history had to respect his eye for business, and he was mightily impressed with Stupak's Stratosphere. The two had briefly considered entering into a casino deal years earlier in Atlantic City, but the Stratosphere had both men excited.

"Every time I drive by this damn place there's more activity going on there and I'm beginning to pay more and more attention to Bob Stupak," Maheu said later. "So I decide to go in one day and there's action, and I figure, what in the hell is this guy's combination? I was intrigued by him. And when he approached me I didn't have to check his business acumen, because I had seen it over the years."

With his inner circle in place, Stupak entered into a consulting agreement with Space Needle Corporation, which operated Seattle's famous observation tower. It was Stupak's plan to eventually have the Space Needle operate Stratosphere—the tower, not the casino. The Seattle company would be brought in to manage the property, food and beverage, retail sales, marketing, hiring, and administration.

But if anyone believed Stupak intended to loosen his grip on his own project, they were mistaken, as a letter in the Stratosphere prospectus clearly notes:

"To date, Mr. Stupak has been responsible for the development of the Tower...Because Mr. Stupak has agreed that the Company will have a right of first refusal with respect to his future gaming, entertainment and recreational ventures (other than expansion of Vegas World), the Company is and will be dependent upon Mr. Stupak's continued active involvement in the Company's business. The Company intends to obtain, and thereafter to maintain, for a period of not less than two years, a key man life insurance policy on Mr. Stupak in an amount not less than $5 million."

Bob Maheu and the Space Needle people were only two of many talents Stupak surrounded himself with. In addition, there was Ned Baldwin, the Stratosphere's principal architect. As the president of Baldwin & Franklin Architects of New York and Toronto, Baldwin's company designed the CN Tower. It couldn't hurt to have the firm that designed the tallest building in the world on your side.

And there was Gary Nelson, architect of the American Center in Phoenix and the Sheraton Tucson El Conquistador Golf and Tennis Resort. Nelson was a respected member of the high-rise building subcommittee for the city of Phoenix.

John Skilling, Chairman of the Board of Skilling Ward Magnusson Barkshire Inc. of Seattle, was hired at Stratosphere expense to represent the interests of the City of Las Vegas. Skilling played an integral role in the design and construction of the World Trade Center, and he reviewed the design and drawings of the Stratosphere.

Frazer Smith was hired as the principal structural engineer of the Stratosphere Tower. As an associate of JAS Cashdan Inc., Smith specialized in the analysis and design of sophisticated concrete structures. He was an expert in earthquake-resistant design.

Dan Cashdan of JAS Cashdan specialized in nonlinear analysis and was one of the state's top structural engineers. Among his engineering credits were Bally's, the Golden Nugget, and the Tropicana. Tony Tschanz was a structural design engineer and an expert at structural analysis. He had contributed to the structural design of the Bangkok World Trade Center and AT&T Headquarters in New York.

As executive director of Ad-Art Inc. of Stockton, California, Charles Barnard's advanced design concepts had helped create the largest signs in the world, including those outside the Golden Nugget in Las Vegas and the Superdome in New Orleans.

Bob Stupak had done his homework and had gathered many of the greatest architects, developers, and managers since Eiffel himself. It was clear Stratosphere was not a typical Bob Stupak production.

Weeks after their meeting, Hantges bumped into Stupak and Phyllis McGuire in a casino in the northern Nevada town of Elko. Bob and Phyllis had been hitting the clubs and even tried to crash a few of the cowtown's legalized brothels. McGuire was playfully appalled to learn that Nevada law prevented her from dropping in at one of the whorehouses for a beer with the working girls. Even her pleas to the sheriff were to no avail.

Stupak invited Hantges to dinner and a show. After dinner, the Gary Puckett show, and a few cocktails, Stupak finally got around to business. He wanted to know what Hantges really thought of the deal, and the securities broker told him.

"Bob, your deal is not going to get done," Hantges said, reminding him why he'd turned down Stupak in the first place. "You're bullshitting yourself. You guys are not going to raise the money. We'd be foolish to participate. It's just not a good deal."

Though Stupak had surrounded himself with men of impeccable credentials, his greatest obstacle remained selling himself to those that mattered most—the public.

Even with the collection of brokerage houses working their clients and pitching Stupak's lengthy list of Vegas World Vacation subscribers, the IPO barely inched toward its $35 million minimum goal in July just as the tower reached the 400-foot level.

"It was pretty obvious that they wouldn't be able to pull it off," Hantges said. "It wasn't through a lack of effort, just a lack of interest. They were calling a lot of old customers. They were pushing. They were working hard. At one point, I said, 'You need to go and make yourself a deal. You need to bring in a partner.' I didn't tell him who to see. Bob knows plenty of people on his own."

By late August 1993, the tower had reached the 500-foot level, the halfway point give or take a few concrete pours. Despite the odds, the small securities firms managed to reach the halfway mark as well. But though he desperately needed it, he was unable to use a nickel of the escrowed IPO money.

In addition to attempting to charm traditional investors, Stupak was hitting up friends and associates to invest in his dream. He worked the poker rooms all over town, trying to coax a few bucks from his low-ball buddies. Then he moved to the casinos' executive offices. Some of the biggest names rumored to be interested in the tower included Las Vegas gaming legend Jackie Gaughan, who owned a half dozen casinos downtown; Si Redd, the video poker giant who was a longtime Stupak ally; Ralph Engelstad, whose Imperial Palace was one of the most profitable casinos on the Strip; and Lyle Berman, whose upstart

Grand Casinos of Minneapolis was setting records on Indian reservations and had big plans for riverboat operations.

But time was of the essence. The $35 million minimum offer had to be completed by November or the deal was ruined.

Bob Stupak had never let the public see him sweat, and he wasn't about to start now.

"It'll be the first thing people see when they fly in or drive in," he told a reporter. "And you can believe me when I say there'll never be another like this in Nevada—there's always going to be other theme parks, but this is an exclusive."

At the time, Bob Stupak could not have known how right he was.

EIGHT

Towering Inferno

With Stratosphere's initial public offering in full swing, public confidence in the project began to rise along with the tower: slowly but steadily.

Bob Stupak's dream continued to draw its share of one-liners—few could resist calling it "Stupak's Stump" and even the "Tower of Bobel"—but by late August 1993 he was beginning to win a few converts and, more importantly, increasing numbers of investors.

The Stratosphere Tower still was not much more than a gigantic stanchion on Las Vegas Boulevard, but by August 28 it had risen to 510 feet. It already was by far the tallest structure in the city, and it had not yet reached the halfway mark in its climb skyward. After the change in contractors, the early delays, and the initially slow public stock offering, the Stratosphere finally appeared destined to meet a completion deadline: summer 1994.

Shortly before 1 a.m. on August 29, all that changed.

It was early Sunday morning when some Vegas World tourists first noticed flames and smoke rising from the top deck of the tower. What they could not know is that the fire had already spread to the tower's stairwell and was making its way down one leg.

At 12:39 a.m., the fire was reported.

At 12:45 a.m., the first engine arrived at the scene. Fire hoses were set up on the roof of Vegas World in hopes that the water pressure would somehow enable them to fight the fire from more than 250 feet below.

Vegas World had hosted its share of torch singers, but this was another sort of flame entirely. For one night only, it was Stupak's towering inferno.

"It was raining fire," said one witness. "The back side was on fire, and within a matter of fifteen to twenty minutes the whole thing was engulfed.

"It was shooting part of the scaffolding onto the casino and down to the ground. Thank God the winds weren't blowing too hard."

A California tourist staying in the hotel told a reporter, "At first I thought they said Vegas World was burning down. When I got outside, I saw it was the big cement tower thing, so I wasn't so worried. Actually, it looked like a pretty good show."

The entertainment aspect was lost on those charged with battling the blaze and herding the tourists and gawking bystanders.

Las Vegas Fire Department engines converged on the structure and found a gigantic torch burning on the site of the old Million Dollar Historic Gambling Museum & Casino, which had succumbed to fire nearly 20 years earlier.

A modern ladder truck can climb several stories, but even the department's tallest fire crane wouldn't begin to approach the flames burning more than 50 stories overhead. The most powerful streams of water fell 30 floors short of the fire.

The crew of firefighters stationed atop Vegas World fared little better. Their best efforts left them not only well below the flames, but also in the path of falling debris.

What access existed was limited to the stairwell and construction elevator used to ferry workers and material. Without a clear idea of the extent of the flames, the firefighters would be foolish to take the trip skyward.

Sparks drifted on the increasing 20-mile-per-hour winds from the upper deck to nearby residential areas, but no spot fires were reported. The simple fact was, as spectacular as the fire was to watch, there wasn't much to burn up there but a stack of cement forms used to frame the daily cement pour. The tower's concrete structure would not be weakened by the fire, no matter how hot it burned. The last of the construction workers departed the site at 4:30 p.m., so there would be no need for a daring and dangerous rescue attempt.

A nearby McDonald's was evacuated at 12:51. The diminutive Aztec Casino next door was cleared minutes later.

Police, who had recently spent nearly $1 million in crowd-control preparation in the wake of LA's Rodney King riots, quickly blocked off traffic on Las Vegas Boulevard from Sahara to St. Louis avenues. Streets were barricaded for blocks around what instantly became the biggest show on the Las Vegas Strip. Two miles to the west, traffic along Interstate 15 slowed to school-zone speed as drivers gawked at the Stratospheric sparkler.

Falling debris threatened to harm the thousands of spectators who gathered from nearby motels and Meadows Village to watch the show. In that rough neighborhood, falling debris was hardly the only thing that threatened to hit them on the head.

Hundreds of tourists, who no longer could complain of not receiving enough excitement from their discount vacation packages, grabbed their belongings and temporarily checked out of Vegas World. They were not, however, evacuated immediately. The hotel was not on fire. It was the debris outside that was potentially life-threatening.

Better to keep them inside. But then the lights went out and the chaos began. Guests hurried to gather up their stuff in the rooms or clear their winnings off the tables before rushing outside. With burning pieces of wood dropping down past the guests' windows, the scramble became crushing. Patrons struggled to see in the darkened hallways. When they located the stairs, they found them flooded with other guests. In the dim light someone easily could have been trampled, but the only serious injury suffered was to Bob Stupak's name.

Some Vegas World employees remained behind to assist with

the evacuation. Although they had been given no fire-safety training, they responded as if they owned a piece of the place.

Comedian Marty Allen, who had become a staple in the Vegas World showroom, worked on his material from the sidewalk.

"They kept saying, 'It's a hot act,'" he said.

By 2 a.m., the blaze was upgraded to a three-alarm fire, but
the firefighters were limited to making sure the burning debris
didn't spread the flames throughout downtown. The lack of wind
probably saved lives and millions of dollars in property damage.

One hour later, the fire on top began to die out, but the blaze
was still strong at the building's lower levels. The top would
continue to smolder until sunrise.

"Letting the structure burn was what we had planned," Las
Vegas Fire Chief Clell West said. "It was going to burn itself out.
Our main concern was that it didn't spread, which it didn't, and
that we didn't have any injuries or fatalities, which we didn't.
We predicted that we would be able to contain the fire within
the structure itself, and that there would be no deaths and injuries."

Unlike the fire nearly two decades earlier, in which officials
offered opinions as to the blaze's origin even before it was extinguished, neither Chief West nor his men and women would
speculate on the cause of the Stratosphere fire.

Where it comes to fire safety, common sense has been in short
supply inside the Las Vegas casino industry.

In October 1960, Beldon Katleman's El Rancho Vegas, the
first resort to open on what would become known as the Strip,
mysteriously burned. Although Las Vegas-based mobster Johnny
Marshal, *nee* Marshall Caifano, was suspected of setting the fire
after Katleman kicked him out of the joint, no one ever was
charged. In fact, those familiar with the construction of the El

Rancho Vegas recalled that the hotel's kitchen vents emptied directly into the building's attic, and the flammable grease buildup was several inches thick in the months leading up to the fire. Luckily, no one was injured.

Exactly 20 years later, the largest hotel disaster in Las Vegas history took place. In November 1980, an electrical fire broke out at the MGM Grand (now Bally's). The resort, then the world's largest hotel with nearly 3,000 rooms, lacked a water sprinkler system that would become a standard fire safety item a few years later. Firefighters risked their lives evacuating hundreds of hotel guests. In the end, 84 people died and nearly 700 were injured.

Only a few months later, another deadly fire, this one at the Las Vegas Hilton, again raised the specter of catastrophe at Las Vegas resorts. The MGM and Hilton fires resulted in numerous changes in the community's fire-code standards.

No one was seriously injured in the Stratosphere blaze, but it attracted plenty of national media attention: 500-foot Roman candles tend to do that.

A day later, Las Vegas Mayor Jan Jones toured the site. Jones had had her share of run-ins with Stupak, but she appreciated a good deal for one of the most troubled areas in the city when she saw it. Given to wearing stylish miniskirts and designer outfits, the mayor sported a hard hat for the occasion and greeted skeptical reporters with confidence. City officials met with area business owners in an attempt to allay their fears, but one fact remained: the stretch of Las Vegas Boulevard that brought them customers was going to be blocked off for some time.

With Stratosphere struggling to complete its IPO, the tower fire provided the worst sort of media attention. The *Los Angeles Times* was typical of the coverage:

GUESTS FLEE HOTEL AS VEGAS TOWER BURNS

The *Reno Gazette-Journal* was more blunt:

VEGAS STRIP: TOWER BURNS

At the time of the fire, Stupak was in Minneapolis attempting to persuade Grand Casinos Chairman Lyle Berman to invest in the Stratosphere project. Berman loved the tower idea, but his young casino company—the fastest-growing outfit in the industry—was interested in more than just another roadside attraction. As great as the tower's potential was, Berman believed the project needed more. If Stratosphere were to compete in earnest with Strip resorts in far better locations, then it would have to gain megaresort status: more rooms, more attractions, and especially, more casino space. That meant an infusion of real money—not just one man's bankroll, but several hundred million dollars.

Grand Casinos not only had credit, it had credibility as well. In addition, Berman and Stupak had shared a poker-playing friendship for two decades. A Stratosphere-Grand affiliation looked like a good fit.

Then came the late-night phone call awakening Stupak with the bad news from his confidant, Andy Blumen.

"My initial reaction was, 'What is there to burn?'" he commented. "I didn't know of any of the details until the next day."

Stupak shrugged and went back to bed. A few days later, he was back before the cameras with a message: The tower project was very much alive.

"It was a small but spectacular fire," he told a group of reporters. The professional poker player tried to show no outward signs that he felt his project was in danger, but he was clearly shaken. He appeared noticeably humbled by the event. "It was a construction accident. It happens all the time. Fortunately, no one was hurt. We're definitely moving forward."

But first, the job site needed a new crane to replace what was now a 25-ton collection of scrap iron balanced atop the tower. Although fire crews had secured the damaged construction crane with chains to prevent the possibility of it breaking loose and crashing onto Las Vegas Boulevard, or worse, the top of Vegas World, the problems created by the gigantic broken erector set were many. Securing it was one thing, removing it quite another.

Engineers would have to construct a 700-foot crane and bolt it to the outside of the tower, then use it to remove the ruined crane piece by piece. That was the bad news.

The good news? As the days passed it became clear to inspectors that the tower had suffered no structural damage. Although a container of plastic material appeared to be at the flashpoint of the fire, the cause of the blaze remained unknown.

With construction delays assured until December, the building schedule was shredded. Stratosphere was still a long way from becoming the ninth-tallest structure in the world.

The top of the tower wasn't the only thing that burned on that hot August night. The initial public offering went up in smoke even faster than the building. If investors were leery of Stupak's big idea before the fire, they ran away in droves afterward.

The sound of investors' checkbooks closing was almost audible. Though the tower was not structurally damaged, surely that fact would be lost on potential stockholders.

Brokers had managed to raise $20 million of the $35 million IPO, but with only a few weeks remaining before the offering's deadline, the odds of completing the deal grew more remote by the day.

Mike Moody, then president of Union Equity Partners, which was selling most of the shares, said of the fire, "It's devastating. It could very well kill the deal. We have two problems here: what will the setback be, and how difficult will it be to raise money in the offering?" Moody wondered. "If this does make it difficult to complete the offering, it will have to be stopped and restructured and done later. The important thing is the shareholders will get their money back if the deal is not completed."

Privately, Moody realized the deal was as cooked as the buckled construction crane.

"I was crushed," Moody said. "I had more than $1 million of my clients' money in the deal. I saw commissions going out the window. And it was going to be awful for the city. A bunch of small brokerage firms were trying to do this deal, and it couldn't have been worse timing."

For the diminutive securities firm already battling Stupak's image problem, it was like being caught in the middle of the ocean in a tiny sailboat with a world of good intentions but not even a whisper of a breeze.

"We were just getting momentum. People were beginning to see the tower take shape," Moody said. "Once the fire hit, it took the wind out of the sales of both the brokers and the investors."

Sales of the IPO were temporarily halted. Although James Quiter of Rolf Jensen & Associates later told reporters that tower safety would exceed local fire codes, the public's confidence in the project had dropped to an all-time low.

Stupak, however, remained outwardly unconcerned about the fire and its effects on the physical structure of the Stratosphere, as well as its financing.

"For a couple of hours it was the best show in town," Stupak told *Barron's* Andy Zipser. "I told them I had a hot deal here."

Zipser was perhaps the first reporter from a national publication to detail the bonanza that Stupak would mine from the best-efforts deal. Investors who jumped in early, he wrote, got their names etched in granite, but Stupak received much more. If the public purchased a minimum of 11.7 million units by November 20, 1993—which would fund Stratosphere with at least $32.4 million and perhaps as much as $54.1 million—Stupak would be in line to receive up to 17.6 million shares of stock at "a price substantially less than the offering price."

As a result, the total stock pool would be severely diluted. Each share of stock would dip to as low as $1.22 in actual book value, according to *Barron's*. Stupak was guaranteed to retain ownership of at least 60 percent of the tower, and minority investors would not share in the hotel or casino profits.

"What they will have," Zipser wrote, "is a 500-foot piece of concrete, four acres immediately adjacent to a section of Las Vegas that is so badly run down the locals refer to it as 'Naked City,' and a handful of Stupak's dreams, including high-speed elevators, lasers, lions, and wedding chapels."

Local newspaper editorial writers, rarely at a loss for words when it came to championing development in Las Vegas, also fretted over the future of the project.

"As hotel-casinos come up with more bizarre plans to attract tourists, even greater attention should be paid to basic safety principles," the *Las Vegas Sun* offered. "The enthusiasm to improve our community with dazzling new attractions must be tempered with common sense."

The fire only confirmed suspicions in the minds of many investors, and that spelled trouble for Bob Stupak.

NINE

Enter Berman

It was not by chance that Bob Stupak was in Minneapolis the night of the Stratosphere fire. What his friends in the financial community had been telling him for months finally had begun to soak in: the best-efforts initial public offering wasn't selling fast enough to meet the deadline for the $35 million minimum. If he didn't bring in a partner, his dream project was in jeopardy.

But who would be daring enough to team up with Bob Stupak?

With more than $20 million already invested, Stupak couldn't continue to build out of cash flow and short-term loans from his casino pals. If the IPO fell short, the deal would be doomed in the unforgiving world of finance. He had to act quickly.

Stupak decided to pursue Lyle Berman as his partner for a number of reasons. First, they were friends and high-stakes poker adversaries. Also, Berman's Grand Casinos Inc. was a meteoric success story in the fiercely competitive gambling industry. Berman had bounced his casino design concepts off Stupak in 1991, and Stupak had opened up Vegas World for his inspection.

"Everything I could do to push him into the deal, I did," Stupak said. "I told Lyle, 'You're in Minnesota, Mississippi, you've got these Indian deals in Louisiana. But it's the difference between the minor leagues and the New York Yankees.

The majors is Las Vegas. If you're not in Las Vegas, you're no-where.'

"Every time he came to town, he'd come to look at the tower. I'd take him up to whatever level we were at. I could see he was intrigued with it. He liked it from the beginning."

Berman recalled the meeting in which Stupak handed him the business plan. Berman was impressed by the market research that had been done; Bob Stupak was not known for letting a few details like structural engineering and design get in the way of a big idea. But this time was different. He appeared to have changed.

"Originally we were just brainstorming, he and I, in my capacity with Berman Consultants," Berman said later. "I was one of the few outside businessmen he knew. By 'outside' I mean beyond Las Vegas, which, you know, is kind of a world unto itself. I was what you might call a 'real-world' businessman."

The decision to enter into a partnership with Stupak was not unanimous. Grand Casinos insider Richard Schuetz, for one, was concerned that Stupak's notoriety might blemish the public's perception of the fastest-growing company in America.

"I'd been in Vegas for a long time and Bob's image wasn't one I thought was conducive to the image that I and others had worked so hard to shape at Grand," Schuetz said. "I just didn't think it was an image, be it right or wrong, that we necessarily wanted to have associated with our very pristine, successful name."

But by most accounts Berman appeared an ideal partner. In one regard, Berman was everything Stupak was not: educated, understated, respected at the highest levels of the industry and on Wall Street. In another light, they appeared very much alike. Both were successful poker players who possessed the courage to take great risks at the tables and in their business lives.

Stupak described Berman as a player with a "quick arm." That is, a fellow not afraid to push his chips to the center of the table at a moment's notice.

"When you play poker with a guy, you get to know what

kind of person he is," Stupak said. "I've got somebody who can match me—and maybe go even higher—as a gambler. Lyle plays poker. Lyle shoots craps. Lyle could sit down and win a few hundred thousand and lose a few hundred thousand. No question about it. He's got gamble in him."

More than that, Berman had the respect of the country's best players.

"Is Lyle a good player? Yeah, he's good," one noted player said on the condition of anonymity. "He's better than Bob. Lyle's probably in the top one percent of all poker players all-around. Whether it's ring games or tournaments, he's good at everything."

Berman and Stupak were born the same year, 1942, but the childhood similarities ended there. While Stupak was knocking around Pittsburgh's South Side as the son of a gambler, Berman was growing up the son of a clothing-store owner in Minneapolis. Berman graduated from the University of Minnesota in 1963 with a degree in business administration.

Instead of embarking on an Australian odyssey, Lyle Berman stayed in Minnesota and entered his family's traditional industry. He went to work for Rodeo Leather Works, which after his takeover was renamed Berman's Specialty Stores. The leather coats and jackets were stylish and profitable, and Berman's management style was full of energy and innovation. Berman's Specialty Stores multiplied at a rapid clip.

About the time Bob Stupak was unveiling Vegas World, Lyle Berman was selling his specialty-store chain with its 27 outlets to W.R. Grace for $10 million. Then Berman made a decision that would change his life: instead of taking the money and striking out in another direction, he remained with W.R. Grace as president and chief executive officer and continued to grow the company. But his interests stretched beyond retail marketing and included founding Computer Network Technology in 1982. Lyle Berman was going places in corporate America.

Berman clearly understood the value of rapid growth in the 1980s. The faster he expanded the business, the more attractive

it became to speculators in the era of junk bonds and the leveraged buyout. In 1987, Berman tapped his contacts in the financial community and reacquired the company, which by then had
expanded to 165 stores, and by 1980s' standards was underval-
ued at $100 million.

Riding the crest of the decade, he sold out to Wilson Suede
& Leather a year later. The price: $200 million.

As a gambler, he had gained a national reputation in the
poker room and had taken plenty of lumps in early forays into
Las Vegas. But his sucker days were over.

"When Lyle first showed up in the rooms, he was a mark,"
one local player said. "He was the one we waited for because he
played much bigger than he should have for his skill level. But
Lyle was so competitive, he hired all these computer analysts
and experts to study the games he played. And he taught himself.

"Then he turned the tables on all the guys who thought he
was easy money. He used to let the big games get started late at
night while he slept in his room. Then, early in the morning,
Lyle would come down and join the game. All these guys were
tired from playing all night, but they couldn't force themselves
to leave without Berman's money. And he'd kill 'em. Lyle beat
the heck out of everyone for a long time until the poker world
snapped to what he'd done. Now, of course, he's known wherever he goes."

Berman was a regular at high-stakes tournaments in Las
Vegas, but now he was coming to the table with genuine capital.

Grand Casinos was created as a management company to
oversee Berman's $3 million stake in a Native American bingo
parlor and slot joint, which opened in April 1991, 90 miles north
of Minneapolis on a reservation owned by the Mille Lacs band
of the Ojibwe Chippewa Indians.

The reservation casino on the western shore of Lake Mille
Lacs at Onamia was an immediate success, and Berman's group
collected the lion's share of the profits. The success of the Mille
Lacs casino helped convince Berman and his Grand Casinos co-

founder, Stanley Taub, to take their company public in October 1991. From there, Berman embarked on a casino expansion plan that impressed the industry's most successful players. In short order, Grand Casinos opened another Chippewa reservation gambling hall in Hinkley, Minnesota, then moved south, gaining two licenses to operate in Tunica, Mississippi, and approval to manage a casino in Louisiana.

Grand Casinos gambling halls benefitted greatly by their exclusive locations. Where it came to casinos, Berman had developed a knack for being in the right place at the right time. He also saw what many traditional gaming executives missed—that to remain prosperous and, indeed, improve their tarnished image, casinos needed to offer more than cards and dice and cheap buffets. Although the Las Vegas Hilton had been the first to devote a section of the hotel to a day-care center in the 1970s, Berman was the first to extensively develop in-house child care as a marketing theme. His Kids Quest Activity Centers offered supervised care and enabled parents to hit the tables.

Those who work for Berman find it impossible to keep up with his 16-hour workdays and the kind of intense focus capable of creating rapid expansion and a seemingly unlimited potential.

"Lyle didn't know the casino business when he started Grand," Schuetz said. "But Lyle's a really smart guy. When you sit down with Lyle, you're fading the I.Q. points. He's a brilliant guy. He comes in at eight in the morning and leaves at 10 at night. He just works feverishly."

With corporate assets at the time well in excess of $300 million, Lyle Berman was a rising star, and it appeared he was taking Bob Stupak with him.

On November 15, 1993, Lyle Berman and Bob Stupak struck a deal. Grand Casinos of Plymouth, Minnesota, saved the IPO by purchasing $28 million worth of stock, and in doing so acquired 43 percent of Stratosphere Corporation, as well as picking up options including an agreement to acquire 75 percent of Vegas World from Stupak for $50.4 million. Grand Casinos did not, however, assume Stupak's liabilities, which included the cost of the Vegas World vacation packages.

Within weeks, Grand Casinos would control 52.2 percent of the Stratosphere project through purchases and proxies. Stupak held 17 percent, but he also possessed the knowledge that his dream tower would be completed and, as the largest individual shareholder of Stratosphere, he would remain integrally involved in the resort. At least, that's what he believed at the time.

"Stupak's much smarter, even though it's a street-corner sort of intelligence, than most people give him credit for," securities broker Tom Hantges observed. "He really had to have this deal. He had to make a deal or he would have been busted. He was building out of cash flow. He never wanted the construction to stop. Being smarter than that, he kept it going, even if it was slowly.

"I think the fire did hurt them. But I would venture to say that even without the fire the best-efforts offer wouldn't have gotten done. The problem with best-efforts deals is that brokers don't like to commit dollars unless they know the deal is going to close. Most brokers like to wait until they see the deal closing. It's the chicken and egg; nobody wants to go first. He had to make this deal or he was done."

Added broker Garren Sepede, "I can't tell you how many people laughed at us. Important people in town, the kind of people with the money to invest, were saying, 'This is going to be a joke. It's never going to work. It's never going to be completed.'

"No doubt, Grand saved the deal, but Bob had a lot to do with that. He went out and found the White Knight. Bob is a very driven, very focused person. He has a vision of the big picture and how it's all going to get done. I've always felt that by hook or by crook, Bob would get the Stratosphere done."

As 1994 progressed, even Bob Stupak's biggest critics had to admit that Stratosphere was materializing. With a new crane in place and construction crews back on the job day and night, the tower was again reaching for the sky. The structure was anchored just 12 feet underground, but its four-legged design made it a marvel of structural stability. It balanced on three legs, each 20 feet by 32 feet, with a supporting center column completing the base. The concrete legs were form cast and designed to support 6,000 pounds per square inch. Wind-tunnel studies had been performed on the tower model, and Stratosphere engineers were eager to boast of its structural integrity and fire-safety precautions.

"The tower is pretty well over-designed," engineer Rick Stone told a reporter. "Nobody wants the damn thing to fall over."

The foundation was a web of reinforced steel and 5,600 yards of concrete. Beneath that was the desert's ultimate foundation, a layer of caliche (lake-bottom hardpan) several feet thick. The base stretched 180 feet in diameter from the center core. Above the base, the concrete legs themselves were 16 inches thick and tapered to a height of 264 feet where they joined the center column.

The one visible flaw was the imperfection of the tower's north leg. It didn't detract from the structural soundness of the project, but it did detract from the public's confidence in the tower. It also gave people a chuckle at Stupak's expense. After all, surely only Bob Stupak could build a 1,000-foot tower with a crooked leg. In fact, Stupak's own Leeman Construction had been responsible for the flaw. The gimp leg was smoothed out before the project was completed. Removing the distraction enhanced visitors' appreciation of the tower's more attractive features.

The Stratosphere climbed 774 feet before again flattening to a base for the tower's 12-story pod, which would feature observation decks, wedding chapels, gift shops, a 400-seat restaurant, and a lounge. The revolving restaurant would be the world's largest; the chapels would be the first wedding facilities in an observation tower.

Stratosphere's laser lights would lend a distinctly Vegas World theme to the tower. With a ring of synchronized lights and lasers shooting downward from the 700-foot level, the pod would take on the appearance of a spaceship.

The tower's daily progress was easy enough to see, but it continued to be met with opposition from Clark County Aviation Director Bob Broadbent, who didn't like the idea and was dedicated to keeping the tower from climbing to Stupak's new proposed height of 1,825 feet, which would include a radio antenna hundreds of feet high. Broadbent contacted the Federal Aviation Administration, local airlines, members of the Las Vegas Convention and Visitors Authority, and the most powerful casino operators in the city in an attempt to pressure the Las Vegas City Council into limiting Stupak's ambition.

Stupak had been battling Broadbent on the height issue since 1991. At that time, a preliminary finding by the FAA found that the tower's proposed 1,012 height created a "substantial adverse impact" on flight patterns in the Las Vegas Valley. The FAA was concerned over any structure above 781 feet. Broadbent suggested the city take out collision insurance and quoted safety warnings from pilots organizations, such as the Air Transport Association and Airline Pilots Association.

In the end, Stupak's record-setting radio-tower-extension plan was killed by the City Council. He would settle for 1,149 feet.

But he intended to make every inch a part of the show. With the tower's financing apparently secure, his promotional instincts went into overdrive. He contacted officials at Intamin, which had developed a thrill ride based on a jet flight simulator, to discuss installing a number of trainers atop the Stratosphere. With 360-degree rolls performed 1,000 feet in the air, it would be a guaranteed hit with the strong of stomach.

"We've customized the ride for this application," Intamin's Mark Messersmith said. "The way it is being mounted, the arms will extend beyond the sides of the building and the passengers will be able to look straight down more than 1,000 feet to the streets below. It will be an amazing sensation. Combine the dives and rolls a person can put the capsule through and the height at which they can do it here and you've got yourself one super thrill ride."

But the Intamin Flight Trainer failed to take off, and in no time Stupak was angling for other action. He contacted Jay Checketts at S&S Sports Power of Ogden, Utah, and flew a private jet full of friends and associates to experience what was sure to be the greatest tower-topping attraction in the world: the Space Shot liftoff simulator. With nine rides all over the world— and a spotless safety record—S&S Sports had developed the technology capable of launching 16 riders strapped into chairs 150 feet up a specially designed 187-foot tower in three seconds at a force of four Gs. The drop, at negative one G, sent the riders halfway back down the pole and gave a sense of free fall. From beginning to end, the ride lasted 30 seconds, allowing hundreds of riders per hour to blast off. Mounted atop the Stratosphere, it was sure to be a winner. In keeping with the Vegas theme, Stupak would change the name from Space Shot to Big Shot.

Despite the Broadbent feud, by the summer of 1994 Stupak was enjoying an unprecedented surge of positive press and public support for the Stratosphere project. With the reliable Berman in place to shepherd the financing and expand the theme, Stupak appeared to be moving toward widespread community acceptance for the first time.

But it's not easy being politically correct when you've made a career out of offending people. It didn't help that Stupak announced the eviction of dozens of tenants from the apartments he owned near Vegas World to make way for construction at his expanding $323 million resort. He offered to pay a few bucks to relocate the 300 residents at 122 and 128 West Boston Avenue. Not surprisingly, his most vocal critic was City Councilman Frank Hawkins, who had barely survived Stupak's sleazy sting operation three years earlier. Perhaps not wanting to jeopardize his newfound public support, Stupak trudged into City Hall, met with Mayor Jan Jones and members of the City Council, and rescinded the evictions until a later date. But he wasn't finished backtracking.

Stupak had feuded with the Culinary Union from the day Vegas World opened. He had fought sidewalk pickets and National Labor Relations Board complaints. The local union's mob associates had tried to muscle him; its in-house instigators had tried to organize his maids, waiters, and bartenders. After 15 years, he finally appeared to be enjoying a truce with the union. But then a Culinary Union button appeared on a maid's uniform. Taking it as a sign of trouble, Stupak overreacted and fired 36 maids merely for wearing the buttons. Even the local anti-labor zealots shook their heads over Stupak's apparent callousness.

City leaders, including the mayor, met privately with Stupak a day after the maids were terminated. Stupak and his counsel, Andrew Blumen, emerged from the meeting sounding every bit like union activists. The maids were rehired. Stupak claimed that the fired workers had walked off the job, but that he was a generous boss and had allowed them to return to their work cleaning rooms and making beds.

It wasn't easy being a benevolent casino mogul. Over the years he had provided turkey dinners for hundreds of homeless people at Thanksgiving and Christmas. Although his Vegas World health plan did not rank among industry leaders, he had personally funded surgeries for some of his longtime Vegas World employees. Still, when it came to public opinion, Stupak was a man forever on the edge of the abyss.

The most painful reversal concerned the thousands of unredeemed Vegas VIP Vacation and Stratosphere Club packages Stupak's telemarketing and direct-mail operation had sold up to 1992. The Gaming Control Board demanded that the investment those customers had made in future vacation packages be protected by Stupak. As part of his forced settlement of the vacation package issue reached with the state's casino regulators, Stupak agreed to set aside Stratosphere stock equal to 150 percent of what the outstanding packages were worth, which amounted to $44 million. To appease the Control Board, Stupak put up 7 million shares of stock. He had the option to pay the total package price in cash, or sell off stock to cover the debt, but he passed in favor of placing the stock in escrow.

It would prove a crucial mistake that eventually would cost Stupak millions.

In late 1994, Stupak attempted to get the regulators to soften their position. Even at 110 percent coverage the packages would be protected, but Control Board Chairman Bill Bible was adamant.

"People paid for these packages," he said. "The money was collected by Vegas World. It is our position that they get what they paid for."

Bible was in no mood to accept Stupak's word, and Stupak was in no position to pay off the packages with cash without driving down Stratosphere stock and investor confidence. In attempting to protect investors, Gaming Control had inadvertently set Stupak on the edge of personal ruin should Stratosphere perform below its lofty expectations. Quite simply, most of Stupak's wealth—which would range as high as $130 million in the days leading up to the resort's opening—was tied up in company stock.

On November 4, Grand Casinos quietly took control of Vegas World and, in effect, the entire Stratosphere project, by completing its deal with Bob Stupak. For $51 million in cash and secured notes, Stupak had become a mere player on the stage that he'd built with his own hands.

"The acquisition of the hotel gives Stratosphere Corporation control of the entire project and is an important step in our total development plan," Lyle Berman said.

With 17 percent of the stock, Stupak was still Chairman of the Board of Stratosphere and its single largest shareholder. But

Grand Casinos controlled 51 percent and, as such, was in charge of the destiny of the tower and the resort.

The project had grown many times since Stupak's Australian brainstorm. Costs soared from $30 million in 1989 to $350 million by the end of 1994. Grand Casinos was in the process of floating as much as $210 million in bonds to finance its increasingly exorbitant plans for the resort on the edge of Naked City, which included not only the thrill rides Stupak had dreamed about, but also a 2,500-room hotel and an eye-popping World's Fair theme that Berman believed would make the project instantly competitive with the Strip's larger resorts.

But it also would be in the similar financial strata: the project was fast becoming one of the most expensive casino-resorts in the history of the city and the first of its size to be built on the edge of a slum neighborhood a $6-$8 cab ride from the heart of the Strip. Including the equity-to-debt incentives to bondholders, Grand Casinos was preparing to take on more than $200 million in debt with an effective interest rate of 20 percent on a substantial part of the notes. It was the kind of rate that would make even a diehard junk-bond junkie break into a cold sweat, but professional poker players learn to be impassive. If Berman and Stupak were nervous, no one was able to tell.

With construction struggling to remain on schedule, the regular addition of new ideas to Stratosphere threatened to push the grand opening into early 1996. Instead of an encased lion's den, Stratosphere would feature a multimillion-dollar aquarium with menacing sharks and fish of many varieties. When Stupak learned the details of the costly fish tank, he was so angry he sent live fish in water-filled plastic bags to Berman and his fellow Stratosphere executives. As if the top of the tower weren't wild enough with the addition of the Big Shot, Stupak forged ahead with plans for installing a roller coaster at the 770-foot level. The good ideas jumped like corn from a hot popper, but

TEN

Coming Through

When Metro Detective Richard Hart's phone rang shortly before midnight on March 31, 1995, he knew the news was bad. As an investigator assigned to the fatal and life-threatening accidents desk of the police department's Traffic Bureau, Hart worked the day shift but was on call all night. After 13 years with Metro, nine of them working fatals, he knew that no one ever called at this hour with good news. By the time he dressed and drove to the scene of the accident at Rancho Road and Mason Avenue, joined there by his partner, Detective William Johnson, the three victims of the motorcycle and automobile smash-up had been transported to University Medical Center. The traffic cops who had blocked off the area were still buzzing about the Harley rider and his long-shot chances of surviving the night.

"Once we get to the scene we look at all the evidence, mark the evidence, determine the path of the vehicles, and take witness statements," Hart said. "We always send somebody to the hospital to check whether there is any indication of alcohol. We determined that there was no indication of alcohol present. Someone said the rider took the brunt of the impact, and that's the way it looked at the scene."

It quickly became clear that the female turning left in the '86 Subaru hadn't seen the motorcycle approaching at high speed. The Harley came right out of the background lighting. Hart and

Williams removed the headlight assembly from the Harley and put it in evidence. It was later determined that the headlamp had been on.

"One of the biggest things when you're riding is that you have to be double cautious," Hart said. "You're a small thing, especially when you're coming straight at someone.

"I determined that the motorcycle was traveling about 63 miles per hour in a posted 35-mile-per-hour zone. That's quite a bit over the speed limit. He was so far back that she couldn't see him. There were a lot of background lights; he could have blended into the background. We attributed the cause of the accident to be speeding on the part of Bob Stupak."

By the time Hart had surmised who was at fault that night, Bob Stupak already had taken eight units of blood at the UMC Trauma Center.

"To look at the wreck, you wouldn't have thought he would live," Hart said. "He flew over the vehicle and landed on his face."

The damage to the Subaru was perhaps the most dramatic statement on the impact of the collision.

"The Subaru was knocked hard out of the driving path, too. In fact, it was turned almost completely around," said Howard McCulley, who worked for Quality Towing and removed the vehicle that night. "With a motorcycle and a car, they're usually more glancing than that. This one was pretty solid. It was easy to clean up, but the car was damaged terribly."

Hart issued a ticket for excessive speed and the lack of an operator's license and closed the case on May 31, but he didn't expect the charges to go anywhere. Stupak had suffered severe injuries. Like several of the paramedics who handled Stupak that night, Hart dropped by the hospital to look in on him and saw family members and Phyllis McGuire maintaining a vigil.

As part of his duties, Hart submitted his findings to the City Attorney's office. Las Vegas City Attorney Brad Jerbic, a former county and federal prosecutor, weighed the facts and the options. Stupak clearly was at fault, but Jerbic knew a speeding ticket was the least of the casino man's worries.

"How much more can you penalize a guy who is in a coma?" Jerbic asked.

Bob Stupak's injuries were extensive and varied. He had suffered injuries as a motorcycle drag racer, but broken knees could not have prepared him for what he was now experiencing.

His face was a broken mass of cuts and shattered bones. His teeth were knocked out, and his throat was cut by the helmet strap. Both arms and his left leg snapped on impact. His pelvis was cracked. Blood filled his lungs, and his skull was fractured in three places. His brain suffered intense trauma and was beginning to swell.

With trauma nurses administering unit after unit of blood and a team of doctors working to keep him alive through the long night, Bob Stupak did not lack for care.

Emergency surgery was needed to stem the blood flow, but not even the hospital's top doctors knew the extent of the damage to Stupak's brain. If they failed to control the swelling, he would die.

"He almost bled to death," UMC Chief Surgeon Hugh Follmer said. "All of us were thinking he might die."

Nevada Stupak, who had crawled to his father's side after the accident, suffered a broken leg. His pain was intense and his shock was understandable, but he had to remain alert. Early in the morning, UMC surgeons approached him with a proposition only he could accept: They possessed an experimental drug that succeeded in reducing brain swelling in some patients, but it was not approved by the Food and Drug Administration. The drug was to be used only if the patient was not expected to live.

Bob Stupak lay in critical condition. While the drug might kill him, he surely would die without it.

Nevada immediately approved its use, and the doctors returned to work, administering the drug and placing him on a ventilator. Bob Stupak entered a coma that would, in theory, allow his badly bruised brain a chance to stop swelling.

As the sun began to warm the Las Vegas Valley on April 1, television and radio stations buzzed with the news of Bob Stupak's crash. Camera crews were dispatched to UMC, a prayer vigil took place at St. Anne's Catholic Church, and the first of thousands of cards, letters, and bouquets for Stupak began arriving at the hospital.

Although he had to nearly kill himself to do it, for the first time in his career Bob Stupak had the sympathetic attention of everyone in Las Vegas.

Eddie Baranski was amazed Stupak was even alive.

"It was the worst-looking thing you've ever seen," he said. "There was no way he could live. His head was swollen to the size of a basketball."

Phyllis McGuire: "I don't know how anyone could have survived. Every bone in his face was fragmented. It was worse than anything you could see in a horror movie."

Stupak was packed in ice blankets and monitored around the clock. Physicians did what they could. For the most part, all they could do was wait to see if he survived the first 48 hours in his comatose state.

Despite the severity of his injuries, over the next two weeks Stupak's condition stabilized. Physicians worked on him every day to repair the damage. Setting his bones and sewing him up were easy compared to the work to come on his head and face. Plastic surgery would piece his cheeks, nose, and mouth back together, but his jaw needed to be reconstructed, and there was no guarantee that he would emerge from the coma mentally whole.

Phyllis McGuire took up a vigil at the trauma center and later followed Stupak to the hospital's Intensive Care Unit, where she read to him daily. She remained by his side for weeks, along with the rest of the Stupak family. Nicole flew in from Australia to be with her father.

Stupak was active even while comatose. Within days, he began twitching his fingers and appeared to be struggling feebly to use his arms. McGuire was ecstatic and rushed to Dr. Hugh Follmer with even the slightest bit of good news.

After a particularly dismal day, McGuire finished reading Stupak the newspaper and whispered to him, "Bob, I'm becoming discouraged. I really need to know if you're hearing what I say."

She will never forget the moment he squeezed her hand. It was then she knew he would survive.

After five weeks, Bob Stupak opened his eyes. He knew who he was, but not where he was. He did not recognize his own son, of whom he always had taken pleasure in saying, "George Washington may be the father of our country, but I'm the father of Nevada."

Phyllis McGuire recalled Stupak's return to consciousness. "Bob was slinging and flinging his arms trying to break out of the restraints. I call him the warrior of warriors. I've never seen anyone fight so hard to stay alive. It was a sight to behold how this man fought warrior-style to stay alive."

Each morning the doctors would quiz him. Did he know his name? Did he recall their names? Did he remember anything about the accident? He underwent more facial surgery, and remained in bed.

Then, slowly, light began to return to his memory. Although he recalled nothing of his accident, he recognized his family, began getting the doctors' names straight, and noticed one person at his side each day, Phyllis McGuire.

Stupak later learned of the tear-drenched prayer vigil at St. Anne's and was sent a videotape of the event from a local television station.

"I didn't know these people, but they cared about me," he recalled later. "They were pulling for me, praying for me. There were hundreds of people who wanted me to pull through."

It was a side of Stupak the public seldom saw.

"He truly believed that everyone's prayers and wishes were what pulled him through," former Las Vegas City Councilman Scott Higginson said. "That's the absolute dichotomy of Bob Stupak. He could be this gambling, drinking guy, and then he would be this guy who cared about his children and was worried about the Man Upstairs."

In post-accident interviews, Stupak often talked about being a changed man who had been given that rarest of gifts in life, a second chance. He read the hundreds of cards and letters, some from politicians, but most from neighbors, Vegas World regulars, and concerned Las Vegans, and was determined to get better.

Within days of emerging from the coma, his restlessness was apparent. Although extremely weak, he began to move around his hospital room using a wheelchair and, later, a walker. His left leg was in a cast, as were his forearms, but he managed to work the walker with his elbows. Each step was excruciating, but with each step he moved closer to the day he would leave the hospital. Finally, he was transferred from UMC to a rehabilitation center, where he underwent daily exercise. His cigarettes-and-whiskey workout routine was replaced by increasingly long walks with a cane to support one side, while McGuire or a nurse held up the other.

At the Las Vegas Rehabilitation Clinic, McGuire saw Stupak make great strides. His memory was returning, he was responding to therapy, and he was improving with each surgery.

"That's where I believe he really woke up," McGuire said. "He was unbelievably determined that he would function again, be whole again. I think what motivated me was the fact I knew what his dream meant to him. I knew how important living was to him. I think that's why I was there. I knew it was a matter of life and death, and it was my privilege to do that."

At the clinic, Stupak continued taking injected doses of human growth hormone smuggled in by McGuire. Growth hormone proponent Daniel Rudman, M.D., of the Medical College of Wisconsin heralded the drug in a 1990 article in the *New England Journal of Medicine*. HGH, as it is called, mimics the hormones produced in the pituitary gland and is considered by many a breakthrough in the science of aging.

He later gave partial credit to the so-called "Fountain of Youth" hormone for his steady recovery, but was far more certain that it was McGuire's dedication, and the grace of God, that enabled him to regain his normal health and personality.

At the rehabilitation center Stupak encountered oddsmaker Jimmy the Greek Snyder, who suffered from numerous maladies. Stupak raved about the growth hormones and told Snyder's friend, Tommy Manakides, to encourage the Greek to try the wonder drug.

"Jimmy," Manakides said, "this is the guy who built the Stratosphere Tower. He was in a horrible motorcycle accident and almost died. Look at him now, and you're still in a wheelchair."

Snyder looked at Stupak and said, "Anybody who rides a motorcycle oughta be dead."

Stupak laughed through his scarred face.

But he was insistent on seeing Snyder get with the program.

"You need to give them to Jimmy," Stupak told Manakides. "If you don't, he's never going to get out of that wheelchair."

Snyder never left his wheelchair and died a few months after their conversation.

Aided by a cane and flanked by nurses, Bob Stupak left the rehabilitation center at 4 p.m. on June 30. He was obviously weak and shaky, but he was moving under his own power. Local television cameras recorded the homecoming and, as she had been every day for the previous three months, McGuire was there at his side.

A day before Halloween 1995, Stupak called a press conference at the North Las Vegas Police Department. His advance man, Dan Hart, declined to reveal the purpose of the gathering, but assured skeptics there was a story in it. In the small department's debriefing room, Stupak appeared in public for one of the first times since his motorcycle accident. He wore a tailored gray suit and dark glasses and walked with a cane until he got near the cameras. Then he handed the cane to an assistant and gingerly approached the microphones.

"This is probably the most important press conference I've ever held," Stupak said, his voice quivering. "I'm here for a simple reason. Tony Bagley is not here anymore. He's never going to be here. But I'm here. I know how nice it is to be alive."

Halloween marked the first anniversary of the murder of second-grader Tony Bagley on a North Las Vegas sidewalk. His mother and 11-year-old sister also were injured in the attack by an unknown gunman. Stupak carried with him two items: a skeleton costume of the type Bagley had worn the night he was killed, and a paper sack containing $100,000 in wrapped stacks of $100 bills.

The costume reminded him of the one he had worn as a boy in Pittsburgh. The money was a reward offer: $100,000 for information that would lead North Las Vegas homicide detectives to the killer's door.

"Somebody just happened to come along and put a bullet in everybody and put a bullet in Tony's head," Stupak said.

For one of the few times in his career, he appeared to have captured the public's attention for a less-than-selfish reason.

"I feel good. This is the first time I've worn a suit and tie in seven and a half months," he said. "I probably wouldn't have done this a year ago. Please keep in your minds that the last thing Bob Stupak needs is publicity. I've had enough publicity."

But he was seeking more in his first press conference in 17 months. His handshake was weak, his eyes sensitive to light, and his energy level low, but he managed to get through the 10-minute question-and-answer session before returning to his cane. Against doctors' orders, he was smoking again. Even a near-death experience, five weeks on a ventilator, a reconstructed face, and a seven-month rehabilitation couldn't kill Stupak's ferocious cigarette habit.

Hart had just started working as a spokesman and consultant for Stupak and initially was leery of his client's motivations. But he became convinced of Stupak's sincerity as he listened to him.

"He used to go on and on about Tony Bagley, about how much it all bothered him," Hart recalled. "There are some criminal acts that are just absolutely inexcusable, especially violence against kids. Bob didn't want that kind of behavior to go unpunished in his community."

Despite his generous offer and well-publicized plea, police failed to arrest a suspect in the Bagley case.

Less than a month later, Hart circulated a press release announcing the creation of the $1 million Stupak Family Foundation to benefit southern Nevada charities, including Jan Jones' pet project, the Mobile Assistance Shelter for the Homeless. Stupak already had pledged $300,000 to build an expansive kitchen for the shelter. The presence of highly respected former two-term Nevada Governor Mike O'Callaghan on the foundation's Board of Directors was a sign that Stupak's respectability was climbing. Attorney Mark Denton, whose father Ralph Denton had bailed Stupak out of many legal jams over the years, also was one of the charitable board's directors.

With Stratosphere stock climbing, Stupak threw his shares around the way tourists had used their Vegas World casino action chips. But weeks before its grand opening, most analysts agreed that Stratosphere was an infinitely superior bet.

Stupak proved a little more each week that he was a new man deserving of a new title.

Multimillionaire had a nice ring to it. By Christmas 1995, Stupak's seven million shares of Stratosphere were worth approximately $77 million. Once the IPO closed, Stratosphere stock was listed on NASDAQ and traded daily by investors all over the world. Share prices had climbed steadily from $5 in January to $11 in December. Stratosphere's 55 million shares were worth $605 million on the market, and even many of the project's staunchest skeptics were scurrying to buy a piece of the surefire success story.

Before the holiday, Stupak turned the Thunderbird Motel into a cafeteria to feed turkey dinners to 3,500 homeless men, women, and children. He strolled through the crowd handing out cash and wishing his guests a merry Christmas. Although television cameras recorded his generosity, it was obvious to those close to him that the publicity potential was only a partial motivation for the display of generosity.

"The happiest I've ever seen Bob was that Christmas when we fed all those homeless people at the Thunderbird," Hart said. "I've never seen him happier."

Hart might have thought twice, however, had he known that conversations between Stupak and Berman were growing increasingly chilled as the days passed. The now $550 million project was beginning to look as if it might be ready to open by April 1996 and Stupak pined for a decision-making role. He floated ideas daily through his small circle of friends at Stratosphere, but no one was listening. He attended meetings of the board of directors and found himself out of the loop, at one point interrupting the proceedings with vaudevillian antics and lounge-comic one-liners.

Meanwhile, he wanted to know about Stratosphere's casino marketing plans. The vacation packages he had used to lure thousands to Vegas World would be honored at Stratosphere, but

Stupak was unsure about future markets. Targeting visitors was far more important in a poor location than in the center of the Strip. The tower was a natural attraction, but how would they fill the 2,500 rooms that would be finished over the next year?

Although Stupak's questions went unanswered, publicly he remained elated by the project's progress. He did, after all, have 77 million reasons to smile. So he continued to announce charitable-works projects, including the dedication of Chester A. Stupak Memorial Park for children in the Meadows neighborhood.

In late January, he cut a deal that was sure to grab the attention of his increasing throng of fans: For a $100,000 donation to the United Negro College Fund, Stupak would suit up and "play" for the Harlem Globetrotters. Of course, with a training table that again consisted largely of coffee and cigarettes, he was in no shape to run the floor with the magicians of basketball. So they would fix it for him to check into the game, get fouled in the act of shooting, and take a pair of free throws. Stupak practiced shooting foul shots a few times at a court outside his Rancho Circle home, then left the rest to the fates and his own fierce streak of competitiveness.

"It's something I really want to do," he said. "Then I'll be known as an ex-Harlem Globetrotter. 'Ex-Harlem Globetrotter Bob Stupak said today...' has a nice ring to it. It's fun. I have a chance to do something I want to do, and forever I'll be a Harlem Globetrotter."

"Bob wanted to buy the franchise," Hart said. "His dream was always to own the Yankees. Then he started wondering about what happened to the Globetrotters. He talked about buying the team, bringing it to Las Vegas to play exhibitions. It evolved from there."

As usual, Stupak managed to turn his New York trip into hot news. He held court at the Plaza Hotel, and his big donation led one television news broadcast and was a front-page story in the *New York Daily News*.

Stupak had long since stopped traveling light. His caravan

to Madison Square Garden included Las Vegas Mayor Jan Jones, public relations specialist Dan Hart, a personal staff that included a cameraman and sound technician, a hairdresser, and personal valet, and a number of other friends.

His pregame meal consisted of whiskey and soul food at a Harlem restaurant, and his practice session consisted of shooting a few free throws and attempting to entice Globetrotters players into a few friendly wagers.

When the big night came, the plan was to foul Stupak and send him to the free-throw line, where he would shoot a pair and politely check out.

Things didn't go quite according to plan. He checked in, took a pass at the free-throw line and dribbled to the basket. Instead of being fouled, he received a clear path to the hoop.

"What do I do now?" Stupak asked, nervously dribbling with more than 10,000 Globetrotters fanatics looking on.

"Shoot the ball," a player shouted.

So he did. He hit the short baseline jumper and was fouled in the process. He went to the line, shot one shot, and made it. He later missed a free throw, but he had scored three points in yet another Globetrotter victory.

What the reporters didn't know, but might have suspected had they fully appreciated Stupak's background, is that he wasn't just contributing to a worthy cause and fulfilling a life-long dream.

He also had a bet worth $250,000 hinging on his ability to make those shots. He had wagered $50,000 at 5-to-1 odds with some poker associates and won part of the bet.

"I had to keep it interesting," Stupak said later. "I mean, the contribution was legitimate, but the bet kept me juiced up."

Stupak was no Pacino, but over the years his reputation as an actor had grown enough so that he was able to request and receive on-screen credits and expanded speaking parts. He also attracted the attention of the casting director of the 1995 Martin Scorsese movie *Casino*. Starring Robert DeNiro in a role based on the life of Frank "Lefty" Rosenthal and a cast that included Joe Pesci, Sharon Stone, and James Woods, the big-budget movie told the story of the rise and fall of Rosenthal and the Stardust Hotel.

Scorsese's crowd planned to cast Stupak in a role that was sure to be a stretch for the outlaw casino operator. He was handed a spot as a member of the Nevada Gaming Commission, an arrangement that was bound to make local casino operators laugh and state regulators wince. It wasn't a speaking part, but he would receive a few seconds on screen in the same movie as DeNiro.

Unlike many of the movie's bit players, Stupak actually had a resume of film credits. So he asked for an expanded role with a few lines of dialogue. Then he demanded one. Then he was replaced.

"I guess I overplayed my hand," Stupak said later, laughing.

In the first week of February, Stupak was named "Mr. Las Vegas" by Mayor Jan Jones and the City Council. The same government entity that had battled him over zoning issues, sign ordinances, and the height of the tower now embraced him as never before. Only Stupak wasn't there to see it. He was having surgery on his jaw. His daughter, Summer, accepted the council's praise on her father's behalf. If Bob Stupak had failed to take over the council by force, he had succeeded in winning it over with charity and a tower project that promised great things for the city.

Stupak's Stratosphere allies, including counsel Andrew Blumen, attended the City Council ceremony to receive more than another proclamation. They were also seeking approval to construct a 70-foot-tall gorilla that would climb 600 feet up the side of the Stratosphere. As many as 30 passengers would ride in its belly and look out over the city.

It was an odd request even for Stupak, but the council wasn't about to turn him down. Not after it had approved the tower's 1,149-foot height and a roller coaster and Big Shot thrill ride at the top. Although their endorsement of the big monkey plan was not unanimous, they weren't about to stop Stupak now. Not with a $550 million resort taking shape before their eyes. Not with the prospects of redeveloping Naked City and the tawdry and careworn section of Las Vegas Boulevard that led to downtown so close to becoming a reality. They had a lot more than tax revenue riding on Bob Stupak's back.

So it was with something more than just a desire for hype that Mayor Jones and the four council members presented Stupak's daughter, Summer, with a trophy and scroll proclaiming Bob Stupak Mr. Las Vegas.

And he took the title to heart. As his physical strength increased, so did his public appearances. Stupak sightings became commonplace again, often in the company of Phyllis McGuire. But it also became apparent to casual observers that Stupak and McGuire were having their problems.

So, with sufficient press notification by Dan Hart, the mayor's former political adviser and Stupak's new press agent, on Valentine's Day Stupak sent 1,001 dozen roses by Ryder truck to McGuire's Rancho Circle mansion.

McGuire wasn't home. She was on a cruise, but her housekeeper, Enice, was there to accept the offering. Stupak also had a present for McGuire's maid: a new Cadillac.

The roses were over-the-top even for a man devoid of the art of subtlety. His Valentine and birthday card ran as a quarter-page advertisement in the *Las Vegas Review-Journal*.

"Happy Birthday to the most exciting and beautiful woman in the world."

Stupak signed off, "With warmest personal regards, I remain, Sincerely Yours, The Chairman of the Board."

If that didn't win over McGuire's heart, perhaps something

else would. To remind her of their many happy times together, Stupak commissioned special videos of them in Las Vegas and all over the world. With sentimental music playing in the background and an occasional shot of Stupak in the hospital bandaged from head to foot, the "Our Love is Here to Stay" theme was clear.

Recapturing the affection of Phyllis McGuire wouldn't be easy, but it was a snap compared to winning the recommendation of the state Gaming Control Board.

ELEVEN

Street Legal

It was a day Bob Stupak had long dreaded: the inevitable trip to the offices of the state Gaming Control Board to take part in the gaming licensure of the Stratosphere.

The tower was built, the thrill rides were being tested, and more than 2,000 construction workers toiled around the clock in an attempt to get the casino, restaurants, and shopping promenade ready for the projected opening in mid-April 1996.

For weeks Las Vegas columnists had predicted Stupak would be battered like one of Mike Tyson's sparring partners by the Control Board, which had seen fit to fine him for his Vegas World Vacation Club packages only three years earlier. In fact, some speculated that the corporation would be approved, but Stupak would be ostracized. At the very least, the Control Board had no intention of enduring even one more of Stupak's business stunts. The hustling casino operator who had been featured on "60 Minutes" and in *The Wall Street Journal* had played his last wild card with state regulators.

The Control Board members had not only recommended six-figure monetary sanctions against Stupak, but they'd also toyed with the idea of ousting him from the industry for good. Although gaming-license revocation is rare in Nevada, it is far more likely to occur when a licensee is deemed an embarrassment to the industry's image rather than, for example, if there's evidence of organized-crime associations.

Although Nevada's regulatory system is touted as the ideal for the casino industry, it is largely a laissez-faire arrangement, due in large part to severe understaffing of the investigative division. Approximately 90 investigators are responsible for plowing through every aspect of operations in all Nevada casinos. In a state with a long tradition of approving slot machines for use in supermarkets, the chances of catching sophisticated cheats and deep-cover mob activity would appear remote.

The Control Board's overworked investigators had no such trouble compiling damning information against Bob Stupak. All they had to do was sit by the phone and wait for a call from a disgruntled tourist who claimed he was misled by the Vegas World vacation package. One thing was certain: Stupak had no friends on the Control Board.

But Stupak and his attorney, Frank Schreck, had been wise in settling up with Nevada gaming authorities prior to the Stratosphere licensing. The fine had been levied and the check for $125,000 had been cut years earlier. Despite what the three members of the Control Board might say in the hearing, that piece of business was officially concluded.

Some Las Vegas reporters were predicting Stupak would be grilled mercilessly by two of his biggest Control Board critics, Chairman Bill Bible and Member Steve DuCharme. But his March 6, 1996, hearing turned out to be more playful than pugilistic.

It didn't hurt that Stupak was represented by Frank Schreck, who lost a gaming case about as often as the Harlem Globetrotters lost a basketball game.

Schreck, the Nevada power broker whose clout in the casino industry is matched only by his strength as a political fundraiser, had represented dozens of clients before the Control Board and Gaming Commission. In some casino circles, he was unofficially referred to as the fourth member of the Control Board. Not only had he helped craft casino regulation legislation and served as a member of the Commission, but he was also capable of overwhelming members who made the mistake of entering a hearing ill prepared.

Schreck handled the introductions of his clients and Stratosphere associates, including Stupak, Lyle Berman, director Robert Maheu, Stratosphere president Dave Wirshing, executive vice president Andy Blumen, chief financial officer Tom Lettero, vice president of compliance Joe Galvin, and corporate director Pat Cruzen. Also in the audience was veteran local attorney Ralph Denton, who had fiercely done battle for Stupak for many years.

Schreck planned a presentation illustrating Stratosphere's features, operations, and financing, but first Stupak wanted to work the room. After all, he was not accustomed to entering a Control Board hearing smiling.

"It's been quite a while since I've been here before this Board," Stupak started, nervously. "I think this is 1996, and the first time was in 1993. It was an experience then. I hope it's an experience tonight.

"...Talk about the Stratosphere Tower and what is planned for the future, I'd like to leave that to Lyle Berman. Lyle Berman fortunately enough is a long-time poker-playing buddy of mine. Lyle Berman is—I wouldn't say he is one of the best casino operators in the world. In my opinion, he is probably *the* best casino operator in the world, and I think the state of Nevada is very fortunate that Lyle Berman and this company are here taking part. So if I may introduce Mr. Lyle Berman."

"That's fine," Bible said. "We may have some questions later."

"Okay," Stupak replied. "I'll be here."

"I knew you'd stay," Bible said.

Berman recapped Grand Casino's meteoric history, reminding the Board that the outfit named America's fastest-growing corporation had been in existence less than six years. Profits from Indian reservation casinos in Minnesota and going public in late 1991 created the sort of cash flow that made investing in the Stratosphere project possible. Berman discussed the company's two Indian gaming projects in Louisiana and two more riverboat sites on the Mississippi Gulf Coast. Grand Casinos was about to open its eighth casino in five years.

"As measured by capacity, Grand Casinos will be the third largest gaming company in the United States when we open Grand Casino Tunica this summer, and we have joined that elite group of gaming companies that have a market capitalization of more than a billion dollars," Berman said. "There are only seven operating companies that have that, and we're one of the seven. So we're very proud of that. We like to say we have come a long way in a short time.

"The tower itself today, the picture of what you see every day when you drive around Las Vegas, is exactly what Bob Stupak designed and dreamed about and really has changed very very little from when we first got involved with it as a project... The base building, however, is kind of what Grand Casino brought to the table."

Then it was Wirshing's turn to charm the board.

"As Lyle described, we're not just building a tower here, we're building a major international destination that we believe is going to appeal to a cross section of the visitors that come to Las Vegas...Part of what has distinguished Grand Casinos, and we believe is going to distinguish Stratosphere, is the commitment that we have to high-quality levels of service, and the emphasis that we're going to place in that area.

Wirshing outlined the company's marketing strategy: target independent travelers, tour and travel, conventions, and holders of the unused Vegas World vacation packages. It made plenty of sense on its face, but resort-industry analysts might have questioned the company's reliance for nearly a third of its customer base on tourists without hotel reservations. The short-selling of the lucrative convention market—Grand estimated that only 5 percent of its customer base would be generated from there—also might have caused eyebrows to raise. But, Stratosphere officials believed, such was the magnetic strength of the great 1,149-foot tower.

"It is an absolutely stunning property," Wirshing gushed. "For me, the best part of the whole project is the fact that literally everyone that's come through, no matter what walk of life they come from, has had their expectations surpassed and just been absolutely overwhelmed, both with the facility at the base of the building and of course the tower, which takes your breath away. It literally has with everybody."

Brian Harris, the newest and least demonstrative member of the Control Board, became curious about Stratosphere's marketing program. The tower obviously was the biggest attraction, but would it market itself?

"...We really believe we're going to get an absolute cross section of everybody that comes to Las Vegas," Wirshing explained. "So is it safe to say we're specifically targeting a certain segment? It really isn't. It's everyone. We have amenities in the tower, as Lyle was discussing, from weddings to amusement rides that obviously are going to appeal to different people."

As far as Wirshing was concerned, it was just that simple. Although he would have found a historical exception in Disneyland, which opened before it was ready for the public and was considered a flop in its early months, the president of Stratosphere Corporation pegged the tower as a sure thing.

Then Chief Financial Officer Tom Lettero addressed the complex issue of the property's financing. Those still leery of Stratosphere's location might have been alarmed at the high interest Stratosphere had promised to pay on the $203 million first mortgage.

"The [mortgage] notes are for seven years with a four-year noncall provision and bearer coupon interest at the rate of fourteen and a quarter percent and contingent interest on nearly eleven percent of EBIDTA [earnings before interest, depreciation, taxes, and assessments] up to a maximum of one hundred million dollars," Lettero said.

Grand also increased the pot by pouring another $33.5 million into the project through the purchase of stock.

And so the bottom-line reality of the sure-thing $550 million tower resort was beginning to take shape. Stratosphere visitors would have to drop a mountain of coins into the slot machines to cover the monthly juice on notes sold at 14.25 percent interest. The deal was a throwback to the heart of the junk-bond era, when high-interest, high-yield bonds fueled the record growth of some companies and drove dozens of others into extinction.

Total funding for phase one was $333.4 million. Phase two entailed the construction of 1,000 more rooms and suites, a pool area, spa, and expanded parking. Grand Casinos' total cash investment in Stratosphere was set at $71.5 million.

Even before the resort was open, Stratosphere expanded its real estate base on Las Vegas Boulevard when it purchased the Sulinda Motel in exchange for one million shares of common stock, which at the time of the March 1996 meeting were worth more than $12 million. At the time, Grand Casinos held 43 percent of Stratosphere stock, Stupak approximately 15 percent. The Sulinda was scheduled to be razed to provide increased parking for the behemoth.

Grand's total financed investment in the Stratosphere project: $467 million, with an additional $50 million investment by the Gordon Simon Company for the expansive retail center, and another $25 million by the Aquarium Company. Throw in a gorilla ride, and the bottom line was slightly more than $550 million—the third largest investment in a resort in Las Vegas history behind the MGM Grand ($1 billion) and the Mirage ($620 million).

Given Stratosphere's location, the half-billion-dollar investment was an amazing act of faith. But no one, not even the members of the still wary Control Board, was willing to doubt that it would be anything short of a stunning success. The critics would be singing the praises of Grand Casinos genius Lyle Berman, the Stratosphere Corporation, and Bob Stupak, too.

Chairman Bible, easily the most astute member of the Board when it came to comprehending complex corporate-finance issues, was intrigued by the mile-high mortgage-interest rate.

"What is the basis for the calculations for the contingent interest?" he asked. "What are the factors?"

Stratosphere's financial experts based their ability to service their debt on the consolidated cash flow of the resort in total, including projected casino revenues as well as profitable hotel, retail, and food and beverage operations.

For his part, Stupak sounded like a man who planned to hold onto as much stock as possible. Perhaps he hoped his old motto, "The Sky's the Limit," applied to his Stratosphere holdings:

"It's my opinion the stock is going to be much higher than it is right now, and it would be sensible to keep the stock and try to liquidate something else" (to ensure that his vacation-package obligations were fully funded).

Stupak again was forced to explain on the record that he had every intention of honoring the terms of his vacation packages, even though he wanted out. In fact, he had instructed his phone-sales staff to offer refunds even if package holders called to make reservations. At that point, Stupak would have done almost anything to free himself of the embarrassing and largely misunderstood program.

"Why are you encouraging redemption? Just to get rid of the liability?" Bible asked.

"Yes," Stupak said. "The quicker the liability is exhausted, the more comfortable I'll feel."

"I think we'd share that feeling with you," Bible said.

"Well," Stupak cracked, "we have something in common."

"We've talked about this on a couple of occasions," the chairman said.

"At least one or two," Stupak deadpanned. "But I mean, I'm sort of glad to be here to respond to this again. But to be quite truthful, I'm sort of glad to be anywhere right now."

Then it was DuCharme's turn to test his Stupak material.

"Have you given any thought to authorizing someone else to be able to release funds from that [escrow] account?" DuCharme asked, just in case he decided to try riding a motorcycle again.

"If it's necessary, but at this stage of the game it's not necessary."

DuCharme said, "You never know what's going to happen."

"I have every intention of staying alive and being around,"

Stupak said.

Bible and DuCharme were kidding on the square. Their rhetoric was playful, but their purpose was a serious one. With the world watching gaming issues more closely than ever, they did not intend to allow anyone, least of all Bob Stupak, to embarrass Nevada's regulatory process.

"What are you going to be doing at the property?" Bible asked. "What will be your duties and responsibilities? You're (on the agenda) today as chairman of the board, as shareholder, and controlling shareholder."

"Well, I think I own approximately seventeen percent of Stratosphere. I just can't help but get this in, but I believe I'm the largest individual shareholder and no one owns more of the tower than I do."

Bible asked, "Are you involved in the day-to-day operations of the property?"

"No," Stupak said.

DuCharme: "I guess more importantly, are you doing the marketing?"

"Well, I certainly hope they listen to me. Again, I'm patting myself on the back. I don't think there is anybody better."

Suddenly, the kidding had stopped.

"Well, as you know, and we haven't really talked about the issue, but the package programs had quite a bit of controversy attached to them," Bible said. "They led in one instance to a disciplinary action. It is very fortuitous that the combination with Grand Casinos and Mr. Berman, I think to a large extent, have prevented what could have been a very major embarrassment for the state of Nevada in terms of those liabilities and those packages not being available for redemption.

"So I think we worked our way out of this particular problem in a manner that protected the individuals that bought those packages. And I think we have a very fortuitous set of circumstances, and where Mr. DuCharme is leading, are we going to see anything like that again?"

"Everything you are referring to is past history," Stupak said.

"Those are things that happened in the past. And then we had a difference of opinion. I'm not looking to go in that direction again."

"You are a tough guy to keep up with from time to time," Bible said.

"You have to keep taking into account that Vegas World went from 90 rooms to over 1,000 rooms and went from about $15 million for the first year to over $100 million for the last few years. That was all done without financing, bank loans. That was all done through vacation clubs. Vacation clubs led to Stratosphere clubs. If it wasn't for those two issues right there, the vacation club and the Stratosphere club, we wouldn't be having a meeting here today. You know, about what's happening in the future.

"I think the best tourist-attraction hotel and casino in the world is going to open up next month. I think all those things come into play one way or the other. There were some goods and bads, some pros and cons. But I think the pros outnumber the cons drastically. Again, that's my opinion."

Stupak had his pride. Although the vacation packages had a scandalous reputation, they were what kept Vegas World's room occupancy up to industry standards despite the casino's deadly location. Stupak did not rule out keeping a hand in Stratosphere's daily business and acknowledged that he had filed an application for individual licensure—not as an operator, necessarily, but perhaps as an adviser. After all, who knew the Naked City gambling game better than he?

But Bible's friendly warning was clear:

"As you know, there've been a lot of issues between the Board and yourself over the years," Bible said. "You certainly have a lot of creative talents, and we just need to keep them deployed in the right direction…I talked a little about your creative energies. I think we have to keep them channeled in the direction of the tower, a little bit less on the side of those packages and things of that nature, because those packages had a lot of controversy attached to them."

In the end, the Board unanimously voted to recommend approval of Stratosphere for licensure.

Bible was most generous in his praise of the project.

"I think you clearly have a home run here," Bible said. "This is going to be a great project for the state. It is going to be a great project for Las Vegas.

"We talked a little bit about some of the negatives that involve some of the prior business activities of Mr. Stupak. I'd like to emphasize that I think he is to be commended for the vision he had in bringing this project to the table. And Mr. Berman is to be commended, not only for the implementation phase, but also for helping the state work out a fairly difficult problem in terms of the liabilities of the packages.

With a unanimous Control Board vote recommending approval of Bob Stupak's license to operate the Stratosphere, the March 21, 1996, hearing before the Nevada Gaming Commission promised to be little more than a prelude to a celebration. In the history of the two-tiered process, the Commission occasionally overruled a Control Board recommendation for denial of a license, but no one could ever remember the Commission overturning a suggested approval of an applicant.

Stratosphere proved to be no exception. Still, attorney Schreck was in his best salesman mode before the Gaming Commission. He had plenty to say about the Vacation Club packages.

"Just another aspect of this, if you look at the Vacation Club itself, people got a lot more than they paid for," Schreck said. "It was absolutely the best deal in town. If you just took the cash, played what you were given and gone and put it on craps one side or the other, you could make as much as you paid for the entire package, then have the two days and all the drinks and the shows and everything. [It] literally was for the person who knew how to use it the best package you could ever get here."

Schreck's lengthy list of well-heeled casino clients, who often chided Stupak for his gaudy grind joint and his outrageous vacation advertisements, might have been surprised to hear the attorney's passion for the Vegas World discount program.

"The people that have them now have an even better package, because instead of going to Vegas World, now they get to stay at the Stratosphere Tower," he said. "So everything in the package has been upgraded.

"If Mr. Stupak had his way, he would refund everybody tomorrow. That is the preferable way for him to deal with this. He would like everybody tomorrow to write in so he could refund it and it would be over.

"Unfortunately, a lot of those people are smarter than that, and they're going to take advantage of the fact that they now get to come to Stratosphere Tower as opposed to Vegas World and enjoy those amenities. So there are not going to be a lot of requests for refunds. These people have a much better deal than they ever bargained for.

"…And if there is one thing I could ever assure the Commission of, it is that the Board and Chairman Bible have made sure that every person that's been a member of any one of those clubs will either get fully reimbursed or have the benefits of those packages until they expire."

In the face of such rhetoric, the Commission couldn't help but place its seal of approval on what all present had decided would be a grand success for Grand Casinos and the Stratosphere. Its members even treated Stupak with warmth. Beyond a few stated concerns about the resort's marketing structure, the commissioners were clearly overjoyed to welcome Grand Casinos to southern Nevada.

A registered Republican, Stupak began turning up at GOP fundraisers for Bob Dole prior to the 1996 presidential election. When Dole's campaign failed to catch fire in the spring of 1996, the gaming industry, led by Mirage Resorts Chairman Steve Wynn, hedged its bets and attempted to court Bill Clinton. Wynn had played an integral role in raising more than $500,000 for

Dole, then managed to schedule a golf date with Clinton.

That led to a $250,000 fundraiser for Clinton in Las Vegas. Stupak and his companion, Phyllis McGuire, were among the guests at the $25,000-a-plate luncheon at the home of *Las Vegas Sun* publisher Brian Greenspun.

"It's the first time in my life that the President has been younger than me," Stupak recalled. "We're in Brian's house. There are not a whole bunch of people there. And who comes walking in but the President of the United States. He talked to me like he knew me for twenty years. There he is, having fucking lunch right across the table from me, the real President. I mean, this is the leader of the free world. He's the Commander in Chief. He's in charge of SAC. He was just a guy like anybody else. It was hard to believe that this was the President of the United States, the real President. It cost a few dollars, but it was worth it."

For a few dollars, he kept his hand in politics without getting burned and appeared finally to have learned the lesson the founders of Las Vegas knew so well. At that moment, his interests transcended politics and even Las Vegas.

Stupak's early 1996 plan to redevelop the dilapidated 188-room Riverside Hotel in care-worn downtown Reno might have appeared a godsend to Reno's City Council. The Riverside, along with the shuttered Mapes Hotel across the Truckee River, had seen better decades. The 188-room Riverside, which had the distinction of being one of the earliest investments of the Teamsters Central States Pension Fund, had been closed since 1987. Plans to reopen it had been few. Monied backers were nonexistent. There was even speculation that owner Peter Eng would raze the building, but for all the talk, it sat year after year in a worsening state of disrepair a few feet from the riffling Truckee River.

It was nothing new in Reno, where city officials' plans to redevelop downtown had run into a series of delays that threatened not only to doom major projects, but drive away small businesses as well. Where Las Vegas elected officials might be accused of being besotted when it came to doling out redevelopment funds and using the city's powers of eminent domain to change the course of development, Reno's council members appeared to suffer from an inability or unwillingness to embrace any plan.

With the Stratosphere making headlines across the nation, Stupak's Reno proposal was simple: revamp the Riverside and add either a tower or at the very least the thrilling Big Shot ride. The twist: At approximately 300 feet, 72 feet higher than the Stratosphere's $2.75 million version, the Riverside Big Shot would be the tallest ever built by S&S Sports Power. In a city that prided itself on the construction of a large bowling stadium complex as a major tourist draw, the Big Shot ranked as a very big idea.

"I don't know if the tower needs to be 300 feet, but I need to be careful—Bob Stupak will do whatever he wants to do," S&S sales manager Ray Checketts told a reporter.

If he'd only known.

With visions of reopening the hotel's cabaret showroom, Stupak picked up the option to buy the hotel from Eng and set to work.

What might have turned into a glorified coming-out party for Bob Stupak in Reno rapidly degraded into a mess that drove him from the deal. In the face of complaints from area business owners, an environmental-impact study was scheduled. With Eng's interest in the project suddenly piqued, the council set a deadline for plans and impact studies of July 1, 1996, giving Stupak's development team little time to gather its material. It also provided insight into the problems businessmen encounter trying to develop projects in Reno.

Steve Falcone captured the underlying community sentiment in a column in the *Reno Gazette-Journal*.

"Making a ride the focus of your presentation only invites Renoites to try to shoot it down and, given the opportunity, there's no sport that Renoites like better than shooting down someone else's ideas," Falcone wrote. "...If I had money to throw around, I would be happy to buy either the Riverside or the Mapes and turn it into a hotel so classy that rich folks from all over the world would fight for the privilege of staying there. And they wouldn't find a single slot machine in the joint.

"But, of course, I don't have money to throw around, and I'd be sort of embarrassed to try to tell a guy who wants to spend his money to buy an aging, rotting hulk of a hotel that he has to accept my vision of the property instead of his own.

"And so far I haven't heard any of those Renoites with glorious plans for the two hotels offer to put up a single nickel to make those plans a reality...Except for Mr. Stupak, who seems to be willing to do what no one else is: put up real money to light a dark corner of downtown, to bring life to a property that's been dead for a decade.

"Sounds to me like it's the best offer we've got, because it's the only offer we've got."

But no one listens to newspaper columnists.

The council's only alternate plan came from the Riverside's owner, Peter Eng, who wanted financial help from the city to raze the building.

As time ran out, the deal became terminally bogged down in a flurry of concerns over whether the Big Shot would create too much noise.

Stupak's attorney, Sam McMullen, was clearly vexed. After watching the Riverside sit silent for nearly a decade, city officials were demanding completed plans from Stupak in a matter of weeks. McMullen told the council that it made little sense for his client to spend several million dollars without a guarantee that he would be able to develop the property as planned.

As a gambler, Stupak understood about a player's run of luck.

Although he had lost control of it, no one doubted that the Stratosphere was Bob Stupak's dream. For Mr. Las Vegas, it was almost too good to be true.

TWELVE

The Curse of Naked City

When Lyle Berman unveiled a life-size, 24-carat-gold-plated statue of Bob Stupak holding a pair of dice, surely it was meant as a testament to their friendship and as a symbol of Stupak's importance to the Stratosphere project. After all, the Stratosphere was Stupak's idea, even if the credit for completing it belonged to Berman. But with six weeks to go before the opening of the resort, the statue quickly came to symbolize not only the financial excess of the project, but also of the two men's costly, gold-plated relationship. For his part, Stupak gave Berman a pair of solid gold dice.

For reporters, Stupak and Berman waxed philosophical about the importance of getting to know a fellow across a poker table, how relationships forged in high-stakes situations gave keen insight into the mettle of men. Privately, they had ceased making more than the most perfunctory attempts at civility. With state gaming regulators calling for Stupak to stay away from daily operations at the casino, the destiny of Stratosphere—all statues and niceties to the contrary—was in Berman's hands.

Besides, weren't statues usually reserved for dead legends?

Like the Pete Bauer character he had played in that decade-old "Crime Story" episode, Stupak would later lament that his ideas still worked, but that no one would give them a chance. Although he was being disingenuous when he staked a claim to creating Double Exposure blackjack, crapless craps, and other casino gimmicks, he had certainly promoted them as none before him. After coming so close to being perceived as a Vegas visionary, he instead had become a gold-plated afterthought. In a town that hates to dwell on its history, he had become a part of the past.

There was more to the game than recognition and respect. If he couldn't have fame, Stupak was determined to at least have fortune. As his seven million shares of Stratosphere climbed in value, early in 1996 he began quietly selling off blocks of stock.

In a business that makes beggars out of prognosticators, the value of stock in companies that have recently gone public follows a traditional arc: a steady climb prior to opening a new property, a sharp drop in the first quarter, a leveling off, then another climb toward opening-day prices. In recent years, Rio, MGM Grand, and Palace Station stocks all had taken similar rides before becoming steadier investments. But those companies were marked by experienced, energetic management teams and vastly superior locations. Stratosphere's operation was as yet unproven. And its most experienced officer, Bob Stupak, was on the outside looking in.

His scarred poker face did not betray his thoughts and feelings. He continued to press forward as a man out to win public opinion both as a philanthropist and an unabashed promoter of the project.

The Big Shot's media debut February 10 held the interest of local reporters and helped generate national attention for the project. Journalists awed by the world's highest thrill ride barely noticed that carpeting was not down in areas of the resort and that construction crews were still pouring hundreds of yards of cement in a round-the-clock attempt to complete the convention area and aquarium site in the back of the building.

Stupak, smoking like a fiend once more, stole the show atop the tower.

"Oh my God, I'm scared. Let's start before I wimp out," he said. "People have doubted me my whole life. But there's nothing I ever started that I haven't finished.

"When you're a kid in school and you want to go to the bathroom, you hold up your hand higher than everyone else to call attention to yourself. And that's what the Big Shot is all about. It calls attention to myself, to the joint.

"And to tell you the truth, it's great to be here to ride it."

If the local media were exceptionally kind to Stupak, a man they had beat like a snare drum for many years, the public also appeared to have finally warmed up to his profile and his project. By early March, more than 25,000 people had applied for 2,500 jobs at the Stratosphere. It looked not only like a winner, but a fun place to work as well.

Even Stupak's old nemesis, Culinary Local 226, appeared to be making progress toward organizing the service workers. It wasn't as if the Stratosphere would have escaped the notice of Culinary officials John Wilhelm and D. Taylor: their offices were little more than a block from the construction site.

On March 15, after numerous delays, the $550 million Stratosphere Tower finally set an opening date it could live with: April 30, 1996. Painters were still dancing on scaffolding hundreds of feet in the air to touch up the tower's makeup. The back portion of the hotel would never be done in time. Ongoing construction on the latest room expansion, scheduled to give the resort nearly 2,500 rooms, would instead give it a half-done look on opening night. But the decision was made. With daily six-figure construction costs soaring and Grand's 14 percent financial package hanging over the deal like a wrecking ball, delaying the opening further was not an option. If they weren't careful, by the time they finished they would be bankrupt.

Stratosphere felt certain that its colorful World's Fair theme would attract corporate sponsorships and millions of tourists. Just as the Eiffel Tower, Seattle Space Needle, and CN Tower had excited film and soft-drink manufacturers, so too did the megaresorts of Las Vegas. The MGM Grand Hotel & Theme Park signed an exclusive soft-drink deal with Coca-Cola in 1993, and the $70 million Fremont Street Experience downtown signed an exclusive contract with Coca-Cola in 1995.

A week before opening, Stratosphere announced its deal with Pepsi-Cola Company. Not only would Pepsi be the official drink of the tower, but the seventh floor of the pod would be renamed the Pepsi-Cola Observation Deck. Shuffle Master Gaming had previously acquired the rights to place the name of one of its popular casino games, Let It Ride, on the Stratosphere's High Roller roller coaster.

Things appeared to be going well, and if Lyle Berman was nervous about the prospects of paying the interest on his $203 million high-interest debt, it didn't show.

"What's my biggest concern when we open? Crowd control," he said to a *Wall Street Journal* reporter. "I think we're going to be absolutely inundated."

As Stratosphere prepared for its grand opening and VIP party, it was obvious to even casual observers that the project was still a work in progress. But it didn't appear to be progressing all that quickly despite hundreds of workers and giant cranes operating around the clock. Although Stratosphere officials had feasted on weeks of mostly positive press, they had failed to send out a clear message that the ever-expanding hotel portion of the resort would not be completed in time for opening night.

In a business in which first impressions count far more than they should, Stratosphere had made a fundamental blunder that promised to reverberate for weeks to come. Finding a casino under construction or expansion was common in Las Vegas, but no operator wants to open before his joint is ready. In recent years, casino bosses had taken to conducting intensive training and intricate rehearsals for thousands of employees. Many operators understood the value of customer service as a way to make first impressions lasting ones, not only with visitors, but with the media as well.

For instance, it would have cost almost nothing to inform the media that Stratosphere's elaborate fire-alarm system, because it featured highly sensitive technology, was almost certain to go off once or twice before the opening. For whatever reason, the explanation was not passed on.

On April 25, less than a week before the Stratosphere opened to the public, kitchen smoke in the 12-story pod did set off the fire alarms. Hundreds of construction workers and Stratosphere employees were evacuated. Not surprisingly, the media descended on the resort. Print reporters worked the bottom floor, while television cameramen shot live footage from helicopters hovering outside the pod. What would normally have been a news note became a big story.

"The bottom line is: there was no problem," a Clark County Fire Department battalion chief said.

His words were lost amid pictures of smoke billowing from the tower.

Despite its high financing, systems glitches, and unfinished construction, Stratosphere had caught fire on Wall Street. Its Nasdaq symbol had become a hot investment. Fueled by Grand's seemingly magic touch within the casino industry and the media's unabashed confidence in the project, Stratosphere had climbed from $4 per share to more than $12 as workers vacuumed the carpets and polished the brass railings in preparation for the opening.

The company's investment brokers gloated.

"Not bad for a company that never had a dollar in revenue," securities analyst David Ehlers crowed. Ehlers had touted Stratosphere in his industry newsletter and magazine columns for months.

"Criticism of this project has evaporated," Ehlers wrote in his *Las Vegas Sun* business column a few weeks earlier. "In its place, we sense a long-term shift in the place Bob Stupak will occupy in Las Vegas' rich history. Stupak, simply, has given Las Vegas an unforgettable memorial to his vision."

"There's a lot of excitement and hype creating interest in the stock," Stratosphere investment specialist Mike Moody said.

Though he was concerned that the share price might mirror the arc of MGM Grand and the like, he remained high on the project. Other analysts were willing to project Stratosphere's stock price at $17 by 1997.

Time magazine gushed over the project and its developers, insinuating that the city's big players would have to go a long way to top the Stratosphere's theme and statement. In an over-the-top town like Las Vegas, Stratosphere was the quintessential exclamation point.

There was little mention in the business media of the fact that Stratosphere's bondholders were due to receive 10.8 percent of the cash flow in addition to their 14.25 percent on the mortgage notes—an effective interest rate of more than 20 percent.

Only *Business Week* refrained from embracing the resort.

"A few things about the Stratosphere are not so glamorous," Ronald Grover wrote. "For starters, the tower is located on the seedier end of the Strip, miles away from the crowds. The effective interest rate on most of its $244 million is a sobering 20 percent. The cost of building Stratosphere ballooned from $67 million in 1994 to $550 million this year, as new attractions and features were added, including 2,500 hotel rooms, a $35 million aquarium, and a $6 million, 70-foot mechanical gorilla that will climb the exterior of the tower, carrying as many as 48 tourists along with him.

"...Now that Stratosphere is built, will the throngs materialize? To make its steep debt payments and cover its operating costs, Stratosphere has told investors that more than 14,000 people a day will pay an average of $5.35 to take the elevator ride to the tower's top. It figures that 53 couples daily will pay an average of $350 to get married in one of its three sky-high wedding chapels. If it meets those expectations, the company says it will generate $244 million in revenues and $81 million in operating cash flow for its first full year of operation. Those numbers are better than Circus Circus...which is better located and has long been among Vegas' most profitable casinos.

"Stratosphere's promoters are certain that the casino's sheer size and bizarreness will be its salvation. 'You can see this tower from the moment you hit town, whether it's from the airport or a car,' notes Stratosphere President David R. Wirshing, a veteran casino manager. No doubt. But will tourists drop enough cash to make Vegas' tallest gamble pay off?"

In Las Vegas, the city that loves a winner to the exclusion of all else, it was a question surprisingly few people were asking.

"I was chairman of Stratosphere and figured I could do things like I did when I ran Vegas World," Stupak told a reporter 72 hours before the grand-opening fireworks began. "I commissioned a company to design a ride and agreed to pay them $2 million. When Lyle found out, he went ballistic. He let me know I couldn't do things the old way anymore."

Even if their relationship had grown tempestuous, no one appeared to notice. Nor was anyone likely to put the self-styled Polish Maverick in a media straightjacket any time soon.

"Every time the stock moves up twelve and a half cents, it's a million dollars," Stupak bragged. Still, he added, "I don't have near the money I need. If I wanted to buy a Gulfstream IV, I couldn't afford it; it costs $25 million and about $5 million a year to run. I'm not saying I want one, but if I did, I'd need more money.

"There's a thousandaire, and I've done that. There's a millionaire, and I've done that. The next step is billionaire, and I've set a personal deadline for the turn of the century. That's my next step."

The kinder, gentler Bob Stupak appeared to have disappeared in a blizzard of Stratosphere stock, but he continued to campaign for the affection of southern Nevadans. He took out a full-page advertisement in the April 28 edition of the *Las Vegas Review-Journal*. The headline was simple:

THANK YOU, LAS VEGAS

Tomorrow, Las Vegas will witness a miracle. The opening of the Stratosphere Tower represents nearly six years of hard work, constant dedication, and unyielding courage from everyone involved with this project. I am tremendously proud to provide Las Vegas with its most magnificent attraction ever.

Personally, I too am grateful, but for more than just the Stratosphere Tower. As you know, on March 31st last year, I was in a terrible accident. It looked like I was leaving Las Vegas for good. For five weeks I was in a coma, somewhere in another world. But I came back. Bit by bit, slowly but steadily, I came back. And I don't intend to ever leave again.

I also learned something new. During those long, laborious months of recovery, I received an outpouring of love and prayers from many of you. I received thousands of letters from people who wanted to let me know that they were behind me, that they believed in me, and wanted me to be well again. And that, more than anything else—more than all the physical therapy, more than all the operations—helped me recover. I learned that the power of love is a healing power. It helped me believe in myself, and brought light to even the darkest moments. Thank you, all of you, for this comeback.

Tomorrow will be a great day...a day of miracles. Being here to share it with my family and friends is another miracle. And when you think about it, neither of these miracles would be possible if it weren't for the love, support and dedication of so many people. The Stratosphere Tower is as much for me as it is for you. It's also for my father, Chester Stupak, who isn't around to see it. Those of you who know me know my father was the greatest influence in my life. Without him, none of this could have happened. And in my heart, I see the Stratosphere as a monument to him, as much as it is a monument to this great community.

Thank you, Las Vegas, for making it all come true. And more than anything else, thank you for believing in me.

With my warmest regards, I remain yours,
Bob Stupak

It was no time for acrimony, no time to reveal the fact that his relationship with Stratosphere's executives was nonexistent. It was not the right time to explain to newspaper readers that control of the resort's day-to-day operations—from the casino marketing strategy to the price of a cup of coffee—had been taken from him. Nor was it the right time to explain that, as part of his deal with Berman, Stupak agreed to depart the chairmanship within 90 days of Stratosphere's grand opening. It was no time to reveal that he had sacrificed his own position in order to make his dream come true. Because the dream was still his.

Special guests had received small plaques requesting their presence at the VIP party and opening preview at the Stratosphere a day before the public was officially to be set loose on the place. Such soirees are common in Las Vegas, and casino operators occasionally try to outdo each other when it comes to the stars on the guest list, as well as the food and drink. Stratosphere's party was marked by a mob of people. Where 2,500 were expected, more than 5,000 appeared with invitations to celebrate the opening of the tower and casino.

Partygoers who used the resort's rear parking garage walked past a massive construction site gone silent for the first time in weeks. There were a few celebrities, politicians, and casino bosses in the crowd, but the interest was in the resort itself: Its theme drew from world's fairs from Paris to Seattle. The 97,000-square-foot casino was dotted with comical characters who represented the carnival atmosphere, the vertical Circus Circus look of the place.

As he had with so many other resort openings, Nevada Governor Bob Miller made his way through the crush of humanity. He braved the long lines and took the elevator ride to the top, but refrained from experiencing the Big Shot.

"I'm sure there have not been so many people this high since the last Grateful Dead concert," Miller joked. "...I can't think of anyone who has defied the odds as often or more successfully than Bob Stupak."

Noticeably absent were most of the city's casino titans. Horseshoe Club President Jack Binion, who had supported Stupak as a friend and business confidant for many years, turned out, as did John Woodrum of the Klondike. But by the time the crowd had begun to feast on hundreds of pounds of fresh shrimp, few other casino executives had appeared.

Celebrities were few, but one stood out: Gary Busey. The award-winning actor, who like Stupak had survived a motorcycle crash and a severe head injury, paid his respects to the Polish Maverick and his big dream.

For his part, City Councilman Arnie Adamsen was giddy. He carried with him a lengthy fact sheet and the knowledge that he had been one of Stupak's few supporters in the project. The rest of the City Council was present, as was Mayor Jan Jones. But Adamsen's brag sheet was the big news of the night and revealed just how much the city's elected leaders believed in Stupak's project:

1. Additional tax revenues estimated in excess of $2.5 million annually.

2. Estimated job creation of over 2,000. Previous employees of Vegas World and residents of the Meadows Village area have been given hiring preferences.

3. New roads and infrastructure in the Meadows Village neighborhood.

4. A new city park, the Chester Stupak Memorial Park.

5. Title to the Stupak Community Center, plus $100,000 toward the construction of a daycare facility at the Center.

6. 15 percent of the incremental property tax revenues to be used for affordable housing within an area near the impacted neighborhood.

7. Generous relocation benefits for all displaced residents ($500-$2,500).

8. Anticipated spin-off development in the immediate area.

The list, though impressive on its face, recalled the many promises made by the casino industry and its political allies when Atlantic City legalized gambling. Gaming lobbyists carried similar lists when they attempted to convert citizens in other states to the tax-revenue, employment, and urban-renewal wonders that materialized when a casino came to town. Unlike the beleaguered Boardwalk, however, which suffered generations-old maladies and vast urban blight, Meadows Village was only one run-down neighborhood in an otherwise booming city.

So it was a moment for optimism, fireworks, and champagne. City leaders could almost feel the changes brought on by the amazing tower on the edge of the barrio.

And not one person had put so much as a nickel in a Stratosphere slot machine.

"Like a lot of people, I've had a love-hate relationship with Bob," Adamsen said later. "But you had to be impressed with his project."

But a funny thing was happening to the Stratosphere on its way to making Las Vegas history. During a massive, $60,000 fireworks display, accompanied by a radio simulcast featuring the music of Pink Floyd, smoke from the pyrotechnics again set off the sensitive alarms in the observation pod. Many Stratosphere workers were unsure whether to conduct a full-scale evacuation or merely direct skittish visitors to the two refuge floors designed to protect guests in emergencies. Some partiers were instructed to use the stairs—all 100 flights—to reach the ground. Still others were told to line up and wait for the elevators, which were understandably busy with the alarms echoing throughout the neighborhood.

The smoke-clearing system worked as designed, vacuuming the vapors from the building, but it was little consolation for the visitors who had been frightened and those who had taken the stairs. Television crews captured it all on videotape.

Before midnight, Stratosphere opened amid celebration and confusion.

Upon the tower's opening, Las Vegas oral surgeon Daniel Orr II, who worked many hours to reconstruct Stupak's shattered mouth and palate, wrote:

"In spite of the magnificent structure I can see so well from my front yard, I don't consider the Stratosphere Tower your greatest accomplishment. I'll never forget the first time we met. You weren't conscious secondary to major central nervous system injury, your head and face were literally swollen to the size of a basketball, you had been totally transfused from hemorrhage of the pelvic area, etc., etc., etc. I remember thinking that Bob Stupak was quite an accomplished individual, but that he was certainly going to die. I avoided talking with Phyllis and Nicole because I didn't want to dampen their spirits. A day or two later, I noticed that you'd begun to fight. How could a man in a coma fight? It's like nothing I've ever seen before. You'd been compromised to death's door, had tubes in literally every orifice and then some, had been tranquilized and paralyzed, placed on a ventilator, and physically soft restrained. A day or two after our first meeting, as you were being slowly weaned off total life support, you chose not to die, but to fight for life in any way you could.

"...There were so many things that could have killed you, Bob, but you beat them all as your strength continued to grow. In my life, I've seen just a handful of true miracles related to my profession, and you are one. I thank you for living, and I thank you for fighting back to the top of the heap here in our humble little village."

More than 18,000 people per day ascended the tower during the first week, but in that short time one minor event came to symbolize the growing list of problems with Stratosphere: on May 9, a 15-pound piece of the High Roller roller coaster came loose and dropped 35 feet onto the observation deck. It was a metal cylinder from one of the motors used to propel the cars around the track. A quick check of the cars revealed that all but one of the cylinders had been properly calibrated. Fortunately, no one was riding the roller coaster at the time, and no one on the observation tower was standing near where the heavy part landed. Still, the story made front-page news and led some television newscasts.

To be sure, not all of the Stratosphere's attractions fizzled. The talented Danny Gans, for one. Signing the handsome impressionist, comedian, and singer showed genuine insight. Gans was capable of mimicking scores of celebrity voices. He was so accomplished that he earned a role as Dean Martin in the television miniseries "Sinatra," and he filled Stratosphere's showroom nightly.

But locals were none too pleased with Stratosphere's center-Strip menu prices at the resort's cafes and restaurants. They also balked at taking the $7 ride up the elevator to the observation deck and paying another $5 each to experience the Big Shot and High Roller. The fact the CN Tower charged $9, the Eiffel Tower $10, and the Seattle Space Needle $8.50 for adults to ride to the top was lost on southern Nevadans who had long since grown accustomed to receiving special rates at "their" hotels.

By the end of the first month of operation, Stratosphere's problems were impacting the bottom line. Its revenues after five weeks were $26.8 million: $19.1 million in hotel revenues and a dismal $7.1 million in the casino. Those numbers were especially telling considering that the tower was an unabashed success, attracting 445,000 visitors. At 80 percent, hotel occupancy was below the Las Vegas average of 93 percent and the traditional 100 percent for just-opened megaresorts, but Stratosphere's $71 rack rate was unprecedented in the history of the location. (Indeed, Stupak had often lamented that he had to give away his rooms as part of his vacation program.) Employees recognized the trend: visitors were coming to the tower, all right, but they weren't sticking around to feed the slots and take on the table games.

Stratosphere President Dave Wirshing was outwardly confident that the revenue figures would improve dramatically once the additional 1,000 rooms were completed, giving Stratosphere the Strip standard of 2,500, but at the moment, the casino numbers were downright perplexing—a full 10 percent below the industry average of 50 percent of total revenues.

Not even Bob Stupak could put an optimistic spin on that one.

"Everything is relatively OK," he said without conviction.

Years after his experience at Vegas World, David Sklansky joined Stratosphere as a gambling consultant. In the wake of the miserable opening, Sklansky said, "The first thing I did was bring up some of the thoughts that Bob and I had talked about. But everybody miscalculated on how little people would transfer their interest in the tower to an interest in the casino."

The Stratosphere was one tall flop in the making, and Grand's lack of a highly developed marketing plan was beginning to take its toll. Locals were grousing about the Stratosphere, but it was nothing compared to the whipping nationally recognized financial analysts were giving it.

"What I think is happening is that the people who are attracted to a facility like that are not necessarily the people who are going to sit down and do some serious gambling," Salomon Brothers analyst Scott Renner told the *Wall Street Journal*.

"The hype moved the stock more than it should have," Dennis I. Forst of Hancock Institutional Equity said. "Frankly, it says more about the securities business than the gaming business.

"In a super-competitive Las Vegas gambling market, no one can simply throw open the doors and expect the masses to rush inside to get a look at another ocean of slot machines. The tower was a magnificent hook, but it alone could not guarantee success."

"The biggest mistake a company can make is to open too soon. First impressions last a long time," Jason Ader of Bear, Stearns & Company said. "Most of the problems are fixable. But these are the growing pains of a young company learning about the business."

Philadelphia-based casino-industry analyst Marvin Roffman, who visited the Stratosphere not long after it opened, was impressed with Stupak's big idea, but underwhelmed by the resort and its location.

"I must tell you I never thought the tower would get built," Roffman said. "I was one of the skeptics. What do I think of the tower? I actually like the tower. I really think it's a wonderful thing.

"Is it an attraction? It's an attraction. But is it going to make money? That's the big question."

Long lines for the elevator to the top, upscale prices, and the obviously inferior location weren't going to help matters.

"The problem is the numbers in the casino are absolutely terrible," Roffman said. "And there seems to be a problem with Mr. Stupak. There's going to be a transition coming up and until that happens we think there's a problem here. I was told by one of the people (at the company) that until he's phased out, they expect to have problems. I have the highest regard for Lyle Berman. He's a very astute businessman and pays great attention to detail."

After climbing to $14—with financial-industry predictions of a higher climb in the coming year—Stratosphere plummeted to $5.81 after one month of operation. Even considering the traditional stock shakeout that occurs after casinos open, Stratosphere was falling too fast to hold onto investor confidence. Its public relations machine simply could not overcome the resort's real and perceived problems.

Perhaps to improve its eventual stake in the market or possibly to offset the crush of negative stories being printed after its opening, Stratosphere officials announced yet another hotel expansion that promised to increase the number of rooms at the resort to 4,000 by 1999. It gave investors something to look forward to, but the future would materialize without the King Kong ride, which was scrapped with little fanfare. Privately, other changes in the resort's design were in the works as well.

From the SEC Schedule 13D filed by Bob Stupak July 1, 1996: "Mr Stupak is also considering resigning as Chairman and as a member of the Company's Board of Directors. In his opinion, because Grand currently owns approximately 42 percent of the common stock and is the controlling stockholder, Mr. Stupak's ability to influence the Company's operations and strategic business decisions is extremely limited. Nevertheless, Mr. Stupak recognizes that until a merger or other form of business combination is consummated, the interests of the Company's stockholders other than Grand may best be served by Mr. Stupak remaining as a member of the Board of Directors where he may continue to exercise some influence on decisions and actions...which he could not do if he disassociated himself from deliberations of the Board of Directors."

All the while, Bob Stupak kept smiling and kept selling his stock as it plummeted back to its original asking price.

"This is going to be the biggest thing ever to hit Las Vegas," Stupak said as the Stratosphere opened. "How can you miss knowing we're around?"

But by then Stupak knew it was he who would not be around much longer.

THIRTEEN

After the Fall

The Stratosphere pod was evacuated again on July 5 after a cardboard box caught fire in an electrical service room on the 10th floor of the pod. Although hotel officials assured skeptics that there was no danger, the tower was shut down the rest of the day. The job of explaining yet another ringing fire alarm fell to Stratosphere's increasingly harried public spokesman, Tom Bruny. In recent weeks, Bruny had gone from conducting light-hearted media tours of the resort to attempting to calm journalists bent on reporting every false alarm and faulty roller coaster part. Bruny's efforts at damage control aside, the Stratosphere was taking a beating in the press and on Wall Street.

It didn't help matters that the resort's radio and television advertising blitz was coming in the wake of the poor revenue returns. Las Vegas residents and tourists can sense desperation at a resort, and Stratosphere ran the risk of frightening off its customers by appearing to try too hard. Adding to its obvious financial woes was the torn relationship between Berman and Stupak. So much for high-stakes friendships. Wrote *Review-Journal* gaming reporter Dave Palermo: "The dismal figures have caused a rift between poker-playing buddies Bob Stupak, who conceived the project, and Lyle Berman, whose Grand Casinos Inc. bailed Stupak's unfinished stump out of impending financial failure. Stupak last week again predicted he will resign as chairman of the board, a threat company executives are hoping he makes good on."

Stratosphere could and did cut its payroll, by terminating 150 workers. Stratosphere could and did make itself more attractive to locals, by dropping the price of its elevator ride from $7 to $5. Casino managers also moved to adjust the payout percentages of the slot machines to make them more attractive to local players, and hotel managers started revamping the resort's pricy restaurant menus.

But no one could snap his fingers and complete 1,000 unfinished hotel rooms. No one could wave a wand and open the three dozen retail shops that were behind schedule. For that matter, no one could force tourists to sit and play slot machines they could operate anywhere in the city from a 7-Eleven to Caesars Palace.

Stupak's personal world was coming apart faster than his tower. He appeared to have exhausted his good fortune and then some. On July 9, Stupak informed the Reno City Council through attorney Sam McMullen that he was abandoning his plans to remodel the Riverside Hotel and add a Stratosphere-like thrill ride downtown. Development in Reno has never approached Las Vegas's blinding growth, and the reason why was clear to Stupak. After requesting the city council to assist him in acquiring the run-down property from owner Peter Eng, Stupak was faced with the possibility of putting up a $500,000 nonrefundable deposit with the city and spending another $500,000 in site plans, only to have Eng back out of the deal.

"We are not interested in going forward under these circumstances," McMullen said. "Stupak is not going into a deal where all of the effort and time will end up for naught."

The city had granted Eng eight years to improve the shuttered property after he acquired the Riverside in 1987. Bob Stupak was realizing he would receive nowhere near the same consideration.

The moment Bob Stupak had been hinting at for months arrived Monday July 22, when he resigned as chairman of the board of the tumbling Stratosphere Corporation. The resort's $11.1 million first-quarter loss was ushered in by predictions of impending bankruptcy from two respected Wall Street firms. In his last official act as the figurehead chairman of the resort he dreamed up, Bob Stupak crafted his letter of resignation and addressed it to his ex-friend, Lyle Berman.

July 21, 1996

Lyle Berman
Chief Executive Officer
Stratosphere Corporation
2000 Las Vegas Blvd. South
Las Vegas, NV 89104

RE: RESIGNATION

Dear Lyle,
You are long aware through personal conversations and formal business meetings of my continuing dissatisfaction with the "Grand" management of the Stratosphere and the methods and results of operations.

My increasing frustration with my inability to have any meaningful say or input with respect to discussions or decisions made by "Grand," the Board of Directors or any management personnel clearly leaves me no alternative but to tender my resignation as Chairman and Director, effective immediately.

Pursuant to the terms of the November 15, 1993 agreement as amended on December 22, 1993, I will be exercising my right to nominate my successor to the Board of Directors. I am currently considering various qualified candidates and will promptly notify you as soon as I have made what I believe is a satisfactory selection.

Sincerely,
Bob Stupak
Chairman of the Board

Stupak sent copies to Stratosphere officers Thomas G. Bell, Andrew Blumen, Patrick Cruzen, Morris Goldman, Ronald Kramer, Robert Maheu, David Rogers, Neil Sell, Stanley Taub, Joe Weller, and David Wirshing.

"He was trying to save face," a Stratosphere executive said after reading the letter.

A day later, Lyle Berman and his corporate crew held a national teleconference to attempt to explain the company's terrible first quarter and assuage the fears of dozens of fretful stockbrokers, many of whom were scrambling to spin their own version of events to investors.

Stratosphere shares dropped from $4 to $3 as stockholders dumped 5.2 million shares onto the market.

Salomon Brothers analysts Bruce Turner and Tim Kelsey spared no body blows and made no attempt to be politically correct in predicting the failure of the property with its bad location and worse debt load.

"With a prohibitively expensive debt structure, bankruptcy may prove the only option," Turner and Kelsey wrote.

If their financial predictions proved correct and the tower generated only half the $80 million projected by company officials, Stratosphere would fail to meet its bond obligations, even with Grand Casinos kicking in up to $50 million in a promised one-time capital infusion.

Bankruptcy "has not been in our vocabulary at this point," Berman told the teleconference of reporters and securities analysts.

Grand's investment in Stratosphere had swollen to approximately $125 million: $75 million in equity and $48.5 in debt through a completion guarantee. The company appeared to have $90 million in cash reserves, but every penny was earmarked toward construction and expansion. Berman had personally purchased $8 million in Stratosphere bonds.

While Stratosphere was reeling, Grand Casinos reported quarterly revenues of $194 million—$1 million more than the same period the previous year.

There was plenty to look forward to.

Simon and Gordon, which was designing and building the Stratosphere's shopping arcade, planned to have 35 stores open by the end of 1996. Phase two would add another 35 stores, giving the Stratosphere one of the larger malls in the city. The Stratosphere was in the process of adding 875 rooms, including 150 suites, as well as a pool area. With an occupancy rate anywhere near the city's standard 90 percent, there would be sufficient traffic flow at the hotel.

Berman's Kids Quest child-care center, a popular trend in casinos across the country, would give parents a chance to gamble without worrying whether their offspring were learning to say, "baby needs a new pair of shoes."

But the improvements were months away.

Berman announced that the casino, which had been so disappointing, would loosen its wagering structure. Odds on craps would be increased to as much as 30 times. Dollar slot machines would return more than 98 percent. With maximum coins bet, select video poker machines would return more than 100 percent. What's more, they would institute crapless craps, double exposure blackjack, and single-zero roulette.

For all his acumen and education, Lyle Berman was beginning to sound a lot like Bob Stupak.

If Stupak sought refuge in a public willing to forgive its favorite reformed huckster, he would be sorely disappointed. Securities & Exchange Commission filings revealed that, while he was busy touting the wonders of the Stratosphere, Stupak was quickly selling off thousands of shares of stock. A shareholder lawsuit would later claim that he sold 471,000 shares in a period of six weeks from May 10 to July 24 at prices ranging from $8.72 to $6.75; the sales amounted to six percent of his stock and netted him approximately $3.6 million, but lesser investors who had believed Stupak's pronouncements of the infallibility of the resort were destined to suffer big losses.

On July 24, Stratosphere stock fell to 2 $^{11}/_{16}$ths after 1.7 million shares were dumped on the market.

Ironically, Stupak's replacement at the head of Stratosphere would have to possess many of the talents of casino promotion that had made Stupak famous. Berman found his man in long-time friend Richard Schuetz, a 45-year-old former blackjack dealer who had bounced around Las Vegas at nearly every level of the casino business for two decades. Schuetz had dealt at Reno's Harrah's casino and had worn a suit at the Golden Nugget, Frontier, and Sands. More recently, Schuetz had served as Grand Casinos' vice president of corporate marketing before resigning to become an industry consultant. He also wrote a lighthearted column for *Casino Executive* magazine. Berman trusted Schuetz.

Although industry insiders respected his intelligence, Schuetz had offended more than one staid corporate type with his sense of humor and less-than-understated demeanor on the casino floor. Still, he appeared to be an ideal choice for the interim position: he was loyal to Berman and was experienced enough to know Stratosphere had to bust loose or it was going to bust out.

The resort's physical maladies—guests found the valet parking arrangement inconvenient, for example—could be corrected. But Stratosphere suffered from other ailments as well. Its group room bookings were nearly nonexistent and casino marketing efforts lagged months behind. It didn't help that the room-reservation number in the phone directory was incorrect, or that Stratosphere's managers failed to sell the rooms months ahead of time. And nothing had changed in the casino—throngs of tourists visited the tower daily, but few stopped at the machines and tables long enough to spend a quarter. They bought more T-shirts than gaming tokens.

The lavish piece of Native American artwork that dominated the entrance was a symbol of the extravagant lengths to which Stratosphere's designers had gone in order to dress up the resort. Although the figure of two Indians reaching for the stars was handsome, it stood in the spot where, in other casinos, slot machines ruled.

"This store is a casino, not a museum," the witty Schuetz

told a reporter not long after taking over. He would need every ounce of his sense of humor in the coming months.

National newspaper headlines pulled no punches. Stratosphere was considered the biggest flop since Bob Snow's Main Street Station debacle five years earlier. Going broke in a boomtown was bound to leave room for criticism—and not merely for the media's favorite whipping boy, Bob Stupak.

The *Los Angeles Times* proclaimed:

HYPE, HOPE AREN'T ENOUGH—
VEGAS TOWER FAILS TO CASH IN

The *Wall Street Journal*, which had all but championed the project from the start, joined in the mugging:

STRATOSPHERE'S STOCK, BONDS
TUMBLE TO EARTH, AS CASINO IS STUNG
BY DELAYS, COST OVERRUNS

The headlines had Schuetz feeling every bit like Rodney Dangerfield. He'd have to hustle to earn Wall Street's respect. Many of the analysts who lauded the tower's can't-miss potential now called it a half-billion-dollar bust.

"One of the problems is this company may have made statements it couldn't deliver on," Schuetz said. "Now this place needs to be fundamentally repositioned. There's no risk to that. What are we going to do? Screw it up?"

With 1,000 unfinished rooms, more than a dozen unfinished retail shops, and a nonexistent aquarium, it was too late for that.

"We're trying to make this an attractive place with what we've got," Schuetz said in late August after the company announced it was halting construction on the resort's phase two projects. The rooms and shops would go unfinished. The aquarium idea was shelved.

But on the casino floor, Stratosphere was changing dramatically. Schuetz made sweeping changes in an attempt to attract players to the slots and tables. Adopting *his* best huckster mode, Schuetz instituted single-zero roulette, which lowers the house's advantage over the player from 5.26 percent to 2.7 percent. At the crap table, he instituted 20-times odds, and later upped the figure to an unprecedented 100-times odds. The move decreased the casino's edge to a microscopic .02 percent of the total action wagered on the pass line and odds. He loosened the slots to a 98 percent return on $1 machines. As a special incentive, Schuetz installed 80 video poker machines that returned more than 100 percent. These positive-return video poker machines were, ironically, the brainchild of Bob Stupak, who debuted them at Vegas World several years earlier.

Then he lowered admission to the tower from $7 to $5 and dropped the price of the buffet. These were desperate moves that would have made Bob Stupak proud.

"Right now, we've been able to generate a lot more interest in the cheese than the trap," Schuetz cracked to a journalist. To another reporter he boasted, "We're showing that we're a dynamic, aggressive property willing to take risks." "Best Place to Gamble on the Planet" was the unofficial motto.

As much as he might have wanted to, Stupak could not stay out of the news. He wasn't making public appearances, but substantial stock transactions connected to him had drawn the attention of small-time shareholders and the Securities & Exchange Commission. Stratosphere's shareholders immediately began accusing him of dumping his stock to the detriment of the company, and that same argument would be made in litigation filed in the weeks to come. What critics didn't know, or failed to acknowledge, was that many of the shares sold under Stupak's name were moved on the market by PaineWebber to attempt to recoup margin-account loans to Stupak. He later argued in an SEC filing that he had no control over the approximately 2 million shares of Stratosphere. When, according to Stupak's filing,

PaineWebber called in the $2.1 million in margin loans on July 22, it made him look like he was abandoning a sinking ship. Although anyone who understood finance would have found it incredible that Stupak—a corporate officer and largest individual shareholder in the company—could have somehow forgotten about the regulations, he appeared to have done just that. Gaming-industry insiders whispered that the stock sale held the potential for a securities violation, but Stupak bristled at the suggestion.

"The only mistake I made was I didn't sell enough stock," he sniped. He also criticized the apparent lack of marketing at Stratosphere.

"There is no place in town that doesn't market, or they couldn't survive," he said as he watched his fortune in Stratosphere stock fall to 3 on the Nasdaq board on the last day of July.

As shareholders watched the stock drop, Stupak continued to sell. Analysts who had talked of Stupak's creativity and Berman's business acumen only a few weeks earlier blamed both men for the stock's nosedive. Especially Stupak, who clearly contributed to the decline of the stock by dumping hundreds of thousands of shares. By mid-August, the stock had fallen to a few cents over $2.

On August 5, Stratosphere shareholders Michael Ceasar and Samuel Tolwin filed a federal class-action lawsuit alleging Stratosphere Corporation, Grand Casinos, Stupak, Lyle Berman, David Wirshing, Tom Lettero, Andy Blumen, and Las Vegas attorney Tom Bell had violated securities laws through misleading practices. Stupak was targeted for selling off 948,000 shares of Stratosphere stock for a profit of more than $8.25 million from December 19, 1995, through July 22, 1996. Clearly, Ceasar and Tolwin were looking to fuel a stockholder revolt after their combined 1,700 shares of Stratosphere dropped in value from nearly $21,000 to $10,000. The suit claimed Stratosphere officials misled stockholders by touting the resort's grand potential while privately selling off stock.

According to the litigation, Stupak went on a selling binge in the months leading up to Stratosphere's opening. He sold 88,000 shares of stock in January for a gain of more than $900,000; 145,000 in February for more than $1.5 million; 120,000 in March for another $1.2 million. In May, he dumped 334,000 shares on the market for an approximate gain of $2.9 million.

The suit quoted a July 30 *Wall Street Journal* article in which a stockbroker lamented the fact that Stupak had sold so many shares while investment experts were still recommending the stock.

"Had I known the chairman of Stratosphere was such a large seller, I would not have made such a recommendation to my clients," the broker said.

Had Stupak violated SEC regulations requiring insiders to disclose their sales in a timely manner?

"Shame on me if I sold cheap in January, February, and March," Stupak told the *Journal*. He denied any wrongdoing.

The day the Caesar-Tolwin lawsuit was filed, Stupak filed another SEC Schedule 13d. It read in part:

"Effective July 22, 1996, Mr. Stupak resigned voluntarily as a member of the Company's Board of Directors. The resignation was not precipitated by the Company or its controlling stock-holder, Grand Casinos, Inc. ...To the contrary, such action reflects Mr. Stupak's inability to conduct the customary functions or exercise the influence commonly associated with his position either as a director or as "Chairman of the Board, " a position which he held from the Company's inception until the date of his resignation. Mr. Stupak also has had significant and increasing concerns over construction management controls and unexplained project costs, marketing approaches and certain other Grand-directed decisions that in his view adversely affected the Company, as well as with respect to the general unwillingness of the Grand-appointed management and the Grand-controlled Board of Directors to consider his advice and opinions."

In mid-August, Stratosphere officials contacted representatives of Donaldson, Lufkin & Jenrette, a respected Wall Street investment banking firm, to analyze its stock predicament and consider its options. None were appetizing. The company could rush out and seek outside capital at a high interest rate, or it could conduct a rights offering, which would enable shareholders to buy blocks of stock at a heavy discount. Even with Grand Casinos' promised $48.5 million construction-completion guarantee, the project still wouldn't be finished.

Then there was Grand's other problem. If Stratosphere failed to generate at least $50 million in cash flow, Grand was on the hook for three years to make up the difference up to $20 million each year. With Stratosphere's junk bonds taking their high-interest hit, confidence in the future of the resort was at an all-time low. So was the stock: 1 $^5/_8$.

Stupak, Berman, Stratosphere, and Grand were hit with a second federal class-action lawsuit on August 29 filed by Harvey Cohen, Dawn Ennis, Robert Buckler, Jeff Wexler, and Union Equity Partners. The complaint: deceptive trading and brokering.

"Fully aware of the risky, best-efforts nature of the offering, defendants secretly structured and conducted the offering so that all of the risk that the offering might not reach its maximum would fall on the investors and the selected dealers, but if the offering became 'hot,' almost all of the reward would flow to defendants and their affiliates, friends, and families," the suit alleged. "...In other words, defendants deceived the investors and the selected dealers into taking on the risk of failure, while secretly denying the investors and the selected dealers the full upside potential in the event the demand for the units exceeded the maximum offering and the units were certain to trade at a premium to the offering price."

Stupak and the others accused scoffed at the allegations, laying them off to disgruntled stockholders who were happy as long as Stratosphere shares were climbing, but were unable to face the reality of the marketplace when the stock plummeted. Still, refuting the allegations would be time-consuming, costly, and would further damage the company's reputation and potential.

Stupak's image in the community mirrored Stratosphere's financial position. Bob the Changed Man had begun to be portrayed as the Same Old Stupak, who flashed a bankroll for charity and cashed in on the media coverage only to withdraw his generosity a few months later.

His $100,000 reward offer for information leading to the persons responsible for the death of 10-month-old Francine Meegan was quietly withdrawn over the summer. In late August, when a key witness applied to receive the reward, it had vanished. Metro's Homicide Bureau backed Stupak's move, but the public impression was that he had reneged on his promise. "It would be our opinion right now that there is nobody qualified for the reward," Sgt. Ken Hefner told a reporter, but the public's impression was that Stupak had broken his promise.

While Stupak was quietly selling off Stratosphere stock, officials at St. Vincent de Paul Management Co. were banking on a 30,000-share gift bestowed by the generous casino man to pay for a new kitchen at the Stupak Mobile Assistance and Shelter for the Homeless. By September, they realized they would have to delay plans for the kitchen after the value of their stock dropped from $405,000 to $56,400 in a few short weeks. Officials said they had no intention of removing Stupak's name from the building.

Days later, Stratosphere Corporation was chided in the press for failing to make good on its agreement to deed Naked City's Chester Stupak Community Center to the city and throw in $100,000 for on-site improvements. City officials deemed the dilapidated 7,000-square-foot building that honored Bob Stupak's father's name one of the worst of its kind in Las Vegas. For her part, Mayor Jan Jones was reluctant to kick Stratosphere— which she had praised only weeks earlier as a triumph of urban redevelopment—for failing to turn over the property.

By September 30, Stratosphere stock had fallen to $1 per share, but Minneapolis-based Cargill Inc. added a wrinkle to the resort's predicament when it purchased approximately $60 million of the company's $203 million first-mortgage notes for 82 cents on the dollar. Given the likely prospect of bankruptcy, Cargill's move was telling. Obviously, experts inside Cargill, the largest private company in the United States, believed the resort would survive a reorganization and eventually right itself.

With an additional $31.5 million from Grand Casinos in the form of a construction-completion guaranty, Stratosphere officials braced themselves for the remainder of the year.

Given its monumental financial woes and the fact that its former chairman, Bob Stupak, rarely let a day go by without criticizing its operators, it was hardly surprising that the statue of the founder of the tower who, according to its inscription, "shaped the destiny of the Las Vegas skyline," was clandestinely removed from the casino and placed in storage in late September.

A month later, still having difficulty filling its 1,500 rooms, Stratosphere Corporation changed its official line and announced that it intended to file bankruptcy in an attempt to reorganize its behemoth debts. The resort would remain open throughout the process and, if its financial cards fell right, emerge in a superior position. A key reason for the announcement: its third-quarter losses were $26 million despite a 49 percent increase in revenue from $23.7 million to $35.3 million. Grand Casinos also took a hit, reporting an 84 percent drop in net income to $3.5 million. A new marketing program at Stratosphere was now essential not only for the tower's survival, but for the well-being of Grand Casinos as well.

It was hardly shocking, then, when word surfaced that Stratosphere had failed to meet its $14.5 million payment to bond-holders due December 16. The company's executive vice president, Andrew Blumen, said, "We're busier than we've ever been in the past." But under the weight of its mortgage interest, the company was not recovering.

Stratosphere stock closed at 1 $1/16$ that day.

As if to underscore the changes to come in the new year, in late December the High Roller roller coaster again suffered mechanical difficulties, losing a wheel with a dozen passengers aboard. No one was injured, but the malfunction scared away tourists and forced another closure of the world's tallest roller coaster. It would reopen with few passengers willing to take the wild ride that mirrored Stupak and the tower's own tumultuous tale.

Life After a Sure Thing

A funny thing happened on the way to bankruptcy for Stratosphere, then the third most expensive resort project in the history of Las Vegas. Company President Richard Schuetz's wide-open marketing strategy, which had reminded many observers of Bob Stupak at his best, began to work. The casino filled up with tourists seeking friendly slot machines and locals in search of the hottest deal in town. Although it would never show a profit without a thorough restructuring of its insane debt load, Schuetz had managed to turn the casino around. In doing so, he gave irate bondholders hope for the future—and made them more amenable to accepting the change that was on the way. But even he wondered on what, exactly, more than a half-billion dollars had been spent, given a hotel that still had 1,000 uncompleted rooms.

"What we did here is a funny thing," Schuetz said. "I really do believe we have the best place to gamble on the planet. That's not hyperbole. That's not an advertising slogan. We can pretty well support that. We've been thrilled with the numbers. That's not to suggest we can be viable given the existing debt structure, which is the whole point of restructuring. I believe the Stratosphere can be viable under restructuring. We're working without a net, but I think we can do it."

By mid-January, Chapter 11 bankruptcy reorganization was imminent. Backed by Cargill's ownership of $60 million of the first-mortgage notes purchased at a 20 percent discount, the majority of bondholders showed a willingness to compromise on the 14.25 percent notes. And after a meticulous look at Stratosphere Tower Corporation under Schuetz's guidance by an ad hoc committee of 57 percent of Stratosphere's bondholders, they agreed to accept 11.25 percent for their notes with a due date of May 15, 2002, a move which over time would save the company millions in interest payments. The company's next interest payment would be due by November 15, 1997.

As a bonus, the new noteholders would receive a 15 percent interest incentive once Stratosphere's cash flow exceeded $60 million, a gesture that could amount to as much as $3 million per year. As part of the deal, the company was tentatively approved under the reorganization to issue $25 million in additional bonds to complete construction projects put on hold by the foundering finances.

But Stratosphere's precipitous fall had more than shaken the faith of some of its stockholders.

"Where's the money?" Las Vegas investor Frank Zohar asked. "That's the first thing. They had $58 million and another $38 million was raised. Where's the money? They opened up the place incomplete. They gave beautiful reports at stockholders meetings, but they didn't tell us they had any problems with construction."

For longtime Las Vegan Christian Schneider, Stratosphere's decline defied even the strained logic of the stock market.

"My friend Fritz Uebler and I are looking at each other and are asking how we could fall for such a scam," Schneider said. "Stupak knew the stock was falling and sold millions of shares. He dumped them quietly while Fritz and I and other people suffered. Now we are asking ourselves why we didn't sell the day after it opened."

For its part, Grand Casinos agreed to convert $50 million due from Stratosphere into a large block of common stock equal to 40 percent of the company. Existing shares would be canceled before the new stock would be issued for $1.31 per share. Previous shareholders would get preference and would receive a warrant to purchase another share for $3.

After the reorganization, Grand Casinos would come away owning 65 percent of Stratosphere. Grand also agreed to contribute another $75 million by June 1997 to complete the 1,000-room hotel addition.

The agreement hinged on approval by a federal bankruptcy judge, but it was clear that Grand Casinos had no intention of abandoning its Stratosphere investment. The rapid reorganization also led Bob Stupak to believe he was duped by his old friends Lyle Berman and former Vegas World counsel Andy Blumen.

"I think Bob trusted a lot of people he shouldn't have trusted," Dan Hart said. "How can they blame this on Bob? How can this be his fault? He did everything he could to modify the course that Grand was taking."

David Sklansky: "The truth of the matter is, if Bob had stuck to his original idea—building a $50 million tower with a minor renovation of Vegas World—then it would have been a home run. If he could have just sold the stock, he wouldn't have had to spend $500 million. But Lyle could not allow that same strategy to have Grand's name on it. They couldn't have a second-rate hotel associated with them. They couldn't have a schlocky casino associated with them. Lyle might have gone overboard, but he definitely had to do a lot of expensive upgrades. Lyle had a big-time casino company that had to be first-class or he couldn't do it. He has stockholders to think about. He had the company image to think about."

On January 9, 1997, Stratosphere officials further modified Stupak's financial connection with the resort when they canceled approximately $15 million in outstanding vacation packages that had been sold during the Vegas World-Stratosphere club era.

The company's letter to package holders infuriated Stupak.

"Several years ago," the letter began, "you purchased the right to visit Bob Stupak's Vegas World Hotel and Casino where in exchange for a payment you made, you received a letter from Bob Stupak which indicated that at Bob's expense he had arranged for you to take your vacation at the new Stratosphere Hotel and Casino when it opened.

"Bob was able to offer you this opportunity because he had made arrangements with Stratosphere to deposit the money needed to pay for these package benefits in an escrow account set up for that purpose. Unfortunately, at the present time, there are insufficient cash funds in the account to pay Stratosphere for the benefits Bob Stupak's company previously sold you.

"In addition to the current unavailability of funds in the escrow, Stratosphere anticipates filing for Chapter 11 bankruptcy protection in the near future. This filing will prevent Stratosphere from providing the benefits previously sold to you by Bob. If Bob and Stratosphere are able to make adequate arrangements, then Stratosphere will again be able to provide its facility for your use subject to approval by the bankruptcy court."

In relieving themselves of the potential financial burden, they put Stupak at the head of the line to be sued by irate package holders. By order of the state Gaming Control Board, Stupak had placed seven million shares of Stratosphere—a $100 million value at its highest point and $7 million at its nadir—in an escrow account. He remained responsible for all refunds for the packages.

Stratosphere, which had been a public relations nightmare up to that point, made itself look even worse by stiffing Stupak's loyal customers.

From the Dow Jones Information Services wire: "Stratosphere Corp. compounded its legal and financial woes this week by abruptly refusing to honor $16 million in presold vacation packages affecting roughly 16,000 customers, mostly retirement-age patrons.

"The decision, which stranded some travelers in Las Vegas, highlights the hotel and casino's embarrassing struggles to remain afloat just nine months after opening.

"...Moreover, the consumers' quandary raises questions about the foresight of Nevada gambling regulators in allowing the vacation packages to be backed by seven million Stratosphere shares."

Indeed, in accepting Stratosphere stock to back the cost of redeeming the vacation packages, the Gaming Control Board set itself up to appear culpable. Had Chairman Bible and members DuCharme and Harris forced Stupak to pay off the packages with cash—or through a personal loan from Berman or Grand Casinos—the issue might have been averted. But it was too late for hindsight.

"All this is being done by Lyle Berman," Stupak told a reporter. "He doesn't give a damn about Las Vegas, doesn't give a damn about Nevada."

Schuetz said the company regretted canceling the vacation packages, but it was a matter of survival.

"I can't afford to offer the packages without knowing I'm going to get paid for them," Schuetz said.

He was also tired of hearing Stupak blame everything on Berman.

"I have a difficult time with the chairman of the board of a corporation saying he didn't have any control," Schuetz said. "I wasn't here, but that makes zero sense to me. If this place had been a success, do you think Bob would say he didn't have anything to do with it?"

Even as they traded barbs and as Stratosphere headed for federal reorganization, Stupak and Grand Casinos were meeting to reach a settlement in the vacation package debacle.

"When I was here in the '80s, there were two people I admired as marketers. One was Andy Tompkins at the Lady Luck. The other was Bob Stupak," Richard Schuetz said. "They both took what at that time I thought were close-to-impossible situations and made them work.

"But the world has changed too much. Bob has been rendered obsolete. The world changed in fundamental and meaningful ways from a legal standpoint and from a social and cultural standpoint, and I don't think Bob can change that much. I don't think he'll come back up to any scale. On the other hand, Bob has incredible survival instincts. He won't go down easy, I guarantee you."

Even Dan Hart, who was so quick to defend his friend and client, didn't like the odds of Bob Stupak making one last comeback.

"I would never be a person who would count Stupak out," Hart said. "I'd never count him out, but I think he's facing one of the biggest challenges of his life."

Mayor Jones, whose relationship with Stupak had gone from adversarial to a genuine friendship, considered the Stratosphere story a loss on many fronts.

"The Stratosphere was the key to the city," she said. "It should have been a winner. Bob liked being a big casino boss. Bob liked being rich, but for different reasons. He liked being able to give his money away. He was more generous than most people realize. He really tried to help, and he was willing to put up his money. Lyle Berman is one of the smartest people I've ever met. I think what's happened to all of them is just a tragedy.

"If I could give Bob back his dream, I'd give Bob back his dream."

Stupak worked for years to overcome the stigma attached to his lack of a formal education. In the end, the men who ran the casino industry knew plenty about business, but little about the spirit of a hustler.

"I think that Bob has had a driving ambition to prove that his eighth-grade education shouldn't stop him from living in the same circles as Lyle and me, Steve Wynn, Donald Trump, and Michael Milken," David Sklansky said. "I think Bob always wanted to prove he was in those people's categories. I think on pure I.Q. he might very well be.

"The big problem Bob has is you can't enter the game as easily as you could in the old days. If you don't have $100 million to throw around, it's hard to get in the game. The sad part about it is Bob had to be almost ruined before he could make a resurgence. He's got ideas to stave off disaster, and I think there's a better chance that he will pull it off than others think."

Ever the optimist, Phyllis McGuire stands by her friend.

"He's not really down," she said. "He saw his dream realized. The dream that he'd had so long is that the tower should be finished. I've never seen him so happy as the night it opened. He's already survived the biggest challenge of his life."

Stupak had been counted out before, but this time he appeared to have taken the ultimate beating. The man who prided himself on always getting the best of it in the end had absorbed the worst. In seeing his dream project come true, he had lost his casino, his bankroll, and the fickle admiration of jaded Las Vegans. He had even lost most of his old friends from the industry that had outgrown him.

"The days of those characters are gone," he said. "There's no more Jay Sarnos around. There's no more me's around. It's all over."

In 1997, he found himself one of the city's neon dinosaurs, perhaps the last of the carnival-style casino operators that once proliferated around town. Las Vegas had indeed changed in meaningful ways, not all of them positive. But those changes didn't bode well for Stupak. Like Adalbert, the patron saint of his misspent youth, Bob Stupak's life's work was destined to be characterized by failure, but his impact on Las Vegas was great.

These days, you'll sometimes find him a few blocks north of the tower on Las Vegas Boulevard at his faded Thunderbird Hotel, planning the comeback even his friends don't believe he will make. He has in mind building a new joint optimistically named The Sky's the Limit Club after his old motto.

Although it no longer makes headlines, he still sees Phyllis McGuire. He still smokes like a fiend, still fails to take his doctors' advice. After a lifetime spent chasing the numbers, he still gambles a little every day.

Like the old dice scuffler of Vegas past once asked, how else will he know when his good luck returns?

Bibliography

Books

Adler, Jerry. *High Rise—How 1,000 Men and Women Worked Around the Clock for Five Years and Lost $200 Million Building a Skyscraper*, HarperCollins Publishers, New York, 1993.

Canadian Encyclopedia, The, Hurtig Publishers, Edmonton, Alberta, 1985.

Charlton, Peter. *Two Flies Up a Wall—The Australian Passion for Gambling*, Methuen Haynes, North Ryde, Australia, 1987.

Demaris, Ovid. *The Last Mafioso—The Treacherous World of Jimmy Frattianno*, Bantam Books, New York, NY, 1981.

Eicholz, Alice, Ed. *Ancestry's Redbook—American State, County &Town Sources*, Ancestry, Inc., New York, NY, 1989.

Epstein, Richard A. *The Theory of Gambling and Statistical Logic*, Academic Press, New York, NY, 1967.

Findlay, John M. *Magic Lands*, University of California Press, Berkeley, Calif., 1992.

Griffin, Peter. *Extra Stuff—Gambling Ramblings*, Huntington Press, Las Vegas, NV, 1991.

Griffin, Peter. *The Theory of Blackjack*, Huntington Press, Las Vegas, NV, 1996.

Guinness Book of World Records, Guinness Publishing, Ltd., New York, NY, 1995.

Hess, Alan. *Viva Las Vegas—After Hours Architecture*, Chronicle Books, San Francisco, CA, 1993.

Johnston, David. *Temples of Chance—How America Inc. Bought Out Murder Inc. to Win Control of the Casino Business*, Doubleday, New York, NY, 1992.

Jones, Alison. *The Wordsworth Dictionary of Saints*, Wordsworth Editions, Ltd., Denmark, 1995.

Klatz, Ronald. *Grow Young with HGH,* HarperCollins Publishers, New York, NY, 1997.

Knepp, Donn. *Las Vegas—The Entertainment Capital,* Lane Publishing Co., Menlo Park, CA, 1987.

Provost, Gary. *High Stakes—Inside the New Las Vegas,* Truman Talley Books/ Dutton, New York, NY, 1994.

Reid, Ed, and Ovid Demaris. *The Green Felt Jungle,* Pocket Books, Inc., New York, NY, 1963.

Salvadori, Mario. *Why Buildings Stand Up—The Strength of Architecture,* W.W. Norton & Company, New York, NY, 1980.

Sifakis, Carl. *Mafia Encyclopedia,* Facts On File Inc., New York, NY, 1987.

Stupak, Bob. *Stupak on Craps,* Hammond Publishing, New York, NY, 1985.

Tauranac, John. *The Empire State Building,* Scribner, New York, NY, 1995.

Turner, Wallace. *Gamblers' Money—The New Force in American Life,* New American Library, New York, NY, 1965.

Venturi, Scott; Brown, Denise Scott; and Izenour, Steven. *Learning from Las Vegas,* The MIT Press, Cambridge, MA, 1993.

Wadsworth, Ginger, and Snyder, Jimmy. *Farewell Jimmy The Greek, The Wizard of Odds,* Eakin Press, Austin, Texas, 1996.

Magazines

Advertisement. "Own a Piece of the Tower," *Parade Magazine,* Aug. 22, 1993, p. 12.

Buntain, Rex. "Stratosphere Rethinks Entertainment Plans," *International Gaming and Wagering Business,* Sept. 1996, p. 10.

Corliss, Richard. "Just What Vegas Needed," *Time,* May 6, 1996, p. 75.

Grover, Ronald and Dale Kurschner. "Vegas' Tallest Strip Tease: Stratosphere is Gambling on Supergimmicks," *Business Week,* May 6, 1996, p. 124.

Smith, John L. "Into the Stratosphere," *Casino Executive,* April 1996, p. 30.

Ryan, Thomas M. "Stratosphere Heralds Vegas' Third Wave," *Casino Executive,* April 1996, p. 26.

Casino Journal, Special City of Las Vegas Edition, May 1996.

Dorn, William J. "Lyle Berman: The Mastermind of Grand Casinos," *Casino Magazine*, Vol. 4, Issue 5, p. 22.

Stupak, Bob. "From the Inside Out," *Gambling Times*, Vol. 6, No. 9, Jan. 1983, p. 64.

Stupak, Bob. "From the Inside Out," *Gambling Times*, Vol. 7, No. 12, Apr. 1984, p. 34.

Di Rocco, Chuck and Ray Poirier. "Tower Adds New Chapter," *Gaming Today*, Vol. 22, No. 2, Jan. 7, 1997, p. 1.

Curtis, Anthony. "What's Wrong with the Tower?," *Las Vegas Advisor*, Vol. 13, Issue 9, Sept. 1996, p. 1.

Curtis, Anthony. "Casinos At Odds," *Las Vegas Advisor*, Vol. 13, Issue 10, Oct. 1996, p. 8.

Curtis, Anthony. "News," *Las Vegas Advisor*, Vol. 14, Issue 2, Feb. 1997, p. 3.

Cohen, Aaron D. "All of the Attractions Are Not At the Top of the Tower," *Las Vegas Business Press*, Jun. 19, 1995, p. 29.

Staff Writer. "'Lady Maverick' Sandy Stupak New World Champion!," *Las Vegas Sports Book*, May 18-24, 1984.

Staff Writer. *Las Vegas Style*, "Standing Above it All," Dec. 1995, p. 14.

Staff Writer. *Las Vegas Style*, "Stratosphere Tower," Jan. 1996, p. 63.

Staff Writer. *Las Vegas Style*, "Stratosphere Offers a New View of Las Vegas," Jun. 1996, p. 21.

Hutchings, David. "The McGuire Sisters, Those Sugartime Princesses of Pop, Have Reunited After a 17-Year Split," *People Weekly*, Mar. 3, 1986, Vol. 25, p. 46.

Brown, Peter H. "McGuire Sings 'Sugartime' Blues; Popular '50s and '60s Singer Blasts 'Lewd' Cable Biography," *TV Guide*, Nov. 25, 1995, Vol. 43, No. 47, p. 38.

Moskowitz, David. "Stratosphere: Towering Problems, Grand Solutions," *Casino Executive*, Sept. 1996, p. 13.

Documents

Candidate Declarations of Campaign Expenditures, May 20-July 3, 1991, by Nicole Stupak.

Complaint, Ceasar, et al. v. Stratosphere Corp., et al., File No. CV-S-96-00708-PMP (RLH), filed Aug. 5, 1996, in U.S. District Court.

Complaint, Cohen, et al. v. Stratosphere Corp., et al., File No. A349985, filed Aug. 29, 1995, in District Court, State of Nevada.

Complaint, Cohen, et al. v. Stratosphere Corp., et al., File No.CV-S-94-003340DWH (LRL), filed Apr. 5, 1994, in U.S. District Court.

County Clerk, Clark County, various files.

Handicapping Stupak: Las Vegas Advisor Special Report, 1992.

Las Vegas Convention and Visitors Authority, Marketing Plan and Advertising Program, 1996-97.

Letter dated June 28, 1993, from Bob Stupak enclosing Stratosphere prospectus.

Letter of Resignation from Bob Stupak to Lyle Berman, dated July 21, 1996.

Nevada Gaming Commission, Minutes of March 1996 Meeting, Mar. 21, 1996.

Nevada Gaming Control Board, Minutes of March 1996 Meeting, Mar. 6, 1996.

Portrait of Achievement: "The Vegas World Story".

Securities & Exchange Commission form 13D of Robert Stupak, July 1, 1996.

Securities & Exchange Commission form 13D of Robert Stupak, August 5, 1996.

Senate Bill 704, *To Establish the Gambling Impact Study Commission,* 104th Congress, 1st Session, April 6, 1995.

Traffic Bureau, Accident Investigations Section, Metropolitan Police Department, Press Release, Rick Hart and William Johnson.

Various Press Releases, Stratosphere and Grand Casinos, Inc.

Newspapers

Advertisement. Tower Facts: Why are McCarran Airport and the FAA Blowing Smoke? *Las Vegas Review-Journal,* May 17, 1994, p. 7A.

Advertisement. *Las Vegas Review-Journal,* Sept. 29, 1996, p. 9A and 11A.

Advertisement. *Las Vegas Review-Journal*, Oct. 2, 1996, p. 7A.

Berns, Dave. Beating the Odds, *Las Vegas Review-Journal*, Oct. 22, 1995, p. 1J.

Berns, Dave. Stratosphere Alarms Triggered by Smoke, *Las Vegas Review-Journal*, Apr. 26, 1996, p. 3B.

Berns, Dave. Stratosphere Boss Learns From Mistakes, *Las Vegas Review-Journal*, Aug. 26, 1996, p. 1D.

Berns, Dave. Stratosphere Offering Gamblers a Better Deal, *Las Vegas Review-Journal*, Sept. 30, 1996, p. 1D.

Berns, Dave. Stratosphere Deadline Quietly Passes, *Las Vegas Review-Journal*, Dec. 17, 1996, p. 3D.

Borders, Myram. McGuire Sister Sues for $60 Million, *Las Vegas Sun*, Feb. 23, 1982.

Burbank, Jeff. Tower Project Gains Ground, *Las Vegas Review- Journal*, Oct. 22, 1991, p. 1A.

Burbank, Jeff. Vegas World to Add 22-Story, 370-Room Tower, *Las Vegas Sun*, Jul. 29, 1988, p. 3B.

Cahill, Bob. Vegas World Shareholders' Meeting 'Unconventional', *Las Vegas Sun*, May 25, 1990.

Caruso, Monica. Neighboring Businesses Keep Faith in Stratosphere, *Las Vegas Review-Journal*, Jul. 28, 1996, p. 6C.

Caruso, Monica. Stratosphere Deals Itself Winning Hand, *Las Vegas Review-Journal*, Oct. 2, 1996, p. 1D.

Chereb, Sandra. Vegas World Averts Closure of Room Tower, *Las Vegas Sun*, May 3, 1986, p. 1B.

Clayton, David. Memories of Landmark Opening Rise from Dust, *Las Vegas Sun*, Nov. 8, 1995, p. 1A.

Cohan, Jeffrey. Stratosphere Stock Drop Stalls Kitchen for Shelter, *Las Vegas Review-Journal*, Sept. 13, 1996, p. 1A

Cohan, Jeffrey. Stupak Center Deal Still Hangs in Limbo, *Las Vegas Review-Journal*, Sept. 14, 1996, p. 1B.

Collier, Lynn. Tall Talk: What's behind the tower Fuss? *Las Vegas Business Press*, May 16, 1994. Page 1.

Cox, Don. Fallout from Failed Stupak Deal Studied, *Reno Gazette-Journal*, Jul. 12, 1996, p. 1A.

Day, Ned. Recent Doings of Locals Could Surface at Mob Trial, *Las Vegas Review-Journal*, Oct. 30, 1985, p. 9B.

Digilio, Don. Refloating a Thunderbird Vintage Stupak, *Las Vegas Sun*, Dec. 27, 1991, p. 3A.

Edwards, John G. Stratosphere Sale Completed, *Las Vegas Review-Journal*, Nov. 5, 1994, p. 8C.

Edwards, John G. Stratosphere Corp. Gets New President, *Las Vegas Review-Journal*, Jul. 30, 1995, p. 1C.

Edwards, John G. Stratosphere Tower Soaring on Wall Street, *Las Vegas Review-Journal*, Apr. 28, 1996, p. 1E.

Edwards, John G. Stratosphere Plans to Keep Expanding, *Las Vegas Review-Journal*, May 23, 1996, p. 12E.

Edwards, John G. Bob Stupak Leaves a Troubled Stratosphere, *Las Vegas Review-Journal*, Jul. 23, 1996, p. 1A.

Edwards, John G. Stupak Sold Stratosphere Stock in Spring, *Las Vegas Review-Journal*, Jul. 24, 1996, p. 1D.

Edwards, John G. Stratosphere Stock Continues to Plunge, *Las Vegas Review-Journal*, Jul. 25, 1996, p. 10D.

Edwards, John G. Stupak Dismisses Failure to Report Sale, *Las Vegas Review-Journal*, Aug. 1, 1996, p. 1C.

Edwards, John G. Stratosphere May Halt Expansion, *Las Vegas Review-Journal*, Aug. 16, 1996, p. 1D.

Edwards, John G. LV Resort Brings in Adviser, *Las Vegas Review-Journal*, Aug. 22, 1996, p. 1D.

Edwards, John G. Man on the Move: Stratosphere Boss is Having Time of his Life, *Las Vegas Review-Journal*, Aug. 27, 1996, p. 1D.

Edwards, John G. Grand Casinos Lowers Its Earnings Projection, *Las Vegas Review-Journal*, Aug. 28, 1996, p. 2D.

Edwards, John G. Cargill Has Towering Stake in LV, *Las Vegas Review-Journal*, Sept. 30, 1996, p. 1D.

Edwards, John G. What About Bob? Stupak Statue Vanishes from Stratosphere Tower, *Las Vegas Review-Journal*, Oct. 11, 1996, p. 1D.

Edwards, John G. Stratosphere Reduces Space, Debt, *Las Vegas Review-Journal*, date unknown.

Ehlers, David. Stratosphere Investors Laugh All the Way to Bank, *Las Vegas Sun*, Nov. 10, 1995, p. 10C.

Ehlers, David. Schuetz Ready to Meet Stratosphere Challenges, *Las Vegas Sun*, Aug. 2, 1996, p. 1D.

Ehlers, David. Growth in Las Vegas Gaming Continues to Defy Odds, *Las Vegas Sun*, Aug. 9, 1996, p. 1D.

Filardo, Lou. The Birth of the Bullet, *Las Vegas Bullet*, Feb. 3, 1988, p. 1.

Flanagan, Tanya. Stratosphere Roller Coaster Comes to a Screeching Halt, *Las Vegas Review-Journal*, Dec. 27, 1996, p. 1B.

Gallant, John. Stupak Sets Sights on Steel Tower, *Las Vegas Review-Journal*, Oct. 5, 1989, p. 1A.

Gallant, John. Tower to Serve as 'Landmark', *Las Vegas Review-Journal*, Oct. 6, 1989, p. 1B.

Gallant, John. Controversy on Tower Plan, *Las Vegas Review-Journal*, Feb. 7, 1990. Page 1B.

Gallant, John. Hawkins, Nolen Easy Winners, *Las Vegas Review-Journal*, Jun. 5, 1991, p. 1A.

Gallant, John. Vegas World Neighbors to be Evicted, *Las Vegas Review-Journal*, Aug. 31, 1994, p. 1B.

Gallant, John. Stupak Rescinds Notices Forcing Tenants to Leave, *Las Vegas Review-Journal*, Sept. 2, 1994, p. 1B.

Gallant, John. Pro-Union Maids Fired at Vegas World, *Las Vegas Review-Journal*, Sept. 8, 1994, p. 1B.

Gallant, John and Marian Green. Council OKs Help for Tower Project, *Las Vegas Review-Journal*, Sept. 13, 1994, p. 1B.

Gang, Bill. Investors Slap Suit on Stupak, *Las Vegas Sun*, Apr. 7, 1994, p. 1A.

German, Jeff. Stupak Debunks Complaints, *Las Vegas Sun*, Oct. 7, 1990.

German, Jeff. Gamers Target Stupak, *Las Vegas Sun*, Jun. 24, 1991, p. 1A.

German, Jeff. Stupak Under the Gun Again, *Las Vegas Sun*, Oct. 22, 1991, p. 1A.

German, Jeff. Same Stupak Surfaces in Ad Campaign, *Las Vegas Sun*, Oct. 22, 1991, p. 3A.

German, Jeff. Stupak Tower Letter Probed, *Las Vegas Sun*, Oct. 23, 1991.

German, Jeff. Casino Plans Downtown are on the Slide, *Las Vegas Sun*, Dec. 12, 1991, p. 3A.

German, Jeff. State Gamers to Hit Stupak in Pocketbook, *Las Vegas Sun*, Jan. 14, 1992, p. 3A.

German, Jeff. Stupak Probe Widens, *Las Vegas Sun*, Mar. 23, 1992, p. 1A

German, Jeff. Rumors Flying as Judge Wolf Returns to Job, *Las Vegas Sun*, Mar. 26, 1992, p. 3A.

German, Jeff. Mo. asks More on Stupak, *Las Vegas Sun*, Mar. 1992, p. 1B.

German, Jeff. Cranking Up His Political Machine, *Las Vegas Sun*, May 31, 1992, p. 3D.

German, Jeff. Stupak Forced to Up Bankroll at Vegas World, *Las Vegas Sun*, Dec. 15, 1992, p. 3A.

German, Jeff. Stupak in Trouble With State Gamers, *Las Vegas Sun*, Mar. 2, 1993, p. 3A.

German, Jeff. Battling Bobs in Showdown at LV Council, *Las Vegas Sun*, May 17, 1994, p. 3A.

German, Jeff. Stupak Ending an Era in Las Vegas, *Las Vegas Sun*, Jan. 29, 1995, p. 3A.

Good, Joshua B. Calif. Man Shot at Vegas World, *Las Vegas Sun*, Dec. 29, 1992, p. 1A.

Good, Joshua B. Stupak: Security Couldn't Stop Murder, *Las Vegas Sun*, Dec. 30, 1992, p. 6A.

Green, Marian. Closing Days at Vegas World Hotel are Sad but Optimistic, *Las Vegas Review-Journal*, Jan. 30, 1995.

Green, Marian. Stratosphere Tower Project Goes Ape, *Las Vegas Review-Journal*, Jan. 11, 1996, p. 1B.

Green, Marian. Culinary Union Officials Discussing Organization of Stratosphere Resort, *Las Vegas Review-Journal*, Feb. 8, 1996, p. 2B.

Green, Marian. Thousands Hope to Climb on Board Stratosphere Resort, *Las Vegas Review-Journal*, Mar. 4, 1996, p. 1B.

Green, Marian. Brand Names Reach for Stratosphere, *Las Vegas Review-Journal*, Apr. 24, 1996, p. 1B.

Green, Marian. Chronology, *Las Vegas Review-Journal*, Apr. 28, 1996, p. 12B.

Green, Marian. Dreaming Lofty Dreams, *Las Vegas Review-Journal*, Apr. 28, 1996, p. 1E.

Green, Marian. Smoke Sets off Alarm, *Las Vegas Review-Journal*, May 1, 1996, p. 1A.

Green, Marian. Stratosphere Recognizes Culinary Union, *Las Vegas Review-Journal*, May 8, 1996, p. 3B.

Green, Marian. No Deals for Locals at Stratosphere, *Las Vegas Review-Journal*, May 9, 1996, p. 1B.

Green, Marian. Broken Part Drops From Roller Coaster at Stratosphere, *Las Vegas Review-Journal*, May 10, 1996, p. 1B.

Green, Marian. Stratosphere's Revenues Below Expectations, *Las Vegas Review-Journal*, Jun. 8, 1996, p. 11D.

Green, Marian. Stupak Reaches for the Stars, *Las Vegas Review-Journal*, date unknown, p. 1A.

Greene, Susan. Tower Has a Big Shot at the Top, *Las Vegas Review-Journal*, Feb. 11, 1996, p. 1B.

Harrison, Carlos. Vegas World Threatened With Lawsuit, *Las Vegas Review-Journal*, Apr. 23, 1985, p. 1B.

Havas, Adrian. City Concludes Vegas World Sign Inquiry, *Las Vegas Review-Journal*, Aug. 22, 1991, p. 3B.

Havas, Adrian. Carpet Merchant Takes on Stupak, *Las Vegas Sun*, Oct. 4, 1991.

Hyman, Harold. Strip Casino Museum Destroyed By Blaze, *Las Vegas Sun*, May 22, 1974. Page 1.

Koch, Ed. Vegas World Seeks OK of 30-Story Tower, *Las Vegas Sun*, Oct. 25. 1989, p. 1B.

Koch, Ed. Stupak's Sign Plan Too Tall, *Las Vegas Sun*, Feb. 7, 1990, p. 1B.

Krauthamer, Jeffrey. What the Stratosphere Misses is Stupak's Las Vegas Savvy, *Las Vegas Review-Journal*, Jul. 26, 1996, Letter to the Editor.

Lalli, Sergio. Vegas World's Stupak to Mail Free Stock in Effort to Draw Local Clientele, *Las Vegas Review-Journal*, Mar. 10, 1987, p. 2B.

Lalli, Sergio. A Look at the Polish Maverick: Stupak's Career Marked by Controversy, *Las Vegas Review-Journal*, May 28, 1987, p. 1A

Macy, Robert, Associated Press. McGuire Finds Little Sweetness in 'Sugartime' Film, *Las Vegas Sun*, Nov. 21, 1995, p. 3I.

McCabe, George. Stupak's Tower a Monument to Vegasness, *Las Vegas Review-Journal*, Dec. 8, 1991, p. 1A.

Mikla, Pete. The Road Back to Stardom, *Las Vegas Review-Journal*, Aug. 9, 1985, p. 1E.

Mikla, Pete. The McGuire Sisters: Stage Comeback Will be Followed by Books and Records, *Las Vegas Review-Journal*, Apr. 25, 1986, p. 5D.

O'Brian, Bridget. Stratosphere's Founder Sold as Stock Sank, *The Wall Street Journal*, Jul. 31, 1996, p. C1.

Orwall, Bruce. Stratosphere Says Bankruptcy Filing is 'Highly Likely,' *The Wall Street Journal*, Oct. 25, 1996, p. B7.

Orwall, Bruce. Bad Bet: Roller-Coaster Ride of Stratosphere Corp. is a Tale of Las Vegas, *The Wall Street Journal*, Oct. 29, 1996, p. 1A.

Pappa, Erik. McCarran Could Lose Millions, *Las Vegas Review-Journal*, date unknown, p. 1A.

Palermo, Dave. Stupak Tower Project Gets 'Wild' Kick-Off, *Las Vegas Review-Journal*, Nov. 6, 1991, p. 1B.

Palermo, Dave. Egyptian-theme Resort Revealed, *Las Vegas Review-Journal*, Nov. 15, 1991, p. 1A.

Palermo, Dave. Vegas World Coming to an End, *Las Vegas Review-Journal*, Jan. 26, 1995, p. 1F.

Palermo, Dave. Minnesota Businessman Rescued the Tower, *Las Vegas Review-Journal*, Apr. 28, 1996, p. 1E.

Palermo, Dave. Stratosphere Revenues Fail to Soar as High as Tower, *Las Vegas Review-Journal*, Jul. 7, 1996, p. 14E.

Palermo, Dave. Lyle Goes From Hero To Goat in Stupak's Eyes, *Las Vegas Review-Journal*, Aug. 5, 1996, p. 1D.

Paskevich, Mike. Stratosphere's Gans Becomes Hot Property, *Las Vegas Review-Journal*, Sept. 1, 1996, p. 1J.

Paskevich, Mike. Duo Basks in Fresh Success, *Las Vegas Review-Journal*, Jul. 20, 1990, p. 1C.

Pledger, Marcia. Landmark Begins Turning to Rubble, *Las Vegas Review-Journal*, date unknown.

Potters, Merilyn. Bob's-Eye View: Stupak Believes Bigger is Better to Attract Tourists, *Las Vegas Sun*, Nov. 20, 1994, p. 1D.

Potters, Merilyn. Tower: It's All in the Details, *Las Vegas Sun*, Nov. 20, 1994, p. 4D.

Russell, Diane. Card Counter Wins Suit Against Vegas World, *Las Vegas Sun*, Apr. 27, 1984, p. 1B.

Russell, Diane. Bob Stupak Seeks Return of Check, *Las Vegas Sun*, Sept. 19, 1987, p. 2B.

Ryan, Cy, Sun Capital Bureau. Stupak Begins Paying His Fine, *Las Vegas Sun*, Mar. 1, 1991.

Scott, Cathy. Stratosphere Has Towering Rivals, *Las Vegas Sun*, May 25, 1994, p. 10A.

Scott, Cathy. Stupak: $100,000 to Nab Bagley Killer, *Las Vegas Sun*, Oct. 31, 1995, p. 1D.

Scott, Cathy. No Reward in Meegan Conviction; Stupak's Offer of $100,000 Was Not Claimed by Witnesses, *Las Vegas Sun*, Aug. 27, 1996, p. 1A.

Scott, Cathy. Making Way for a Resort, *Las Vegas Sun*, date unknown.

Scott, Cathy. Stupak Still Recovering from Motorcycle Spill, *Las Vegas Sun*, date unknown.

Shemeligian, Bob. Craps-Lover Chester Stupak Dies in Las Vegas, *Las Vegas Sun*, Dec. 18, 1991, p. 3B.

Shemeligian, Bob. Strange Day, Indeed, at Vegas World, *Las Vegas Sun*, Feb. 2, 1995, p. 1D.

Shemeligian, Bob. 'Sugartime' Story Panned by McGuire, *Las Vegas Sun*, Nov. 27, 1995, p. 3L.

Smith, John L. Latest Publicity the Kind that Even Stupak Doesn't Want, *Las Vegas Review-Journal*, Oct. 1990, p. 1B.

Smith, John L. Other Worldly Planet Stupak Drifts Off to Cosmic Afterlife, *Las Vegas Review-Journal*, Feb. 5, 1995, p. 1B.

Smith, John L. Stupak Courts a Dream to Shoot Hoops with the Globetrotters, *Las Vegas Review-Journal*, Jan. 31, 1996, p. 1B.

Smith, John L. Mr. Las Vegas, Stupak, Getting Monkeys Off His Back, *Las Vegas Review-Journal*, Feb. 8, 1996, p. 1B.

Smith, John L. Man With the Tower Turns to Flowers for his Valentine, *Las Vegas Review-Journal*, Feb. 15, 1996, p. 1B.

Sprigle, Ray. Cops Can't Help But Know Who Racketeers Are, *Pittsburgh Post-Gazette*, Jul.11, 1950. Page 1.

Sprigle, Ray. The Law Doesn't Fool With Chester, *Pittsburgh Post-Gazette*, Jul. 20, 1950. Page 1.

Sprigle, Ray. Don't Buy Those Dishes, Lady, take a Number, *Pittsburgh Post-Gazette*, Jul. 21, 1950. Page 1

Sprigle, Ray. Carl Kelly-Dibassi Is Genial Host, *Pittsburgh Post-Gazette*, Aug. 2, 1950.

Sprigle, Ray. Don't Think the Numbers Racket Isn't an Efficient, Well-Organized Business, *Pittsburgh Post-Gazette*, Aug. 3, 1950. Page 1.

Staff writer. Heat is off Numbers Men, Fines $10 to $25, *Pittsburgh Press*, Feb. 10, 1936.

Staff writer. State Police, DA Swap Blasts, *Pittsburgh Post-Gazette*, Feb. 2, 1958. Page 1.

Staff writer. Judge Alpern Quizzes Panel After Verdict, *Pittsburgh Post-Gazette*, Aug. 14, 1958.

Staff writer. Private Phone Stalls Bribe Trial, *Pittsburgh Post-Gazette*, Sept. 11, 1958.

Staff writer. Stupak Trial Near Jury, *Pittsburgh Post-Gazette*, Oct. 2, 1963.

Staff writer. Stupak Faces Court in Gambling Case, *Pittsburgh Post-Gazette*, Jan. 11, 1964.

Staff writer. Million Dollar Gambling Museum, *Las Vegas Review-Journal*, Mar. 13, 1974.

Staff writer. Arson Probe Begun in Casino Blaze Here, *Las Vegas Review-Journal*, May 22, 1974. Page 1.

Staff writer. Blaze's Origin Mysterious, *Las Vegas Sun*, May 30, 1974. Page 3.

Staff writer. Wallpaper Worth Saving, *Las Vegas Review-Journal*, Jun. 2, 1974.

Staff writer. Gambling Museum Given Tentative Okay to Relocate, *Las Vegas Review-Journal*, Jul. 4, 1974.

Staff writer. Insurer Charges 'Torch,' *Las Vegas Review-Journal*, Jun.18, 1975.

Staff writer. Insurance Firm Claims Casino Blaze Was Arson, *Las Vegas Review-Journal*, Jun. 18, 1975.

Staff writer. Casino Owner Sues, *Las Vegas Review-Journal*, Jul. 23, 1975.

Staff writer. Lovell Denies Conflict of Interest, *Las Vegas Review-Journal*, Jul. 25, 1975.

Staff Writer, UPI. Winston Firm Denies Bilking McGuire Sister, *Las Vegas Sun*, Feb. 24, 1982.

Staff Writer. McGuire Jewelry Suit Dismissal is Sought, *Las Vegas Sun*, May 22, 1982, p. 12A.

Staff Writer. McGuire Offers $1 Million Reward for Jewels, *Las Vegas Sun*, Jun. 25, 1982, p. 1B.

Staff Writer. McGuire's Suit Near Settlement, *Las Vegas Sun*, Aug. 31, 1983, p. 2B.

Staff Writer. Tar Pot Blamed for Vegas World Fire, *Las Vegas Sun*, Nov. 20, 1984, p. 4A.

Staff Writer. World's Tallest Sign Coming to Vegas World, *Las Vegas Sun*, Nov. 10, 1985, p. 1D.

Staff Writer. Vegas World Addition OK'd, *Las Vegas Sun*, Dec. 5, 1986, p. 5C.

Staff Writer. Labor Department Suing Stupak, *Las Vegas Sun*, Dec. 16, 1986, p. 3B.

Staff Writer. Unions Picket Stupak's Vegas World to Protest Hiring Practices, *Las Vegas Sun*, May 31, 1987, p. 3B.

Staff Writer. Vegas World Begins Building Tower, *Las Vegas Sun*, Aug. 2, 1988, p. 3B.

Staff Writer, Sun Capital Bureau. Stupak Agrees to Pay Fine on False Ads Rap, *Las Vegas Sun*, Feb. 28, 1991, p. 7D.

Staff Writer. Stupak Asks Judge to Oust Major Portion of Lawsuit, *Las Vegas Review-Journal*, Jan. 8, 1992, p. 1F.

Staff Writer. Stratosphere Corp. Sets April 30 Opening, *Las Vegas Review-Journal*, Mar. 15, 1996, p. 1B.

Staff Writer. Stratosphere Trims 150 Workers from Labor Force, *Las Vegas Review-Journal*, Jun. 29, 1996, p. 1C.

Staff Writer. Stratosphere Pod Evacuated in Fire, *Las Vegas Review-Journal*, Jul. 6, 1996, p. 2B.

Staff Writer, AP. Stupak Quits as Stratosphere Chairman, *Reno Gazette-Journal*, Jul. 23, 1996, p. 1E.

Staff Writer, AP. Grand Casinos, Stupak Blame 'Style Differences' for Breakup, *Reno Gazette-Journal*, Jul. 24, 1996, p. 1D.

Staff Writer. Stratosphere Halts Growth, *Las Vegas Sun*, Aug. 30, 1996, p. 1A.

Staff Writer. Casinos Up Odds on Craps Insurance Bets, *Las Vegas Review-Journal*, Sept. 23, 1996, p. 1D.

Staff Writer. Stratosphere Loan, *Las Vegas Sun*, Oct. 2, 1996, p. 1E.

Stearns, John. Riverside Suitor Sports Colorful Past, *Reno Gazette-Journal*, Jan. 15, 1996, p. 1A.

Sterngold, James. The Stratosphere in Las Vegas Comes Down Out of the Clouds, *The New York Times*, Jun. 28, 1996, p. C6 .

Stutz, Howard. Gamers File Two Complaints Against Stupak, *Las Vegas Review-Journal*, Oct. 4, 1990, p. 1A.

Stutz, Howard. Grumbles Brought Stupak Action, *Las Vegas Review-Journal*, Oct. 5, 1990, p. 1B.

Thompson, Gary. The Dreamspinners: Bob Stupak, *Las Vegas Sun*, Apr. 26, 1996, p. 8D.

Thompson, Gary. Stratosphere Stock Plummets Amid Losses, *Las Vegas Sun*, Jul. 22, 1996, p. 1A.

Thompson, Gary. Stratosphere Leads Gaming Stocks Tumble, *Las Vegas Sun*, Aug. 14, 1996, p. 1A.

Tobin, Alan. Casino Bosses Indicted in Tip Scam, *Las Vegas Review-Journal*, Apr. 9, 1992, p. 1B.

Velotta, Richard N. High Roller: Stratosphere Track Will be World's Tallest, *Las Vegas Sun*, date unknown, p. 1E.

Vogel, Ed. Vegas World Plan Modified, *Las Vegas Review-Journal*, Dec. 8, 1994, p. 13D.

Vogel, Ed. Stratosphere Bond Sale Extension Approved, *Las Vegas Review-Journal*, Dec. 21, 1994, p. 12E.

Voyles, Susan. Stupak Gets More Time On Riverside, *Reno Gazette-Journal*, Jul. 7, 1996, p. 1C.

Voyles, Susan. End Looms Today for Stupak's Riverside Deal, *Reno Gazette-Journal*, Jul. 9, 1996, p. 1A.

Voyles, Susan. Stupak Folds on Riverside Deal, *Reno Gazette-Journal*, Jul. 10, 1996, p. 1A.

Waddell, Lynn. $125,000 Fine for Stupak?, *Las Vegas Sun*, Feb. 27, 1991, p. 3A.

Waddell, Lynn. Ex-workers Ask Stupak for Apology, *Las Vegas Sun*, Apr. 17, 1992, p. 1A.

Waddell, Lynn. Going Up, *Las Vegas Sun*, May 21, 1993, p. 6B.

Waddell, Lynn. Vegas World Says Goodbye, *Las Vegas Sun*, Jan. 30, 1995, p. 1A.

Waddell, Lynn. Stratosphere: Sky's the Limit, *Las Vegas Sun*, date unknown.

Weatherford, Mike. Back at Work: Tony Martin Recalls the 'Old Days,' *Las Vegas Review-Journal*, Sept. 23, 1988, p. 1E.

White, Ken. Local News Shameless Promoters, *Las Vegas Review-Journal*, May 8, 1996, p. 11E.

White, Ken. Nothing Amusing About Ride Safety, *Las Vegas Review-Journal*, Sept. 5, 1996, p. 3E.

Williams, Janet. Mob Boss John LaRocca Dies, *Pittsburgh Press*, December 4, 1984, Page B4.

Winship, Frederick M., UPI. McGuire Sisters' Comeback Stint Apparently Successful, *Las Vegas Sun*, Nov. 13, 1986, p. 1D.

Zipser, Andy. Towering Inferno: Despite a Fire, Stupak Pushes his Las Vegas Dream, *Barron's*, Sept. 6, 1993.

Notes on Sources

Bob Stupak hated the idea of a book being written about him at this point in his life. Frankly, the guy tried everything to prevent it, from offering a $10,000 bribe to jokingly threatening to have a few friends of friends in the "Outfit" come and work a little kneecap persuasion on me. Eventually, he cut out the petty payoff chatter and gave me what I really wanted: information about his incredibly colorful life.

At his home in Rancho Circle, Stupak keeps a huge library of videos capturing his eccentric stunts. He has been featured on television broadcasts around the world and has amassed a personal documentary series worthy of a special place in the archives at University of Nevada-Las Vegas. While other casino bosses have been busy guarding their past, Stupak has chronicled much of his on film. He also has collected literally thousands of news clippings and magazine articles touting his casino and himself.

After a few persuasive tactics of my own, Stupak relented and allowed me some access to the library. It was a gold mine that also jogged his memory. Although I doubt anyone would want to sit through a 24-hour Stupak film festival, much of the material in his library captures a spirit that once thrived in Las Vegas and now, unfortunately, is part of its past.

Author's Note: Being afraid of heights, it wasn't easy to take a seat on the Big Shot thrill ride atop the Stratosphere Tower. Standing there next to Stupak, who had survived a near-death experience on a Harley-Davidson, compelled me to give the ride a try.

Information for the Prologue was collected from personal experience, the files of the *Las Vegas Review-Journal* and *Sun*, and a host of magazine sources.

Prologue: Gathering facts for this section proved difficult, as Stupak declined to allow access to his physicians and rehabilitation specialists. Still, University Medical Center officials parted with what information the law allowed, and officials with Mercy Ambulance, the Metropolitan Police, Las Vegas Fire Department, and Quality Towing helped flesh out the section. Interviews with paramedics Bryan Alexis, Ian Adams, Tricia Wacker, and August Corrales gave me a picture of the accident scene I otherwise would have been denied. Corrales on severe accidents: "It's all a matter of timing, timing in terms of getting the patient to the trauma center. Bob Kenney did a great job alerting the trauma center that this patient was coming in very soon. What surprised me is that some people knew who he was before we knew." Police officers at the scene were able to identify the owner of the vehicle and determine that the bloody mess was indeed Stupak. Months after the accident, Wacker recalled with a sense of awe how easily the paramedics moved through the chaos: "It was actually very organized as far as scenes go. It was just an amazing call from beginning to end. My supervisors had everything under control when we got there. We really worked together as a team."

Chapter One: Interviews with Bob Stupak proved invaluable in this chapter, as did the research assistance of librarians in Las Vegas, Melbourne, and Pittsburgh, especially at the Carnegie Library, where the Ray Sprigle series and numerous other clips on Chester Stupak were unearthed. Interviews with John Woodrum and other casino operators also were helpful.

During World War II, Chester worked at a Pittsburgh battery plant and an oil company, but his contribution to the war effort did not prevent him conducting dice games on a regular basis. He had a far bigger future in craps than in factory work. Bob Stupak on his father: "I learned a lot from him about dealing with people and gambling. I wish I could find another owner like him, one who would actually run a gambling casino. There are none out there, including the Horseshoe. They won't even gamble with the best of it. At the MGM, they're afraid of their own shadow. They're always sweating a game out. It's the corporate thing. They have to answer to people who don't know anything about gambling. They're afraid of the games."

Articles by James Rutherford, Sergio Lalli, Jeff Burbank, Marian Green, and Gary Thompson were doubly useful. Thanks also to police sources in Australia and at Scotland Yard, whose wish to remain anonymous will be respected.

Pittsburgh boxer Billy Conn was managed by Milton Jaffe. Jaffe would later own a piece of the Stardust Hotel.

Chapter Two: City of Las Vegas fire and business-license sources provided valuable background on Bob Stupak's first foray into the Las Vegas casino scene. Files at both local newspapers, as well as the reminiscences of Stupak and former Gaming Control Board chief of enforcement Gary Reese, provided insight.

Here is where Stupak's ability to grab the attention of the press first began to be recognized in Las Vegas. Of course, he had been pulling the same hyperbolic stunts for many years by the time the Million Dollar Historic Gambling Museum opened. Casino owner John Woodrum's perspective again was valuable.

Chapter Three: In a city whose casino bosses are by and large no longer candid with potential critics, the unpretentious way Bob Stupak described how he finagled his first series of bank loans was nothing short of remarkable.

City officials were helpful in piecing together the background for this chapter, as were sources inside the Gaming Control Board who prefer to remain anonymous.

An 11th-hour interview with David Sklansky, who has authored an armload of gambling books and was a key insider at Vegas World, greatly improved the material. Sklansky is one of a handful of truly superior minds working in the numbers end of the casino business.

Interviews with Alan Brown, Howard Grossman, Jackie and Michael Gaughan, and a host of other casino men helped bring life to the story.

Documents obtained from sources inside the Metropolitan Police Department and the Gaming Control Board helped bring the mob anecdotes into perspective. Metro officer Frank Smaka, who walked the beat in Naked City in the early days, provided experienced insight into the neighborhood's most dangerous era.

Stupak on the cost of doing business at Vegas World:

"It costs the bigger casinos in Las Vegas a couple hundred thousand dollars a day to operate. I pay millions of dollars a year in casino taxes and fees, just to operate Vegas World. The expense figures are so frightening that we calculate everything on a daily basis and we prorate them. I'd be scared to go over the annual figures. Somehow an electric bill of $1,000 a day sounds a lot better than $365,000 a year.

"The hotel rooms, restaurants, and bars are just auxiliary operations. It's the gambling in the casino...that carried the major load.

One promotion that could only have happened at Vegas World, but didn't, was Stupak's idea of developing a drink called Lucky Juice, which not only promised to refresh but also to provide drinkers with a Vegas World gaming chip in the bottle cap. Not bad for 69 cents a pop. After a few weeks, the plan fell as flat as a week-old Coke.

Chapter Four: Thanks to writer Roger Dionne, who ghosted *Stupak on Craps* and collected many of the hundreds of Bob-as-huckster stories. Newspaper researchers from Melbourne helped collect the Australian material. Particularly candid interviews with Richard Schuetz, Steve Miller, Scott Higginson, and Stupak pal Eddie Baranski are greatly appreciated.

Police reports were valuable in fleshing out the amazing world of Chris Karamanos, who appears to have lived several lives at once.

Reporter Ken White of the *Review-Journal* is a former *Bullet* staffer and was able to lend his insight into life on Stupak's wild weekly.

Stupak struggled for years to stop smoking. At one point, he determined to force himself to quit his four-pack-a-day habit by offering $300,000 to anyone who caught him puffing for the period of one year. As always, there was a public-relations angle to work. He had billboards placed in Hollywood and Las Vegas advertising the $300,000 pitch. He wouldn't admit breaking down after a few months, but he would remind skeptics that no one ever collected the reward.

Chapter Five: For perhaps the first time in his life, Bob Stupak conducted intensive research into something that interested him: the economic power of towers throughout the world. For this book, I attempted to conduct similar research and found several books on the subject invaluable. Mario Salvadori's *What Makes Buildings Stand Up: The Strength of Architecture*, John Tauranac's *The Empire State Building: The Making of a Landmark*, and John M. Findlay's *Magic Lands* were especially helpful.

Findlay: "One basis for Disney's impact resided in the absolute control its designers had over the grounds, which permitted them to organize environs around a few selected themes. Disney and his associates laid out the park so that the whole and its constituent parts—Adventureland, Fantasyland, Frontierland, Tomorrowland, and Main Street U.S.A.—conveyed carefully selected messages. Success inside Disney's walls encouraged imitation outside. Both in the immediate vicinity of Orange County and in urban areas across the country, the theme park exerted a powerful influence on urban form. ...Although many in the region were reluctant to admit it, Greater California dominated the Far West demographically, economically, and culturally. This warm, weird, and exceptionally creative corner of the country produced, besides Disneyland, Stanford Industrial Park and Sun City, such other magic kingdoms as the Las Vegas Strip, Dodger Stadium, the Los Angeles freeway system, the planned community of Irvine, and the San Diego Zoo."

Disneyland is the world's best known theme park, but few people realize it was carved out of the Anaheim, California, orange groves in 1954 and was designed not as a permanent carnival, but as a supermarket for promoting Disney's products. The attractions were the hook for T-shirt sales and cartoon promotions. Disney understood the power of his images.

Bob Maheu's *Next to Hughes* and Michael Drosnin's *Citizen Hughes* were valuable, too. Interviews with Stupak, Howard Grossman, and City of Las Vegas officials were also useful. Newspapers in Australia, Pittsburgh, and Las Vegas provided background for this chapter.

Chapter Six: The journalism of John Gallant and Cathy Hanson was invaluable in this chapter.

The *Las Vegas Advisor* newsletter conducted a series of in-depth interviews with Stupak on the relative value of the vacation packages. Those interviews remain the last word on the subject.

Political consultant Dan Hart also provided his insight into Stupak-the-political-animal after having worked for the embattled Frank Hawkins, Mirage Resorts Chairman Steve Wynn, and the boss of Vegas World.

Not all of the vacation package news was bad. While consumer reporters and state attorneys general feasted on the Vegas World vacation packages, feature writers with an appreciation for the big hustle and the city's seductively surreal atmosphere appeared to appreciate Stupak's schtick. They weren't fooled by the coupon come-ons and the near-empty promises; the Vegas World deal was so bad it was good, and for low-rollers it wasn't the worst bet in the city. It tended to bring out the gonzo journalist in newspaper scribes from the *Washington Post* and *Rocky Mountain News* to the *Milwaukee Sentinel* and the

Village Voice.

In a Washington Post feature titled "Sure Bet Gone Bust in Las Vegas," Bob Garfield wrote, "Gamble? Not me. Gambling is for chumps and rubes. I like a sure thing. That's what caught my eye about the ad for Bob Stupak's Vegas World, and that's why I headed west. And that's how I succeeded in bringing Las Vegas to its knees. Maybe you've heard of this place, the renegade casino for Everyman. Let Caesars Palace and the Mirage draw big-money players, through glitz and ersatz opulence. Stupak targets low-rollers with low-cost vacation packages—and that's what struck me as an opportunity."

Mim Swartz described Vegas World thus, "...But it's easy to spot the place, which has a space theme: An astronaut floats on the side of one hotel tower, rockets marked 'Stupak' jut up here and there, and orbiting celestial bodies flash off the reflective building. Even for brassy Las Vegas, this place is brazen. It's more audacious inside. Moons and half-moons and spacecraft dangle from the ceiling that blinks with tiny lights to resemble star-studded outer space. Walls are covered with mirrors, giving the claustrophobic casino the illusion of being bigger than it is. Bubbling lights gurgle everywhere. This casino makes you break out in giggles."

The point would, of course, be lost on sticklers for accuracy in advertising. By this time, Stupak and Stratosphere needed all the good news they could get as the City Council attempted to use its much-criticized power of eminent domain to acquire 22 acres of real estate around Vegas World for use in the Stratosphere project. But a series of setbacks at district court, most before Judge Don Chairez, sent the Council reeling.

Chapter Seven: Interviews for this chapter include Scott Higginson, Tom Hantges, Garren Sepede, Joe Milanowski, and especially Phyllis McGuire. Tom Hantges: "He really believed his old-boy friendship with Berman was going to bail him out. When Bob and Lyle started knocking heads almost immediately over issues Bob figured Lyle would defer to him on, their relationship deteriorated. These guys right now hate each other. Bob sold his soul. It quickly became evident that once he made the deal he was no longer in charge."

More on Bob Maheu and Operation Mongoose: The scheme began as a serious attempt to kill Castro and was hatched by Meyer Lansky, whose island gambling empire had been devastated by the change of power in Cuba. Florida mob boss Santos Trafficante was enlisted in the plot. Plans were drawn and redrawn. First, the mob considered dispatching a hit squad to Cuba for a bit of machine-gun work reminiscent of Capone's Chicago. But no, too messy. Perhaps a member of his inner circle could be persuaded to poison Castro's food or one of his famous cigars. Maheu's crew even toyed with the idea of slipping Castro a mickey that would make the hair in his macho beard fall out, but that idea, too, was scrapped. No guns or gunmen ever came ashore in Cuba.

In fact, evidence exists that Trafficante and other mobsters conned the CIA out of thousands of dollars and invented many of the tallest tales associated with the plot. Chicago boss Sam Giancana, for one, saw Operation Mongoose as an opportunity to endear himself and his associates with the highest levels of the American political machine. "While the CIA had been advocating the 'elimination of Fidel Castro' as early as 1959, it was the mobsters themselves who volunteered to come aboard for such good works," Carl Sifakis wrote in *The Mafia Encyclopedia*. "Actually, the mobsters were more interested in getting the intelligence agency in their hip pockets for their own reasons. Most important of all, most Mafiosi involved in the plotting engaged in a scam, never really trying to kill Castro and instead robbing the CIA of untold sums of money." As he had so often in his incredible life, Bob Maheu found himself in the middle.

Chapter Eight: The night Stratosphere turned into a Roman candle won't soon be forgotten by Las Vegans. Superior reporting by Shaun McKinnon, Dave Palermo, Jeff Burbank, and Cathy Scott helped paint the scene of the blaze. Superior reporting by Andy Zipser helped flesh out the story of the tower's financing. Interviews with Mike Moody, Sepede, Hantges, and Milanowski are much appreciated.

Chapter Nine: Thanks to Richard Schuetz and David Sklansky for lending their perspective here. The journalism of Dave Palermo, Jim Rutherford, and Gary Thompson was incorporated into this chapter.

A note on Berman: Of the many casino men I have watched and written about over the years, none I can recall have made as big an impression in as short a time as Lyle Berman. The expansion of Grand Casinos, quite frankly, is one of the underrated stories in the history of the industry. There is no such thing as an overnight success, but this casino company is the next closest thing. Whether it will establish itself in the big leagues of the business remains to be seen.

Chapter Ten: Metro detective Richard Hart's experienced views are greatly appreciated. Thanks also to Metro detective William Johnson, City Attorney Brad Jerbic, Nevada Stupak, Phyllis McGuire, Dan Hart, Mayor Jan Jones, and reporters Pauline Bell, Dave Berns, Marian Green, Dave Palermo, Cathy Scott, and Gary Thompson.

Chapter Eleven: Transcripts from the Gaming Control Board provided the body of this chapter. Articles from *the Reno Gazette-Journal, Las Vegas Review-Journal,* and *Las Vegas Sun* also were of service.

From the Nevada Gaming Commission meeting regarding the Stratosphere fire: "What was the cause?" Commissioner August Gurrola asked during the March 21, 1996, meeting that ended in a unanimous vote to license Stratosphere.

"You would have to ask the man upstairs," Stupak said. "Only thing I know for sure, it wasn't lightning. That is the only thing that the fire department could tell me. Outside of that, we have no idea."

"Were there any, in the construction at that time, were there any fire code violations?"

"I'm not completely familiar with it," Stupak said. "I have some knowledge. Perini Construction at that time was in charge of the construction. They had a contract. That area was fenced off. Only Perini people had the keys and went in and out of there. I'm not sure what was up there or what happened. I used to take trips every once in a while with people coming from out of town just to see what it looked like that high up. But I'm not familiar with how they did it or what the cause was."

Chapter Twelve: A crush of humanity crowded into Stratosphere for the opening-night festivities. Unlike most casino VIP openings, which are limited to casino bosses, business leaders, and the press, Stratosphere's unveiling featured a mass of people from all walks of life. From the carefully coiffed to the literally unwashed, it appeared half the city was there. Most of the top casino bosses, however, were not. The work of reporters David Ehlers, Susan Greene, and Marian Green was helpful here, as well as interviews with City Councilmen Arnie Adamsen and Gary Reese, Mayor Jan Jones, financial experts Mike Moody and Marvin Roffman, and a host of others.

Stupak to reporter Gary Thompson, at the height of giddiness as Stratosphere was set to open: "I just turned 54, but I was sick last year so that doesn't count. I've got a lot of things left to do. In 1972, I bought an Orange Julius stand at 725 Las Vegas Boulevard because I thought the Strip would expand north of the Sahara. I was dead wrong. But I'll bet you that by the end of the century, there'll be four major joints between the tower and downtown Las Vegas."

Chapter Thirteen: Interviews with Stupak, Hart, Schuetz, and Jones. Articles from the *Reno Gazette-Journal, Wall Street Journal, Las Vegas Review-Journal, Las Vegas Sun,* and *Los Angeles Times* helped flesh out this breaking story.

Stupak: "I didn't know the place was going down the fucking tubes. New York-New York is $480 million. Monte Carlo is $360 million. Where did the money go?"

Epilogue: Interviews with McGuire, Sklansky, Schuetz, Jones, Hart, Stupak, and Eddie Baranski defined the picture here.

An interesting question was raised by Stupak once he got wind of the "Rise and Fall" subtitle of the book. "This ain't the Roman Empire," he said. "I mean, there's no question in my mind I'm making a comeback." Ever in search of the best of any situation, Stupak said he didn't mind the "Rise" part, but he loathed the "Fall." After all, what is a gambler if not a man capable of making a comeback with a few lucky rolls of the dice?

Now here's a challenge Bob Stupak won't be able to resist: You make a big-time comeback and I'll update the book and adjust the subtitle. You can bet on it, Bob. And it won't cost you a nickel.

About Huntington Press

Huntington Press is a specialty publisher of Las Vegas and gambling-related books and periodicals, including the award-winning consumer newsletter, *Anthony Curtis' Las Vegas Advisor*. To receive a copy of the Huntington Press catalog, call **1-800-244-2224** or write to the address below.

Huntington Press
3687 South Procyon Avenue
Las Vegas, Nevada 89103